# Memoirs of a Cold War Warrior

"I thought you'd got the message...?"

## Keith Harvey

Connor Court Publishing

Copyright © 2021 Keith Harvey

ALL RIGHTS RESERVED. This book contains material protected under International and Federal Copyright Laws and Treaties. Any unauthorised reprint or use of this material is prohibited. No part of this book may be reproduced or transmitted in any form or by any means, electronic or mechanical, including photocopying, recording, or by any information storage and retrieval system without express written permission from the publisher.

CONNOR COURT PUBLISHING PTY LTD
PO Box 7257
Redland Bay QLD 4165
online@connorcourt.com
www.connorcourtpublishing.com.au

Cover picture: 'Weg's Day' cartoon, William Ellis Green, original cartoon in possession of the author.

ISBN: 978-1-922449-48-1 (pbk.)

Cover design by Maria Giordano

Printed in Australia

*Dedicated to my wife, Mary, my partner in life who worked with me and supported me in these endeavours.*

*For Thomas, Maria and Julia, Audrey, Molly, James and Deon*

*And for all those who kept the faith.*

*And in memory of my great great grandfather, Arthur Young Harvey, a progressive farmer from Aberdeenshire, Scotland and my great great uncle, Arthur Young a utopian socialist who struggled to create a better world*

# Acknowledgements

I would like to thank Alice Stinear for reading an early draft of this memoir and giving helpful advice on its content. I would also like to thank several others who also made detailed comments on later drafts, especially my wife, Mary, and also Michael Easson who has a particularly sharp eye and a broad and deep historical knowledge. Rodney Cavalier also offered input on several chapters, supplying an alternative viewpoint to mine on many issues. However, the views expressed in the book and any remaining errors are mine. The illustration on the cover is by the late Melbourne cartoonist 'Weg' [W.E. Green] who gave me this version of his drawing. Its use as a cover design for the book was suggested by Lachy Rees.

*"I thought you'd got the message…?"*

# CONTENTS

1. Nineteen Eighty-Four — 7
2. The Monash 'Soviet' — 27
3. Rope and Cordage days — 61
4. 30 days that shook the Trades Hall — 91
5. Working for the man, at home and abroad — 107
6. My Cold War in the warm Pacific — 133
7. Winning the Cold War and losing the Clerks Union — 155
8. For two are better than one: Social Justice at work — 183

Appendix: The Spectre of Communism — 219

Notes — 236

Index — 255

# 1

# NINETEEN EIGHTY-FOUR

*"The Split was an Australian manifestation of the Cold War...The sudden collapse of the Soviet Union and the discrediting of communism in 1989-91 has rendered almost incomprehensible many aspects of the Cold War to 21$^{st}$ century generations...the ideological threat presented... now tends to be discounted. But it was real...". - Graham Freudenberg*[1]

I have been a member of the Australian Labor Party [ALP] since the 13$^{th}$ of February 1984. I had first joined the Party nearly a decade earlier in late 1974 but as a result of events in 1978, I allowed my membership to lapse in the late 1970s.[2] I applied to re-join the Party in February 1984. I was then employed as a Research Officer in the National Office of the Federated Clerks Union of Australia [FCUA]. In 1984, the Victorian Branch of the FCUA, of which I was a member, along with the Victorian branches of three other Unions, applied to affiliate with the ALP. At the same time, several of their officials and other individuals, including me, applied for party membership.

This event was immensely significant in the history of the Australian labour movement. The four Victorian Unions – the FCUA, the Shop Assistants Union [known as the SDA], the Federated Ironworkers Association [FIA] and the Amalgamated Society of Carpenters and Joiners [the ASC&J] had left the ALP in the bitter split in the ALP in the mid-1950s. Some of these unions became associated with the Democratic Labour Party [DLP] and some of their officials became DLP members and officeholders. The split in the Labor Party was well before my time and the full history and complexity of these times are beyond the scope of these memoirs. Some context is necessary, however [and some more detail is in the Appendix].

The ALP split over the issue of Communism and the role of the ALP Industrial Groups and the Catholic Social Studies Movement [the "Movement" which later became the National Civic Council, or NCC] in the fight against Communist influence in and control of Australian trade unions. The Split's immediate trigger was the action of the then ALP Federal leader H.V. [Doc] Evatt in October 1954 denouncing the work of the Movement in the ALP. The Split had disastrous consequences for the ALP, sundering the party and ending a Labor government: the Cain Government in Victoria. It left the Federal ALP marooned on the Opposition benches until December 1972 despite all DLP-aligned state and federal lower house members losing their seats within two election cycles of the Split.

The division of the Labor Party pitted colleagues, friends and family members against one another. It detached many traditional working-class Catholic voters from the ALP in some States and, through DLP preferences, delivered formerly Labor votes to the Liberal Party. It could be argued that the preponderance of Catholics on the federal Coalition frontbench in recent years is a consequence of the 1950s ALP split. The history of the Movement and its leading figure, B. A. [Bob] Santamaria, has been much written about – there are numerous books and articles, many of them critical of the Movement/NCC, its ideology, methods and strategies.[3]

The history and character of the ALP Industrial Groups [as distinct from the Movement] is less well known and documented and consideration of the Movement and the Groups is often blurred. Nevertheless, they were two separate organisations and, while membership and leadership overlapped, the two organisations had different characteristics. The Movement was a specifically Catholic organisation, although non-Catholics could be part of its work [and were] and it was initially overseen by a Committee of Bishops.[4] The Industrial Groups were non-religious, and many Protestants and non-believers were active in them. Only ALP members could be members of an ALP-endorsed Industrial Group.

It now seems fashionable to decry and deplore both the work of the anti-communist Industrial 'Groupers' and of Santamaria's Movement. I am not one of these critics, although I have not been a supporter the NCC for nearly 40 years for reasons set out later. Despite the significant and unfortunate consequences of the ALP Split, the work of the anti-communists in the union movement and in the ALP was important work carried out, in the main, by people with the best of motives and with integrity, courage and faith. This memoir is written in part as a response those who have written what I consider to be unfair and unjustified criticism of the work of the NCC and the ALP Industrial Groups.

More importantly, while this memoir tells only one person's story, it is also written to acknowledge the selfless work of those who dedicated their lives to fighting against totalitarian communism and to preserve personal freedoms in Australia and the world. Many of these people are unsung and unknown to the world at large. Their work deserves recognition, not disdain. This is not to say that everything done in the name of this work was perfect or that everyone lived up to the vocation. Many people fell by the wayside: some became disillusioned, worn out or were treated badly. Others became disaffected for little or no reason and turned on their colleagues. In my opinion, even B.A. Santamaria betrayed both the work he had started as well as many of his colleagues who had sacrificed much in the anti-Communist struggle. This tale is another story.[5] But, for the most part, the people who carried out this work did so for the best of reasons and for little or no reward. They kept the faith.

Anti-communism has been criticised as a conservative or reactionary movement, but was in many ways economically, industrially and politically progressive. The anti-communism of the ALP Industrial Groups and the NCC was a working-class movement. In late 1935, early 1936 B.A Santamaria founded and edited a magazine called the *Catholic Worker*, directed to employees who fitted this description.[6] The *Catholic Worker* opposed both capitalism and communism from the perspective of religious faith and human rights. Anti-communists in Australia opposed and actively contested wherever they could the oppression of workers and other citizens in totalitarian States. The work of the Industrial Groups and the NCC was grounded in the practical realities of challenging and seeking to defeat those who wanted to use the Australian trade union movement to maintain Soviet totalitarian communism and seek to impose the same political system elsewhere in the world. This local work, based in worker organisations, was in no way akin to either the hysterical anti-communism of Senator Joseph McCarthy in the United States nor the self-serving anti-communism of political conservatives who sought only to preserve capitalism in the interest of the monied classes. Both of these forms of anti-communism discredited the work of genuine anti-communists.

The fall of communism in the Soviet Union and Eastern Europe has shown the work of genuine anti-communists to be on the side of human rights, including trade union rights, democracy and freedom. Recently, anti-communism has been attacked for allegedly using the same methods as those of the Communists:

> *An important Santamaria strategy was to use the communists' own tactics against them. Such was his urgency, he wrote in a report to key Catholic bishops in 1944 that the Movement needed a national campaign "modelled completely on the Communist Party" and its organising principles. God's crusade and knights. Stalin's methods.*[7]

This allegation that anti-communists used communist methods appeared in the Melbourne Age *Good Weekend* magazine in 2016 principally written as a critique of the SDA, one of the four unions which re-affiliated with the ALP in 1984-5.[8] In my opinion, this allegation is absurd. This theme was expanded on in 2017 when Mark Aarons, a former member of the Communist Party of Australia, published a book, co-authored with John Grenville, a former FCUA Federal Secretary, which sought to make this same claim in a greatly extended format.[9]

The Aarons/Grenville book was titled *The Show* – a code or nickname for the Movement/National Civic Council – and has as the title of its first chapter the same words used in *The Age* article: *Modelled Completely on the Communist Party* in reference to the Movement. These words are drawn from a 1944 document written by Santamaria for the Catholic Bishops in which Santamaria did say that it was necessary to meet the Communist challenge by creating an organisation 'completely modelled' on the Communist Party.[10]

*The Show* then uses this document as the base and theme for its subsequent argument. Santamaria's choice of words was poor, but this document does not support the Aarons thesis. Immediately after this phrase is used, Santamaria's document goes on to clarify what it means:

> *That is to say, we will make our qualifications for admittance very high, admitting only people who are ready to do active work for the movement and*

*to pay a membership fee of 26/- [$89] a year.*[11]

Charging a membership fee of whatever level does not make an organisation 'completely modelled' on the CPA nor Stalinist, nor does anything else recounted in *The Show*. The suggestion that the Movement or the ALP Industrial Groups used 'Stalin's methods' is completely at odds with the historical record. The tactics of Stalin and the Bolsheviks in Russia included bank robbery, mass arrests, torture, show trials, banishment and the creation of a massive system of concentration camps containing millions of inmates, as well as judicial and non-judicial murder. The Movement and the Industrial Groups did none of these things. Rather, they opposed at every turn the perpetrators of such outrages and those people who either supported such tactics or sought to excuse or explain them away.

The Movement and the Industrial Groups certainly took the fight up to the Communist Party in the union movement and elsewhere. To do so, it was necessary to be organised and to face a disciplined and committed force with similar dedication. But the analogy with the tactics of the Communist Party holds no force beyond this point. In Australia, since it did not have access to instruments of State power, the Communist Party had to content itself with ballot-rigging in union elections, violence and attempted intimidation.[12] The Industrial Groups, by contrast, fought for 'clean' and fair union ballots in the face of bitter opposition from the Communist Party and its allies. The Movement and the Groups fought for legislation to ensure fair and democratic elections which would allow the will of union members to be reflected in the outcome of elections.[13]

Until the Split in the ALP, the Movement and the Industrial Groups worked for the election of ALP members to positions in trade unions and as members of parliament. The forces of the Communist Party worked against the ALP. It is clear in my mind who was using Stalin's methods and who was using democratic and legal means to ensure rank and file control of the union movement.

The Communist Party of Australia [CPA] was founded in 1920 and sought influence and the means of making revolution principally through penetration of the Australian trade union movement. Australian unions had formed the ALP in the 1890s to win social change by peaceful means: political and industrial. The Labor Party sought gains for workers through legislation, through State ownership of key enterprises and through statutory authorities. Especially important were policies encouraging unionism and the unique Australian policy instrument of conciliation and arbitration leading to the making of industrial awards and agreements. Control of the unions meant control of votes at ALP conferences as well as in the Australian Council of Trade Unions [ACTU] and its Branches in each State.

From its inception until World War Two, the Communist Party sought its goal of a revolution on the Soviet model alternately through a united front with the ALP or by confrontation with the ALP to wean workers away from the 'reformist' or gradualist path of change. Since the unions were very influential in the ALP and since they were working-class organisations they were a natural focus of communist organisational activity. The strike weapon might bring about the circumstances favourable to revolutionary change. In any event, penetration of the unions meant influence in the corridors of ALP power, especially when the ALP was in office at either a State or Federal level. In his memoirs, Eric Aarons, one-time National Secretary of the CPA, indicated the Party's influence on the left-wing of the ALP:

> *Historically speaking, the Labor Party left had no coherent ideology; what it did have was, in the main, derived from the communists.*[14]

At times, the CPA employed the tactic of having secret members who were also ALP members – especially during the 1930s. Some of these secret dual members were elected to key positions in affiliated trades unions, peak trade union bodies and in the ALP itself.[15] For example, John ['Jack'] Hughes who held senior office in the Clerks Union in NSW and federally, as well as in the NSW ALP, was one of these secret members for a period.[16] At other times, he spoke openly of his Communist Party membership.[17]

Hughes played a key role in the Communist Party in Australia. In his memoir, Eric Aarons recounts that in 1951, he 'received a call to visit John Hughes in his office at the Clerks' Union of which he was then federal secretary. I was elated to hear that I had been chosen to lead a group of young Australian communists to study for an extended period of time in China.'[18] Hughes was clearly a key CPA operative having organized this three-year study tour with the new Communist leadership in China from his office at the Clerks Union. The CPA and its officials in Australia were at this time very much part of an international operation. They were in a close partnership with the USSR led by CPSU Secretary Joseph Stalin then still in power in Moscow and with the new Communist regime in Beijing led by Mao Tse Tung.

Several years ago, in some old files of the FCUA National President John Maynes, I found a typed copy of a letter from L.J. [Jack] McPhillips, then Acting National Secretary of the Federated Ironworkers Association [FIA], to a number of Communist Party members in various trade unions. McPhillips was a CPA member in charge of the Party's work in the union movement.[19] The letter was dated '4th September, [19]50' and advised these key Party members that the former National Secretary of the FIA, Ernie Thornton, had taken on a key role in the Asian-Australasian Bureau of the World Federation of Trade Unions. Thornton was by this time based in Peking and McPhillips was writing to ask his contacts to keep Thornton 'fully informed' about decisions taken by their unions, including where possible, Minutes of meetings. This information 'to be of real importance and value' should be sent 'as promptly as possible and this is of course by <u>Airmail</u>'. [Underlining in original]. Thornton's address in Peking was given as 'Mr. E. Thornton, 1 Chen Woo Miu, Peking, 20, CHINA'.[20]

The Chinese Communist Party had come to power in 1949, proclaiming the creation of the People's Republic of China on 1st October 1949. Within a year of this event, Thornton, a senior Australian Communist had been located there, working for the World Federation of Trade Unions [WFTU] which was dominated by Communist-controlled unions. Hughes replied to the letter from McPhillips on the 8th September 1950 agreeing to provide the requested information 'and other information and material' which would be 'sent airmail' as requested.

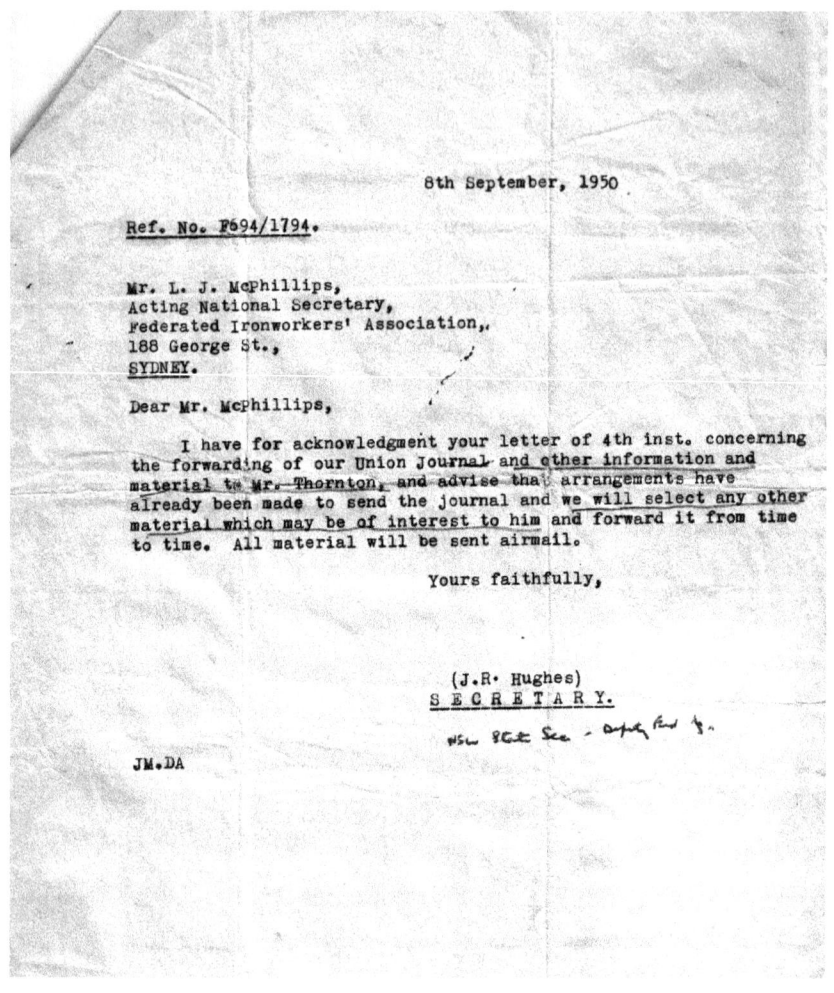

*Carbon copy of letter from Jack Hughes to L.J.McPhillips.
Copy in the possession of the author.*

I was struck when reading this letter to think that within a year of the Communist government establishing itself in China, a senior Australian communist would be based there, blatantly carrying out work for a Communist front organisation which had already been disavowed by the independent unions of the Western world, including the ACTU. Even more striking were the 'with compliments' slips still pinned to the copy of this letter. Hughes's reply to McPhillips had been copied to the Soviet Embassy, both to Vladimir Petrov no less, as well as to the Soviet Ambassador [and to an organisation based in Indonesia]. A few years later, on the 3rd April 1954, Petrov was to become a household name in Australia, when he sensationally defected to Australia, revealing himself to be a Colonel in the Soviet intelligence service [rather than doing his nominal job of 3rd Secretary in the Embassy]. Petrov was a senior KGB agent at the Soviet Embassy in Canberra. His espionage activities and those of the Soviet Union in Australia were to be the subject of a Royal Commission. And FCUA Secretary Jack Hughes was routinely, it would seem, copying him into union correspondence, along with other Soviet diplomats in Australia.

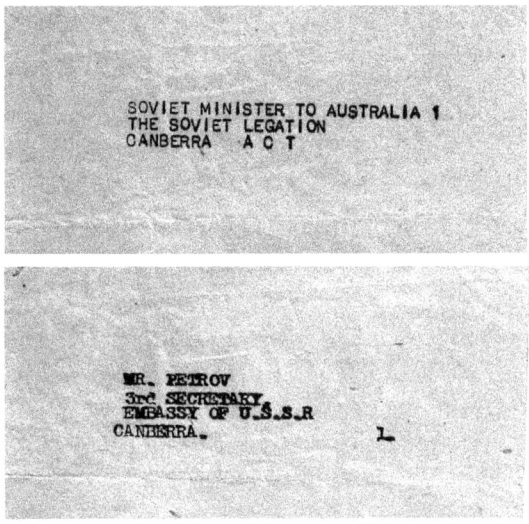

*"With compliments" slips attached to the Hughes letter.*
*Copy in the possession of the author.*

I mention this letter to highlight the political character of those officials in the immediate post-war period who were in control of the Clerks Union nationally. Hughes and his supporters were not just left-wing militants or progressive activists. Rather, they were senior 'card-carrying' CPA operatives, willingly undertaking the work of the Soviet-led communist movement internationally, activities that had been rejected by the ALP and the ACTU.

Communist influence had been waxing and waning in Australia since the formation of the Communist Party. But Communists were strongly entrenched in the union movement and Communism waxed during World War Two when Hitler attacked Russia and the war became the 'great patriotic war against fascism' for the Soviet Union and Communist parties around the world. By the end of the War, communists were in a strong position in the

Australian trade union movement.

To counter this threat, the ALP authorised the formation of ALP Industrial Groups to win unions back to the Labor Party. The formation of Industrial Groups within Victorian unions was authorised by the Victorian ALP at Easter 1946. An ALP Industrial Group was established in the Victorian Branch of the Federated Clerks Union of Australia [FCUA] in September the same year. John Maynes was the Group's first President [21] and one of several prominent and successful anti-Communists who emerged at this time.[22] By 1952, the Industrial Group in the FCU had wrested control of the Union away from the Communist Party and its supporters in most Branches and federally.[23]

When I began working for the Clerks Union in 1979, John Maynes was Victorian and National President and the dominant personality in the Union. I became a member of the Clerical Workers Industrial Group [CWIG], the successor of the Clerks ALP Industrial Group formed in 1946. The CWIG consisted at the time of Movement supporters in the Victorian Branch of the Union, full-time officials and employees as well as honorary officials and rank and file members of the Branch. In 1983, I became an elected member of the Victorian Branch Executive of the FCUA. Since August 1979, I had been a full-time employee of the Union's Federal Office.

The creation of the ALP Industrial Groups in the 1940s ultimately led to significant victories by several Groups in various unions, including in the Clerks Union and most of its Branches and in the Federated Ironworkers Association. The success of the Groups led some union officials and ALP officials to become concerned about the growing strength of the Groups and their influence within the ALP. Labor Party cooperation with the Groups and the Movement was abruptly ended when Federal leader 'Doc' Evatt, having lost the 1954 election, denounced the Movement and its influence in the ALP.[24] The Industrial Groups were then dis-established at the March 1955 ALP Federal Conference. In Victoria, where the Groups were in control of the Central Executive, the Branch resisted, and the ALP Federal Executive sought to assert its control over the Victorian Branch.

This led to two competing delegations being credentialed to attend the ALP Federal Conference in Hobart in early 1955. By a narrow majority, the Federal Evatt-aligned delegation was seated. This action split the party in Victoria. Expulsions of those loyal to the 'old' Executive followed and this also split the Victorian Parliamentary Party, then in a rare period of office in Victoria under Premier John Cain, Senior [who himself had been involved in the Industrial Groups]. Those who had been expelled or were loyal to the 'old' Executive crossed the floor of Parliament on a motion of 'no confidence' moved by Opposition leader Henry Bolte and the Cain ALP Government fell. The ALP remained in Opposition in Victoria until 1982, longer even than their federal counterparts, when John Cain Junior led the party back to office.

The Federal Party also split in 1955 but since it was not in office the consequences were not so severe, although the Party remained in Opposition until 1972 due in considerable part to the DLP's preferences being directed to the non-Labor parties. With the Groups out of the way, the Communists again made gains in the union movement. Shorn of its anti-communist wing in Victoria, left-wing forces and policies dominated the party in Victoria. Thus, the Split had several serious effects on the ALP, especially in Victoria. It deprived the party of part of its natural and core constituency. The dominance of the left also damaged the party's general appeal to voters. Anti-Catholic sectarianism was the order of the times, although many Catholics remained in the ALP in NSW and elsewhere. However, it seems to me that the left subsequently and deliberately sought to encourage the adoption of policies designed to keep Catholics out of their natural party by adopting policies on issues such as State Aid to non-government schools, abortion, etc. that were anathema to Catholics.

This was still the environment in the trade union movement when I first started work in it in December 1972, as an Administrative Officer for the Australian Rope and Cordage Union, an affiliate of the Victorian Trades Hall Council. It continued to be the case when I began working for the Clerks Union in August 1979. I was then working directly for John Maynes, still a key figure in what remained of the now non-ALP Industrial Groups and the Movement/NCC. Just a few years later, in 1984, moderates in the Victorian ALP and nationally had had enough of being a permanent minority in the Victorian Branch of the ALP. Jim Maher, National President and Victorian Secretary of the Shop Assistants Union, said that the initial approach came from ALP Prime Minister Bob Hawke.[25] Hawke said that it was time to end the Split, nearly 30 years after it had occurred. I – and many others – agreed.

## THE WORLD IN 1984

Although much had changed in the world since the tempestuous years of 1954-5, much was still the same in the labour movement in 1984, thirty years later. Today, a further 37 years on it is now hard to imagine this since so much has changed since the mid-1980s. In 1984, the issues that energised me when I first went to university were all still present. In 1970, the Russian dissident Andrei Amalrik published an essay in which he posed the question: 'Will the Soviet Union survive until 1984?'[26] Clearly, the date was chosen because of its allusion to George Orwell's novel, *Nineteen Eighty-Four*.[27] As 1984 began, the USSR still existed and showed little sign to the outside world that it was in difficulty. Communism still dominated half the world. While certain small changes had taken place in the Soviet Union, when Yuri Andropov died in 1984, he was replaced as the Communist Party of the Soviet Union [CPSU] General Secretary by Victor Chernenko. The aging heirs to Stalin and Lenin were still in place presiding over a totalitarian and unchanging one-party State.

The existence of the Gulag Archipelago so vividly described by the leading Russian dissident Alexander Solzhenitsyn was still largely unacknowledged. Solzhenitsyn's novel of concentration camp life, *One Day in the Life of Ivan Denisovich*, had been published in the West as early as 1962-3.[28] Solzhenitsyn's major work – *The Gulag Archipelago, Volumes 1,2 and 3* – occupied more than 1800 pages in total. I had read them all by 1984, together with all his other published works as well as the memoirs of many other Soviet dissidents and victims of the Gulag. One of the most remarkable and eye-opening books I read about the Gulag was that by Evgenia Ginsburg. Ginsburg was not a dissident. She was a card-carrying member of the Communist Party of the Soviet Union [CPSU]. She became one of the victims of Stalin's purges in 1937, arrested without cause, tried and convicted [of course] and eventually sent to a Gulag labor camp in the remote Magadan region of Eastern Siberia.

Her accounts were startling and compelling to me even though, or perhaps because, she had been a part of the system up until her arrest. She wrote two volumes of memoir: the first, *Into the Whirlwind*, was published by Penguin in paperback in 1968. I bought my copy at the Monash University Student Union bookshop while I was a student. I still have it. The second volume, *Within the Whirlwind*, was not published in the West until 1981.[29] I remember one story in her books vividly. While in the Gulag labor camp in the Magadan region she recalled being marched out to work one day past a group of prisoners who had been forced to stand, barefooted, on a frozen pond. It transpired that they were Christians and were being punished because they had refused to work that day because it was Easter Sunday – one of the holiest days of the Christian calendar. Ginsburg thought their attitude ridiculous since she had no religious faith. I found it inspiring.

One startling fact about the Soviet camps is that they were not simply a means of repressing political opponents: the Gulag was equally a forced labor program driven by economics and designed to provide slave labor to develop industries and exploit resources in remote regions of the USSR. This awful fact should have been of considerable concern to free trade unions in the West, but inexplicably for many – and especially for those on the left – it was not. Rather, it was ignored or sought to be explained away.[30] Volume One of the Gulag Archipelago was first published in paperback in Australia in 1974 and all volumes were available by the end of the 1970s. The truth about the Soviet Union was available to all who wanted to know about it in 1984.

Solzhenitsyn thought he was revealing news of the Gulag to the West for the first time but was surprised when he was eventually expelled from the Soviet Union to learn that considerable information about it was already available in the West, but had been largely ignored. I recall, without being able to find it again, a footnote referencing such published information in one of his works saying sardonically, 'Is this another book you have not read Bertrand Russell?'[31] It has been estimated that at least 18 million Soviet citizens had been arrested and passed through the Gulag and its various components.[32] Many of them died in the process and this is not the entire extent of deaths caused by the rule of the Communist Party of the Soviet Union. Stalin's 'Great Terror' of the 1930s also contributed as did the collectivisation policies forced on rural workers in the early 1930s.[33] The Gulag camps were particularly associated with Stalin – the Allies' belated ally in World War Two – but were established by Lenin shortly after the 1917 Revolution [34] and while they were begun to be dismantled by Stalin's successors, they continued to exist into the 1980s. Mikhail Gorbachev – grandson of a former camp inmate – began to finally dismantle them completely only in 1987.[35]

The bleak life the Soviet Union imposed on its citizens still resembled the dystopian world depicted by George Orwell in his novel *1984* and the tactics and double-speak described in *Animal Farm* remained as true as ever. The Chinese Communist Party ran its own forced labor system in China, known as Laogai. The existence of this extensive slave labor system was gradually exposed by a few brave activists and in particular by Harry Wu, a former camp inmate who made his way to the West. In his autobiography, Harry Wu estimated that between 1949 and 1996 fifty million people had been sent to prison camps that make up the Laogai.[36] Today, as many as one million Muslim Uighurs are estimated to be in special prison camps in the Xinjiang region in China.[37]

In 1984, the CPSU still controlled all aspects of Russian society. Workers and citizens were not free. The Berlin Wall was intact. Parts of the Gulag still existed. As we sought to end the Split in the ALP, efforts by Polish trade unionists led by Lech Walesa and Solidarity to free Poland from Communist party rule and Soviet domination had been suppressed and Walesa was under arrest. Nothing appeared to be changing. The Communist Party still ruled China with the same ruthlessness as Mao [and still does today in 2021] and in Viet Nam, the Communist Party was still consolidating its control over the whole country after the collapse of the South in 1975. Vietnamese 'boat people' continued to escape by sea looking for freedom in Australia and elsewhere. The Cold War between the West and the Communist World, despite the Sino-Soviet split, continued to rage and although the Communist Party had also split in Australia and eventually wound itself up, many left-wing union leaders still supported the foreign policy aims of the Soviet Union and China. The repression of working people behind the Iron and Bamboo curtains was continuing.

## ENDING THE SPLIT

I was interested in doing what I could to bring about an end to these injustices. However, in 1984 it was time to end the Split in the labour movement. My experience in the union movement by this time had put me firmly on the side of working people. I had never joined or been interested in joining the DLP which had by this time lost all its parliamentary representation and had officially wound itself up in 1978. Unions and unionists belonged in the ALP. No other party offered anything to working people and their families. The Liberal/National Parties governed in the interests of big and small businesses.

I happily applied to re-join the ALP Victorian Branch, along with other individuals and the four Victorian unions. I had not changed my view about Communism and intended to continue the struggle against it wherever I could. I was no longer a supporter of Santamaria or the NCC as will be seen from a later chapter. My basic values had not changed.

The four unions were not welcomed back into the Labor Party with open arms. The Victorian Branch of the ALP was dominated at the time by the Socialist Left [SL] faction. While there were individual Branches where the Labor Unity faction was strong and which welcomed our applications for membership, the SL faction was determined to block the re-affiliation of the Unions and keep out 'undesirable' individuals.

My application to re-join was dated 13 February 1984. It took more than a year for this application to be accepted. The Victorian Branch set up a 'Committee of 10' to examine the applications from individuals and summonsed us all to appear and give an account of ourselves. While this inquisition was postponed at least once, the individual applicants for membership eventually fronted the Committee in November 1984 and answered its questions. The main charge was that we were DLP or NCC supporters or members. However, most ALP party activists knew that by this time the NCC itself had split and that many of the industrial supporters of the NCC were no longer associated with it. The added charge therefore was that we were associated with something called the Industrial Action Fund [IAF] which had been created by the industrial activists who had left the NCC.

Some of our number had been members of the now-defunct DLP which was no longer standing candidates against ALP endorsed candidates.[38] Since I had never been a member of the DLP and had only ever been a member of one political party - the ALP - as early as 1974, I thought that I was on solid ground to re-join. However, my earlier membership proved to be more of a hindrance than a help. I also had something of a history and profile having been the centre of a bitter dispute in 1978 when I was appointed to a position at the Victorian Trades Hall Council [VTHC]. In any event, the main charge was that we were all secret NCC or IAF members, both organisations now having been proscribed by the Victorian Branch of the ALP. Members of proscribed organisations could not be members of the ALP.

I cannot recall the specific questions I was asked by the Committee of 10, other than why I had dropped my membership of the ALP in the late 1970s. I answered this question by saying that I was disappointed in the action of many ALP members in actively supporting my dismissal from my job at the Trades Hall in 1978. The Socialist Left faction of the Victorian ALP mounted a considerable campaign to prevent the applicants being able to join or re-join the Party. The material and 'evidence' presented by various members of the faction to the Committee of 10 was quite extensive. Gerry Hand, MHR, put in a detailed statement to the Committee on the NCC and IAF. In this statement, he named me twice [along with several others] as a member of the NCC and the IAF. The source of this information was given as three individuals, including John Grenville, a former Federal Secretary of the FCUA.[39]

Another submission was prepared for the Committee by three other members of the ALP, including Julia Gillard, later to be Prime Minister. This submission focused on the work of the NCC in student politics and in the applicant unions and was supported by many attachments and statements. It had nothing to say about student politics at Monash University in which I had been active but on page 33 it briefly stated that I had been a 'guest speaker at an NCC Youth Camp' in 1975 attended by someone [named] who also attended the camp.[40] I left Monash University at the end of 1972. I do not recall being present at the alleged event nor do I recall knowing the person who made this statement.

All my Clerks Union colleagues who appeared before the Committee of 10 were determined to tell no lies. We had the feeling, however, that some Labor Unity leaders expected that we would 'tell the appropriate lies at the appropriate time.' If so, we had a different conscience. We also knew that whatever we said would have little effect on the result as the vote to accept or reject us would occur on factional lines. This proved to be so. In December 1984, the Committee of 10 agreed to recommend the admittance of six individuals to party membership. Of another 14 applicants, three were rejected by a 5-4 vote and for the remaining 11, including me, the vote was tied four all [two members of the Committee of 10 being absent from some meetings].[41]

In my case, there was a note at the foot of the decision suggesting that I might be encouraged to 'apply again' after the next ALP State Conference. The reason for this, it later transpired, was the fact that I had previously been an ALP member and therefore it was possible that I had been a member of a proscribed organisation [the NCC] at the time that I was an ALP member, contrary to party rules. Apparently, a few members of the Committee had the view that I was 'evasive' when asked about this. Undoubtedly this was true since I had no wish to lie. The suggestion was therefore made that I be asked to re-apply after the next State Conference at which time the Rules of the Party would be changed to require applicants to declare whether they had ever been members of a prescribed organisation.[42] This would have forced me to make a formal declaration on the question and given me little wriggle room.

However, the State Conference was deferred, and nothing happened on this score. Ultimately, our individual circumstances as applicants mattered little. Despite the tied votes and my 'apply again' status, in January 1985 I received a letter from ALP Victorian State Secretary Peter Batchelor saying that the Administrative Committee had determined that my application for membership had been rejected, or at least 'could not be proceeded with.' My $20 membership fees were refunded.[43] The four Unions all duly appealed this decision to the ALP National Executive and in May 1985 Peter Batchelor was obliged to write again advising that the National Executive had granted me, and my 13 colleagues 'provisional membership' of the party dating back to the date of my application for membership in February 1984.[44] The provisional membership was subsequently confirmed as full membership.

Elements of the Socialist Left wanted to defy this decision of the National Executive, but wiser heads prevailed. The April 1985 State Conference agreed to implement the decision to re-admit the four Unions. This led to the re-affiliation of the four unions as well as the admittance of the disputed individuals. I was not asked to attend the first conference at which delegates from the four unions were credentialed. Michael O'Sullivan and Frank Lee were two of the three Clerks Union delegates and ran the gauntlet of the tomato throwing delegates from an extreme left sub-grouping of the SL. This sub-faction later became known at the 'Tomato Left'. Leading the SDA delegation back into the ALP was Jim Maher. In 1955, he had moved the disaffiliation of his Branch of the Union from the ALP because of the Split and was pleased to lead the Branch back in. I think that he was the only person who had both left the ALP in 1955 [or was expelled] and who re-joined in 1984.[45] Jim Maher said that he regretted the Split and its effects and was proud to be able to play a role in healing it.

The four re-affiliated unions had the voting strength to elect one member of the Victorian Branch's powerful Administrative Committee. I was chosen as our candidate and was duly elected at the June 1985 conference. This was an awful experience. It was the worst time to be joining the Administrative Committee. I caucused with Labor Unity then led by Bill Landeryou. The meetings were a nightmare. The Committee met every second Friday night from about 6.30 pm. It was not a great way to spend a Friday night. Numbers were tight and no one was able to leave until the meeting ended. The first four meetings I attended averaged a 12.30 am [Saturday morning!] finish.

The meetings dragged on through interminable adjournments mainly because the Administrative wing of the Party was in dispute with the Cain Labor government which was trying to de-register or otherwise rein in the militant Builders Laborers Federation [BLF], led by pro-Peking Communist Norm Gallagher. The 'oppositional' tendencies of parts of the industrial left of the Victorian ALP which have been noted by Paul Strangio[46] were still evident when I joined the Administrative Committee in 1985, notwithstanding Federal ALP intervention in the Victorian Branch in 1970. This struggle pitted the 'faceless' men and women of the party machine against the ALP Government. The battle of wills between the party's administrative and parliamentary wings was reaching fever pitch when I joined the Committee.

One of the most interesting meetings occurred in July, early in my term. The Administrative Committee met on Friday the 26th July, during the Nunawading by-election campaign. Labor held the seat in Melbourne's eastern suburbs and was hoping to keep it.

The timing of this meeting could not have been worse for me. Our third child had just been born. My wife was still in hospital. I had taken leave from work to mind our other two children and had to ask a neighbour to babysit them for the duration of the meeting. The meeting was important for the future of the State ALP Government and every vote on the Admin Committee counted. To put pressure on the Cain Government, the Socialist Left [SL] faction was threatening to convene a special conference to discuss the Government's moves against the BLF. At the very least this would have been embarrassing for the Government and electorally damaging.

The SL moved for the convening of the special conference during the Administrative Committee meeting and declared that there could be no compromise on the issue. After considerable and unsuccessful discussion to resolve the issue it was decided to adjourn the Committee meeting 'for five minutes' so a discussion could be held with the Premier. John Cain was at an election function in Nunawading and could not speak to representatives of the committee from the venue. At this time, mobile phones did not exist and contact had to be made by a land line. Eventually, we were told, the Premier of Victoria was driven to a nearby phone box for late night negotiations with the Administrative Committee.

If a press photographer had been aware of this, I imagine that the effect could have been similar to the photo of federal leaders Calwell and Whitlam standing outside an ALP Federal Executive meeting in 1963 which led to the use of the electorally-damaging term the 'faceless men' of the party machine.[47] However, no one captured an image of the Victorian Premier being 'leant on' in a phone box in the suburbs of Melbourne.[48] Nor did this conversation resolve the issue. The 'five-minute' adjournment eventually ran from about 10 pm until nearly midnight [by which time I was more concerned about my neighbour than the future of the State government] when the SL blinked and agreed not to proceed with the special conference. They demanded instead that at the next ordinary conference a cross factional committee be set up to work out ways in which the party machine could exert its authority over the parliamentary party. This did not occur.[49]

While my neighbour said nothing when I eventually got home, I knew she would not have been pleased by the lateness of the hour. There was nothing interesting or satisfying for me in ALP administrative and factional politics, then or since. I was pleased to be able to extricate myself from this role in late 1986, early 1987 when I went overseas for an extended period with my family. I happily handed over this role to the SDA's Michael Donovan and never sought it again. I am glad to have re-joined the ALP and been part of ending the historic split. I have remained a party member ever since but have never been enthusiastic about factional activities which seem to be more about personality, power, and pre-selection, than about policy and principle.

When I was on the Administrative Committee in 1985-6, there seemed to be only one other person on the non-left side who was interested in policy rather than pre-selection. This was David Cragg, then an active member of the Labor Unity faction of the ALP and later to be Assistant Secretary of the Victorian Trades Hall Council. This period taught me that my main interest was in the trade union movement and the condition of workers, not in party politics. A properly functioning trade union movement is a vital social institution and is under threat. A properly functional ALP is important to both working people and Australia as a whole.

Unions set up the ALP to win by parliamentary means things which they could not achieve through industrial methods. This is still a vital objective. Both the industrial and the party wings of the labour movement have been gravely damaged by people who have seen the labour movement as a means of achieving personal power and/or financial benefit. These individuals, as well as conservative politicians and self-interested employers and free-market economists, are enemies of the labour movement today. In 1984, I was concerned by the influence of the extreme left on the labour movement and by the continuing repression of workers and citizens in Communist countries. How did I come to this position and how did I find my way into both wings the labour movement, as well as into contact with the NCC and the Industrial Groups?

# 2

# THE MONASH 'SOVIET'

"Every action, in the middle of the twentieth century, presupposes and involves the adoption of an attitude with regard to the Soviet enterprise". Raymond Aron [50]

The exact origins of my strong anti-Communist views are now lost to me. Nowadays, I can say with much more confidence what I am for as well as what I am against. But my initial political awareness was triggered by opposition to Communism. This position emerged during my secondary school years and was confirmed by my experience at university. Over the years, people have come to an anti-communist position in a variety of ways. Some of the strongest anti-communists were once communists or at least very left-wing and it was their experience of communism that drove them passionately into the opposite camp. The intellectual and writer George Orwell was such a person. His experience of Stalinist communism in the Spanish Civil War, where he was fighting for the Republican cause against Franco and in alliance with Communists, opened his eyes to the reality of Leninist and Stalinist communism.[51]

In Australia, there were a number of notable anti-communists who had once been active on the left. The Ironworkers Union's Laurie Short was perhaps the best-known example amongst Australia's union leaders.[52] Victorian Denis [Dinny] Lovegrove was another.[53] Catholics were naturally anti-communist since communism proclaimed atheism. Catholics were thus automatically opposed to communism in a fundamental and irreconcilable way. Many political conservatives claimed to be opposed to communism - since it was anti-capitalist - except when this stance conflicted with the opportunity to make a dollar or two in business by selling something to or manufacturing products in a Communist country. This phenomenon continues today, particularly in relation to doing business in China.

None of the usual categories fitted me. The household I grew up in was not religious. My parents were nominally Christian but practiced no religion. I went to secular government schools for both primary and secondary education. My father considered himself to be Anglican. My mother's nominal religion is unclear but neither of them went to church other than for a wedding or a funeral. I have recently discovered that I was baptised in the Presbyterian Church and this may explain why my sister and I were sent to a local Presbyterian Sunday School when we were young. My sister went to a well-known Baptist girls' school from Grade Five. When I was partway through secondary school, my parents suggested that I should go to a local Uniting Church school, but I successfully resisted it. I sometimes described my religious upbringing as ABC: 'Anything But Catholic'.

Presbyterian Sunday School made little impression on me. Except, that is if you ignore the somewhat odd lesson from a teacher who decided one Sunday morning to prove that life after death could not exist. His teaching method was to plug an electric cord into a wall socket. He turned on the switch and the class all nervously agreed with him that there was life [power] in the cord. He then switched off the power and pulled the cord out from the wall. We now all agreed that there was no longer power [life] in the cord and the implication appeared to be that that was how our bodies would be after death. I doubt that this was orthodox Presbyterian teaching! Of course, I may have missed some other point that he was trying to make but this image has stuck in my mind for 50 years while nothing else from Sunday school has. In any event, religion made little impression on me and my parents offered no resistance when I decided to drop out of Sunday School at the point where we had the opportunity to go on to become adult members of the Church at the age of about 16. I was a Scout [although I did not enjoy most of it] and dropped this as well to join a youth group. There was more resistance to that since my mother had been a highly active Girl Guide leader.

Politics was not a topic of discussion in our home. Dad was a clerical worker in the public sector and not union-minded at all. Mum was at home most of the time I was growing up but at one stage worked part-time in a clerical capacity. Both my parents served in the Australian Army during the Second World War: Mum was in the Women's Army as a soldier and Dad initially joined the 'home defence' militia and then transferred as a soldier to the 2nd AIF. Dad served overseas in an active war zone on Tarakan in Borneo in 1945. I knew that both voted Liberal and had done so all their adult lives. They were anti-labor rather than active Liberals. The ALP was the party of the unions, with which neither of my parents had an affinity. Dad took all the 'how to vote' cards from the party activists at a polling place when he went to vote, except that of the Communists if they were standing a candidate. This attitude may have rubbed off on me, but I doubt it. Politics meant little or nothing to me until late secondary school. We were a lower-middle-class family with limited disposable income. Holidays were rare and the family car was a 1952 FJ Holden until the mid-1960s.

My main interest at school was humanities and history in particular. We did not have a TV until I was in my 'Intermediate' year [1967] at school – when I was about 15. Everybody else at school seemed to have had television since late primary school. I knew little of popular TV shows. We did not even have a proper radio in the house. There was a homemade record player with a radio tuner in it that my uncle had put together many years before. It dated back to before to the Second World War. I had extremely limited access to this radio, but I was able to listen to the Argonauts, a popular radio show for young people, but not much else. The dial on the radio did not move from the two local ABC frequencies. Commercial radio was not favoured in our house. Consequently, I read everything that came to hand: from Enid Blyton to the *Boys Own* magazine to the *Popular Mechanics* magazine. The last-named was a bound collection of back copies given to me by a family friend. I was not interested in mechanics, just in reading! I read everywhere: at the breakfast table, while waiting for the shower to warm up [yes, really] and under the blankets, if a torch was available. I took a book with me everywhere and kept a list of everything I read.

My primary school opened a library when I was in Grade 6, the final year of primary school. Then, I borrowed a book each Monday, returned it on Wednesday, borrowed another to return on Friday and got another for the weekend. My only reading rival at school was a girl who borrowed a book every weekday. Our classmates were presumably watching TV! The suburb we lived in had only one small library accessible to me by bike while I was at primary school. Starting secondary school was wonderful because my new school was in the next municipality and it had a much bigger and better library which I was now eligible to join. Weekly trips there added greatly to the availability of reading material. Regular local fetes and Christmas and birthday presents added to my collection of books.

Somewhere amongst this mass of reading material, I must have read something that showed to me the awful reality of Communism. At this time, the Soviet Union, the eastern European bloc and China were all tightly controlled totalitarian societies. Despite the Cold War raging and the existence of the Berlin Wall, the Soviet, as well as the Chinese, Communist parties and their allies in the West largely managed to maintain the myth that behind the iron and bamboo curtains, worker and peasant paradises existed. This was the era in which Communist writers like Australia's Frank Hardy could write books such as *Journey into the Future* extolling the virtues of Soviet life.[54] This book began with the now infamous quote from American 'fellow traveller' Lincoln Steffens who, after returning from the Soviet Union wrote: 'I have seen the future, and it works!'.

In the 1960s, many of the works of Alexander Solzhenitsyn and other Russian dissidents [which I devoured in the 1970s] had not yet been published in the West. These dissident writers later laid bare the realities of the Soviet regime for a Western audience. Even when I studied Chinese politics at Monash University in the early 1970s, little seemed to be known about the realities of Mao's brutal regime. The so-called 'Great Leap Forward' [1958-61] was largely being treated as a positive event rather than as the humanitarian and economic disaster that it was, partly because independent and reliable information was hard to obtain. Estimates have now put the number of deaths by starvation in this horrific three-year period at 40 million or more. The famine that resulted from these economic policies of Mao was man-made, although this has never been acknowledged by the Chinese Communist Party [CCP], which still talks falsely of three years of 'natural disasters.'[55]

Mao's 'Cultural Revolution' which began in 1966 and in many ways continued until Mao's death in 1976 was little understood when I was at university in the early 1970s. Jung Chang has estimated that as many as 10 million Chinese people died as a result of state-sponsored killings between 1966 and 1976.[56] Jung Chang was part of a later generation of Chinese writers and activists yet to come who would be able to expose the crimes of Mao, his Red Guards, and those of the Chinese Communist Party which still holds all political power in China today.

This information about the realities of life under Communism was not yet known to me in these clear terms in the late 1960s but somewhere I had grasped that there was something wrong about Communism. It had no attraction for me at any stage. A little later I came to detest the saying 'If my son is not a communist at 20, I will disown him; if he is still a Communist at 30, I will disinherit him.'[57] I never saw any value in youthful stupidity and complicity in the subjugation of others. Immaturity is no excuse. I was firmly anti-Communist by my final year at high school, in 1969. I cannot put this down to the influence of any teacher. Some of them were woefully inadequate for their jobs and poorly or completely untrained and none made any lasting impression on me. In Matriculation [as year 12 was then called] I did a subject called Social Studies. I do remember the teacher, who we thought was a former Anglican minister. He was not a conservative and I recall getting a poor mark for an essay I wrote on the Viet Nam war. I imagine that the essay was not a particularly sophisticated effort and in it I supported the South Vietnamese side over the Viet Cong and the Communist North. I do not think the teacher liked my line of argument in the essay which he described as 'propaganda'. In the end-of-year exams, I got a D - the lowest pass - for Social Studies for which I cannot blame the teacher since all our exams were marked externally; that is, not by our teachers at school.

In the 1966 federal election, Australian voters had strongly supported the Coalition Government taking Australia further into the Viet Nam war on the side of the Americans and the non-Communist South. By 1969, opposition to the war was growing, particularly because of the existence of conscription. This issue had entered not only into wider society but even into our school. Some students' mothers were known to be active in or sympathetic to the Save our Sons [SOS] movement and a draft resister was invited to speak to students, somewhat controversially for the time.[58]

Being anti-communist meant being pro-democracy and pro-human rights and it was from this perspective that I drew my political inspiration and guidance, such as it was at that stage. I did develop a limited interest in politics in Year 12. That was the year of the 'Don's party' election held in October 1969.[59] Gough Whitlam was now ALP federal leader and the Viet Nam war was becoming a more significant concern for many Australians. I remember taking a precious night off from studying for Year 12 exams to attend a 'meet the candidates' night at The Avenue Uniting Church in Blackburn. This was wonderful entertainment. It was a public gathering; the hall was packed and the people there were very vocal. The seat [Deakin] was a Liberal one and stayed that way in the 1969 election. I later had a hand in winning this seat for the ALP at the 2007 'WorkChoices' election.

I do not remember who the 1969 candidates were or what they said. I only recall a slightly deranged citizen berating the Liberal candidate with the words: 'Could you imagine Jesus with a rifle or St Paul with a .303?' I presume this was a reference to the war in Viet Nam although it was a little hard to tell. It was great fun. I enjoyed the night though mainly as a spectator. I had no real partisan involvement. I was only 17 and did not expect to be able to vote for another four years.[60] I did not expect to be involved in political events of any sort. This changed when I went to University in 1970.

In year 12, I started to think about what sort of career I might have. Since I was interested in the humanities, reading and writing, I considered journalism. I applied for a reporter cadetship with the Melbourne *Age* newspaper. From my interview, I only remember one question which was which cartoon strip I liked reading. I cannot remember my answer, but it may not have been the correct one as an offer of a cadetship did not eventuate. To put off further career decisions, it seemed best to go to university.

## THE MONASH 'SOVIET' [61]

> *Content warning: Many Australian memoirs containing tales of student life in the 1960s or 1970s are full of drugs, sex and rock and roll, together with extreme political activity that drew the attention of the security services and thus produced an ASIO file. What follows contains none of these elements. Since I did not attract the attention of the security services, I do not have an ASIO file from which to reconstruct these memoirs – a research tool that has proved useful to those on the extreme left in writing their stories.* [62]

I chose to go to Monash University for mainly practical reasons. We lived in the Eastern suburbs of Melbourne and my sister was doing her final year of Science at Monash in 1970 so I had transport to and from the university with her. My year 12 results were just good enough and the right combination of subjects to get me into Arts at Monash. However, they did not get me a Commonwealth Scholarship. As this was before the Whitlam Government abolished university fees, the lack of a scholarship was a problem. Students had to pay upfront tuition fees as well as compulsory 'Union' fees, which paid for certain student facilities [and funded student politics, as it turned out].

My parents very kindly agreed to pay the fees and thus I did first-year University on what was known as a 'Daddyship'. At the end of the year, my marks were good enough to get a Commonwealth Scholarship for the remaining two years. However, in both years, while my fees were paid, I had virtually zero disposable income. In my second and third years, I made a little money driving some other students to and from the campus each day in the Morris Minor my sister had passed onto me. At the time it cost about 80 cents to fill the tank with petrol and I was able to make a small profit. I never had a job at any stage during my university years, even during the long vacations. My first months at university were tough as I knew virtually no one there. My only friend from my 'alma mater' - Box Hill Boys High - who was at Monash was doing computer science and our lunchtimes hardly ever coincided. It was lonely and not particularly enjoyable in these early months despite the status and excitement of being at university.

While my best subject at school and my main interest was history, I decided at Monash that I would do a double major in politics and economics. The choice of politics shows a growing interest in this subject. Economics was supposed to be the 'meal ticket'; that is, the choice which would help in getting a job after university. I choose to do this double major in the Arts Faculty rather than in the separate Faculty of Economics and Politics [ECOPS]. This was possible under the Arts faculty rules at the time [they were changed later] and this strategy had the attraction of being able to avoid doing Economic Statistics in first year which was compulsory for students in the ECOPs Faculty. This was short-sighted since not doing Statistics meant that I had and have little or no grasp of this key element of economics and most serious economics papers mean little to me. In any event, other than macroeconomics which Monash taught in first year, economics did not interest me greatly and I had no desire ultimately to work in this discipline.

Political theory and practice did interest me. Politics in first year was an *Introduction to Democratic Theory* with Professor Herb Feith. I was keen to believe that democracy was a system that worked for all people and all cultures. There were two major challenges to democracy at the time. The extreme left supported communism and the so-called 'dictatorship of the proletariat', rejecting bourgeois democracy as another form of capitalist class rule. The authoritarian right suggested that some peoples and cultures needed authoritarian dictatorships and could not handle democracy. I rejected and still reject both positions. I was also disappointed to find that we spent a lot of time in lectures and tutorial groups considering the views of some Western academics [e.g., C Wright Mills] who claimed that western democracy was a myth and seemingly democratic nations were run by elites [or in the interests of the 'military/industrial complex' or some such thing] and not 'by the people, for the people.'[63]

On one level, it was possible to agree with Winston Churchill that 'democracy was the worst form of government, except for all the rest' but I thought and still think that democracy appeals to and reflects the best in all humanity. I became interested in learning more about Marxism and communism to critique and oppose it. In third year, I even enrolled for a subject called *Revolutionary Theories and Movements* taught by Alistair Davidson, who I believed was then or had been a member of the Communist Party. This was a mistake. I was the only non-left student in the class and the only one not 'with the program.' We spent a lot of time that year considering the work of a relatively obscure Italian Marxist called Antonio Gramsci in whom Davidson was interested. I became concerned towards the end of the year when there was a proposal from the students in the class that the 'bourgeois' system of student assessment by written essays and exams should be scrapped and replaced by a system of student peer assessment; that is, by the 'student collective' that was my tutorial group. I am sure I would have failed this form of assessment. Fortunately, academic conservatism eventually prevailed, and I passed the course by writing one long essay on Gramsci and answering four exam questions.

When I started university in 1970, Monash was relatively new. It had opened its doors only in 1961 and grew slowly. By the end of the 1960s, it had a reputation as a radical university, due largely to the activities of Albert Langer and the Monash Labor Club. In 1970, Albert Langer was not a Monash student. He had been a student in previous years, and he was trying to return to do post-graduate studies. The university was trying to avoid this happening and this matter became one of the issues of the year. I understand that the Labor Club was originally established as an ALP aligned club but had since been taken over by supporters of the Maoist aligned Communist Party of Australia - Marxist-Leninist [CPA M-L], led by Albert Langer himself, his wife Kerry Miller, Michael Hyde and the late Jim Bacon [later ALP Premier of Tasmania].[64] It is beyond my purpose to detail the history of the Labor Club. Others have done so.[65] Suffice to say that in 1970 the Labor Club had no affiliation with the ALP and the political situation at Monash was polarised between the extreme left and just about everyone else.

It is completely inaccurate to describe student politics at Monash as a 'Soviet' since the dominant political force was Maoist. 'Soviets' were the name given by Lenin's Bolsheviks in Russia to the worker councils through which they sought to control industrial and other enterprises in Russia. 'All Power to the Soviets' was their slogan. After the 1917 revolution, Russia was renamed the Union of Soviet Socialist Republics – the USSR – but the worker soviets quickly lost all power to the central organs of the State which were controlled by the Communist Party. Maoist communism was a more agrarian form of communism but equally controlled by the highest levels of the Communist party. The Labor Club leaders would have liked student politics to be more of a peasant/worker/student collective on the Maoist model. However, there were few peasants at Monash [despite its nickname "The Farm'] and the sons and daughters of graziers [who largely went to Melbourne University] did not qualify. The Maoists did create a 'Worker/Student Alliance' in 1970 but only one Monash worker was ever identified as a member.

Labor Club activists dominated the scene in the late 1960s, although there was active opposition from the anti-communist right. In the 1970s, rivals to the Labor Club also appeared on the left, claiming to be 'New Left' but often associated with other Communist parties, notably the more mainstream Communist Party of Australia [CPA]. The CPA was drifting away from the Soviet Union in the wake of the suppression by the Soviets of the 'Prague Spring' in Czechoslovakia in 1968. The pro-Soviet Socialist Party of Australia also existed but was not a force on campuses being mainly an industrial communist party based in the unions, especially the Building Workers Industrial Union [BWIU]. The Maoists were strong in the Builders Labourers Federation [BLF] as well as active on campuses.

In 1970, student politics was done differently at Monash. It was run not as a representative democracy – that is via an elected Students Representative Council [SRC], as at other universities – but by 'mass meetings' of students. The traditional SRC had been replaced in the late 1960s by the Monash Association of Students [MAS]. This development could be viewed in either of two ways:

- as a radical direct participatory democracy on the classical 'Athenian' model in which all students participated equally, or

- as a means by which the left activists could control the outcomes simply by being the ones prepared to outlast all the others at the 'mass' meetings until they had the numbers to pass their resolutions.

In practice, it operated largely in the second manner. Mass student meetings were held at lunchtime but tended to drag on. For those students not 100% involved in student politics, and whose courses had high numbers of contact hours, the prospect of sitting on the lawn between the Union building and the 'Ming Wing' [66] all afternoon discussing the latest developments in Upper Volta was not attractive and they went back to their lecture and tutorial rooms at 2.15 pm. Arts faculty students with fewer contact hours and the ability to cram at the end of the semester were more likely to stay as did the almost professional and hard-core activists from the left. The left was active, organised, and prepared to speak up and to try to see off any opponents.

The main issue at Monash in 1970 and the following years was the Viet Nam War, then at its height. Every other issue seemed to hang off this one. Australian soldiers were still heavily engaged in Viet Nam and remained so until the Whitlam Government was elected at the end of 1972. A Liberal Government had introduced conscription for army service in 1964. Young men were required to register for 'the draft' [national service] as they turned 20 which was the age of most second- or third- year university students.

The system worked this way:

> Under the National Service Scheme, twenty-year-old men were required to register with the Department of Labour and National Service (DLNS), they were then subject to a ballot which, if their birth date was drawn, meant the possibility of two years of continuous full-time service in the regular army, followed by three years part-time service in the Army Reserve. As part of their duty, national servicemen on full-time duty were liable for 'special overseas service' including combat duties in Vietnam.
>
> As the number of men eligible for call-up far exceeded the number needed for military service, the bi-annual ballot determined who would be considered for national service. The ballot resembled a lottery draw, even to the extent, in the case of the final five ballots, of being fully televised. Numbered marbles representing birthdates were chosen randomly from a barrel and within a month men whose numbers had been drawn were advised by the DLNS of whether they were required for participation in the scheme or not. Those failing

> to register without an acceptable explanation were automatically considered for call-up as well as being liable to a fine...
>
> Men who failed to comply, who misled the medical board and who made false and misleading statements were liable to prosecution and if convicted were sentenced to prison for a period equivalent to that which would have been spent on national service. Fourteen men were thus prosecuted, until 1968 they were incarcerated in military prisons. Later, they served their time in civilian gaols.
>
> Between 1964 and December 1972 when the Whitlam Government suspended the scheme, 804,286 twenty-year-olds registered for national service, 63,735 national servicemen served in the Army and 15,381 served in Vietnam. Between 1966 and 1971 Australian infantry battalions were typically comprised of an even mix of regular soldiers and national servicemen. Some 200 national servicemen lost their lives in Vietnam.[67]

When my turn came, I registered for national service and was watching the televised ballot when my birthday marble was drawn. An official letter later summonsed me to attend a medical examination in the army recruiting centre in Flinders Lane in Melbourne. Sometime later, I was told that I had not passed the medical test [and would not be called up] and that if I wanted to know more, I should consult my GP. I never did. Nothing has turned up in my health status since that was likely to have caused me to fail the test on medical grounds. Perhaps the army had enough or fitter candidates than me. In any event, any call up to active service may well have been academic as most university students were granted deferments until they finished their studies, which in my case was the end of 1972 when the Whitlam Government came to power, abolished conscription and withdrew Australian forces from Viet Nam. Incidentally, my school friend who was at Monash did not register for national service. He was active in the draft resistance movement at Monash but was not, to my knowledge, known publicly as a draft resister. During my second and third years at Monash, I drove him to and from university every day in my car. I knew his birth date and that he had not registered for the ballot. That was his decision, of course, and I respected it. We remained friends throughout our time at Monash despite some tense times and remain so today.

The existence of national service was almost enough on its own to guarantee a permanent student majority against the Viet Nam war and conscription.[68]

Opposition to the war had been growing for some time in the West.

Australian university students were aware of protests against the war in the US some of which had resulted in the deaths of students [e.g. at Kent State University in May 1970]. Anti-war and peace sentiments were strong and growing. The ALP, led by Gough Whitlam, opposed the war. In May 1970, the largest anti-war protest took place in Australia in Melbourne. An estimated 100,000 protesters in Melbourne's Bourke Street were led by left-wing ALP Parliamentarian Dr. Jim Cairns. Many of the marchers were university students.

The Monash Labor Club was not anti-war, nor did it support peace, in my opinion. It supported a Communist victory in the war. This is not just my view but a fact [and attested to by key members in what they said then and later]. Monash became known not for its anti-war sentiment but for its willingness to support victory by the Viet Cong [or National Liberation Front] and North Vietnamese forces. The student body at Monash had been persuaded by the Maoist Labor Club to donate money to the Viet Cong/NLF, which were portrayed as freedom fighters representing the people of South Viet Nam rather than as agents of the communist North. This became an official policy of the Monash Association of Students.[69]

This had occurred as early as 1967, well before I went to Monash. Initially, funds were raised for medical aid to the Viet Cong/NLF, but subsequently, funds were raised as 'unspecified support' for these forces against whom the Australian armed forces were in active combat.[70] The implication was that these funds could be used to purchase arms and ammunition with which to fire on Australian soldiers. This decision was widely attacked in the media and led the Government to introduce the Defence Forces Protection Act 1967, one justification for which was the actions taken by Monash students led by the Labor Club.

Senator John Gorton [later Prime Minister] in introducing the Bill in the Senate said:

> *Recently, however, we have seen a new development. The Labor Club at Monash University announced that funds would be collected for despatch to the so-called National Liberation Front in South Vietnam. Some of the funds collected, it was announced, were to be collected for use by the enemy in unspecified ways...*
>
> *Thus some Australians have attempted to go beyond exercising their right to criticise the Government's actions, and to persuade the Government and the nation to alter its attitude, and now seek to act by raising funds, in Australia, to be sent to assist the enemy against whom our Australian troops are presently engaged in combat.*[71]

That the Viet Cong/NLF was not independent of the North Vietnamese regime was confirmed by Mark Aarons in his family history, *The History File*. Speaking of his father, Laurie Aarons, who became General Secretary of the CPA in 1965, Aarons junior writes:

> In March 1965, Laurie met with a senior official of the South Vietnamese National Liberation Front (NLF) in Prague. Notionally an 'independent' force, the NLF was in fact directed by the North Vietnamese.[72]

Money was both collected for the Viet Cong and successfully delivered. In his memoirs, Michael Hyde describes how this money was passed on during a visit to Cambodia.[73] The sum donated in this way at this time was a relatively modest $500 [not insignificant then] and was handed directly to representatives of the NLF in Phnom Peng. The Labor Club was aiding not only forces fighting Australians but taking an active and partisan stand, supporting one side in the conflict, not peace.

The Labor Club did not support the ALP's position on the war. The ALP's opposition was led by future Deputy Leader Jim Cairns. Many Monash Maoists hated him with a passion: they called him 'Jimmy Jesus' – supposedly a powerful insult – and attacked the ALP for its bourgeois and therefore not radical enough position on the war. The ALP was diverting anti-war sentiment away from its revolutionary purposes, or so their line went. The Labor Club felt threatened by others getting involved in – and leading – a campaign the Labor Club wanted to run itself. Supporting a genuine and just peace is a legitimate position. Supporting the forces against which Australian soldiers were fighting and at whose hands they were dying, in my view at least, was completely wrong.

While the South Vietnamese regime was a long, long way from being democratic, the North Vietnamese regime was a totalitarian Stalinist regime. In my opinion, there was no virtue in either supporting victory for the Communist forces in Viet Nam or a unilateral withdrawal by the West which would abandon the South Vietnamese people to a Stalinist fate. The mass exodus of people from South Viet Nam after the fall of Saigon later confirmed my opinion as did [in April 1975] images of Soviet-supplied North Vietnamese tanks attacking the city rather than it being taken by Viet Cong units. Since I was anti-communist and pro-democratic, I was appalled by student politics at Monash and looked for a way to get involved and to fight against the totalitarian forces I saw arrayed there.

## MONASH DEMOCRATS, a.k.a. THE DLP CLUB

The search for a group at Monash which was opposed to the Labor Club did not take long. There was only one such group. The Monash Labor Club [as noted above] was in the hands of Communists, moderate ALP supporters having left it, and a later ALP Supporters Club had not yet been re-formed. There may have been a Liberal or Young Liberals club, but if so, it was well known for being a social club that had no interest in and no impact on student politics. The only group that was taking the fight up to the left at Monash was the Monash DLP Club, also known as the Monash Democrats or the Democratic Labour Club. The DLP Club had a presence on campus and a voice. The club published a weekly flyer known as *Free Speech*, cutely taking its name from the left-wing Free Speech Movement at the University of California at Berkeley in the United States.

*Free Speech* had been created and first published in 1966 by John Bailey, a mature aged student studying at Monash. *Free Speech* Vol 1, No. 1 was published on 12$^{th}$ July 1966. It was typeset, properly laid out and printed on good quality paper. According to Bailey, it was established because the then editor of *Lot's Wife*, the Monash student newspaper, refused to publish a reply to published criticism of an earlier article of Bailey's on the question of the Spanish Civil War. It seems remarkable now that in 1966 that there would still be a debate about this issue from the 1930s, which was the political issue of an earlier generation. Students in the 1960s had other concerns.

By 1970, *Free Speech* was interested in the issues of the day and offered an alternative to the views of the Labor Club expressed in their weekly publication known as *Print* when I was at Monash.[74] The DLP Club also had activists prepared to get up at student meetings and argue against the proposals of the Labor Club. I sought them out, attended one of their meetings and volunteered to be Club Secretary – at my first meeting. It was not hard to get a guernsey in this way – activists were thin on the ground. After I volunteered to be Secretary, I recall being asked my name. Someone else wondered at the wisdom of electing someone as Secretary whose name was not previously known. But I got the job, there being no other interested party!

Those who understand something of the history of the DLP itself may be surprised by the type of person who was a member of the Monash DLP Club at the time. There may have been some Catholics who were members, but I am struggling now to think of any. The members were certainly not sons or daughters of typical DLP members. Rather, they were like me: secular, agnostic, anti-communist. Members were from all political backgrounds other than Communists: Liberals and Labor alike and non-aligned or independent.[75] After student politics, the Club's members ended up in a variety of political parties, or none. We had one thing in common: opposition to the dominant left at Monash and a willingness to have a go at opposing it.

The socio-economic background of the members of the Democrats was generally lower middle class and even working-class [although there were not many students from working-class backgrounds who could afford to go to university at the time unless they could get a studentship from the Education Department or some form of cadetship]. I think it is fair to say that the students on the pro-communist left much more frequently came from well off backgrounds.[76] We had to endure their taunts as 'running dogs of the capitalists' as they feigned an alignment with the working class while living off mummy's and daddy's money. I expect that they were purging their upper-middle-class guilt at our expense.

Prominent among the Monash Democrats at the time I joined was Mark LaPirow, with whom I was to become good friends. Mark had an Australian mother who had married an American. He had been raised in the USA and spoke with an American accent. This added to the left's infuriation with him. Mark was very willing to speak at mass meetings and put a lot of time and effort into written publications and activism. He became very well known on campus and, surprisingly, in a left-wing environment, managed, at least once, to top the poll for election to the Public Affairs Committee of the MAS, much to the frustration of the left. In my view, Mark could have gone on to a career in Australian politics but chose the law instead after university. His university image was enhanced by the fact that he rode a motorbike which did not impress everyone, including my parents when he arrived at our place. You could be forgiven for thinking that Mark had modelled his image of 'The Fonz' from the American sitcom *Happy Days* except that the show did not begin its run until 1974. Mark should have sued the producers for stealing his image.

Student politics at Monash operated in three or four ways. The student association funded the production of a newspaper – *Lot's Wife* – which covered student and wider social issues. The editor or editors were paid and effectively worked full-time on the production of the paper. The content of the paper was generally left-wing as might be expected but it did publish letters and occasionally articles critical of left-wing positions.

## 'POWER GROWS OUT OF THE BARREL OF A GESTETNER' [77]

*Free Speech's* form of publication had been widely imitated by other political groups later in the 1960s. The Labor Club had initially created *Left Hook*, which later changed its name to *Print*. Considerable effort went into the production of these broadsheets [foolscap size] and their distribution to students. I later became Publications Officer for the Democrats and was responsible for a while for getting *Free Speech* out each week. The University administration later also decided that it needed a broadsheet to communicate with students. They called it *Sound*, which it may or may not have been.

While Monash had abolished its Student Representative Council [SRC] before I arrived, there were a variety of student-elected committees of importance. These included the ostensibly non-political Administrative Committee [AE] the job of which was to administer the Students' Association. There was a three-person Editorial Committee advising the editors of *Lot's Wife*. There were student representatives on a range of university bodies and collectively these were known as the Committee of Representatives [or COR]. The most obviously political body was the 15-member Public Affairs Committee [PAC] whose charter was specifically to adopt positions on the political issues of the day. Lastly, there were at Monash general meetings of all students that had the final say on issues if enough students could be persuaded to attend meetings. These were open-air meetings held at lunchtime in the space between the Union building and the 'Ming Wing' or upstairs in the Union building, depending on weather conditions.

Student activists had to play a role in all these bodies and the Monash Democrats were the only organised anti-communist group looking to oppose the Labor Club in all these forums. The left also had another vehicle for student [and wider] political activities: 'direct action' – which meant both demonstrations and direct confrontation with government authorities. The issues of the day were, of course, the Viet Nam War, the closely related issue of conscription, apartheid in South Africa [particularly because of the Springboks rugby tour of Australia in 1971] and – at Monash – disciplinary measures taken by the university in response to direct action taken by Labor Club activists.

In July 1970, the left at Monash tried a 'new' tactic to provoke dissent: they decided on a physical occupation of the Monash University Careers and Appointments Office, allegedly in response to its recruitment of students to work for Viet Nam war contractor Honeywell. I say a 'new' tactic, but it was far from new. It was an imitation of overseas student protests, both in the USA and in France in 1968. Michael Hyde, one of the leaders of the Labor Club in 1970, had been trained in activism in the USA:

> *Having spent 1964-1966 living in the United States during the famous student revolt at Berkeley, California, Hyde had been trained in student activism through his involvement with the Students for a Democratic Society (SDS) and various other civil rights groups at Pasadena City College.*[78]

There is little doubt in my mind now [or then] that the tactics of occupation were designed to provoke a reaction from the university authorities to supply further opportunities for escalation of the protests. The Monash Democrats said this at the time in the pages of *Free Speech*. The July Monash Careers & Appointment office occupation lasted about three days. It would have a big impact on my future working life although I played no part in it. The occupation eventually led to several students who had been identified at the end of the protest being charged with breaches of university discipline. They were eventually expelled or suspended.

*Student protesters occupying the Administration building at Monash University. Image used with permission, David Taft, Monash University Archives, Image IN7102.*

The expulsions and suspensions issue dragged on for most of the second half of 1970 and into early 1971. A second occupation occurred later in the year, as did efforts to intimidate the University Council into rescinding the disciplinary measures [an action that was at least partially successful]. Much nonsense was written about this by both the left and by some sections of the right, by the Liberal party and the media all seeking political gain of one sort or another. The occupations were not endorsed by mass meetings of students in advance or later. Rather, the students repudiated them. The university authorities did not handle the protests well. I am sure that the Vice-Chancellor Louis [later Sir Louis] Matheson thought he was a 'small l' liberal university administrator. Unfortunately for him and others like him, appeals to liberal values or attempts to manage in this way had no success. The extreme left opposition neither shared these values nor wanted to work in this 'bourgeois' framework. They wanted confrontation and for the university to be forced into taking a hard line so that the sympathies and support of the general student population could be aroused and then mobilised into further action.

In early 1971, the disciplinary charges appeals process was drawing to an end over the summer 'long vacation'. [The charges were eventually dropped in the New Year by the Vice-Chancellor]. A letter from a Reverend Hyde – the father of Michael – about the penalties imposed on the occupying students appeared in the Melbourne *Age*. I thought it got the facts of the situation completely wrong and sat down at home to pen a reply. Mark LaPirow turned up at my home while I was drafting this letter and he beefed it up. He is responsible for the "Maoist Mystagogue" tag applied to Michael Hyde, but the letter was otherwise mine and it was subsequently published in *The Age*.[79] It read:

> Other ways to show dissent
>
> Sir, Although I don't have the credibility rating of a Methodist Minister, I do have something that the Reverend Hyde [12/1] doesn't: a knowledge of the facts concerning the Monash occupation.
>
> Mr Hyde claims that "no violence was done to anyone". In truth, in the inaugural occupation of 1970 in the careers and appointments office [at which the Maoist Mystagogue Michael Hyde was charged], a 60 year old staff member was kicked and injured in the leg, the injury required medical treatment and took several weeks to heal. Other minor incidents occurred and damage,

including thefts, was hardly minimal.

The claim that "the seven were obviously preselected victims" is not borne out by the facts. The occupation started on Tuesday June 30th, but not until 3 pm Thursday July 2nd, was the office placed out of bounds. At 3.45 the same day officials entered and directed the occupiers to leave; none of the twenty then present left. At 4.30 a group left quickly, concealing their faces.

At 7.30 eight students still present disclosed their names and another student was identified. Two other people were identified from photographs taken at the time; one discontinued studies at Monash and the other was not a student. These students selected themselves for discipline by being in the office at the only time when a positive identification was possible.

Occupation is not the only way dissenting students can express opposition. Anyone who is familiar with Monash knows of the eternal [and infernal] rallies, student meetings and broadsheets which constantly disseminate their propaganda, as well as the more formal channels including direct representation on the University Council.

What I as a student object to, and what other students object to, is a group of self-appointed Messiahs dictating what other students may see and hear. This is what the question of Monash is about.

Actions such as these have no place in the university and neither have the people who perpetrate them.

KEITH HARVEY (Blackburn)

My version and understanding of these events and the charges relating to the occupation of the Careers and Appointments Office appear to have been confirmed by Michael Hyde's recent 'memoir' *All Along the Watchtower*. This book, unlike the earlier *It is Right to Rebel*, appears to confirm that a small number of students remained at the end of the occupation to effectively make themselves the only ones who could be identified and charged. [80]

## THE NATIONAL CIVIC COUNCIL

I was pleased that my letter was published. It had an unexpected effect. The letter was noticed in the offices of the National Civic Council [NCC] which took an interest in student politics. While the membership of the Monash Democrats was in no way typical of what might have been expected, the NCC had some contacts with students at Monash. Up until this point, I had no understanding of, or connection with, the NCC or the DLP, nor any family or other association with either organisation. But, from this time on, because of this letter, I became involved with the work of the NCC in student politics and later in the trade union movement.

The Monash DLP Club was completely self-governing. When I joined it, I knew nothing of its history. History did not matter at the time. What mattered was the fight. Allies were to be welcomed. It appears that the Monash DLP Club, which, despite the name, was not affiliated with the DLP, may have been started by John Bailey, whom I have never met. Gerard Henderson in his biography of B. A. Santamaria says that in 1965 he [Henderson] joined the Melbourne University DLP Club and through that met John Bailey 'a mature age student at Monash University.'[81]

Bailey at this time ran weekly meetings of students from both Melbourne and Monash University which were attended, according to Henderson, by Santamaria so it is likely that Bailey had had a key role in establishing the Monash DLP Club. Nothing resembling these meetings was occurring to my knowledge in 1970, but I came to be in contact with other students with similar views at other universities and with the NCC and, eventually, with B. A. Santamaria himself. I think it is fair to say that such students were part of a loose network known as '*Peace with Freedom*' and I became part of it. Nonetheless, the Monash DLP Club remained an independent force and was quite different from other similar student groups due to the eclectic, self-starting and independent nature of its membership. We ran our own show at Monash and did all our own work on campus with no outside help of any significance, other than as mentioned below. Having joined the Monash Democrats and become Secretary in 1970, I became fully involved in its work in 1971 and 1972, my last two years at the university. Apart from anything else, this changed my social life since I now had many friends and much to do.

In the first week of university in 1971 – Orientation or 'O' week – Mark La Pirow and I were manning the Democrats stall in the Union building. All the various Clubs and Societies set up stands to attract new members. We were approached by a prospective member, a female first-year student from the country. She and I married in 1975. Thus, the Monash Democrats [or perhaps, more correctly, the activities of the Labor Club!] were responsible for both my later personal and working life. It was through this new personal relationship that I became aware of Catholicism and I met many Catholics through my new 'significant other'. This led to me becoming for the first time seriously interested in religion and directly to my reception into the Catholic Church in January 1975. So perhaps I should thank the Democrats and the Labor Club for this as well. God works in mysterious ways...

Speaking at student general meetings was not my strong point. Others were much better and much more courageous than I was. Speaking at mass meetings of students in opposition to positions taken by the left was not for the faint-hearted. I had a chance to develop my debating skills later in an almost equally difficult environment, the weekly meetings of the Victorian Trades Hall Council. In 1971, after the discipline issue died somewhat, the issue of the Springboks tour became a prime issue [while Viet Nam was ever-present]. The Democrats took the position that banning sporting tours was not an effective way to end apartheid. I now think we were completely wrong about this, and the isolation of South Africa from sporting and other contacts was an important tool in forcing the hands of the whites-only government to negotiate with Nelson Mandela and the ANC.

However, we saw it differently at the time. As Democrats' Secretary, I wrote to Mrs. Helen Suzman, at the time the only anti-apartheid MP in the South African parliament. She was an extraordinary woman in her own right. In his autobiography, *Long Walk to Freedom*, Nelson Mandela talks of meeting Mrs. Suzman in jail on Robben Island in 1967:

> Then Major Kellerman appeared to say that Mrs. Helen Suzman, the only member of the liberal Progressive Party in Parliament and the lone parliamentary voice of true opposition to the nationalists, would be arriving shortly. In less than fifteen minutes, Mrs. Suzman – all five feet two inches of her – came through the door of our corridor ... Mrs. Suzman was one of the few [parliamentarians] if not the only, member of Parliament who took an interest in the plight of political prisoners...She was the first and only woman ever to grace our cells. [82,83]

PARLIAMENT OF THE REPUBLIC OF SOUTH AFRICA

HOUSE OF ASSEMBLY,
CAPE TOWN.

14th May 1971.

Mr. Keith Harvey,
Monash University Democratic Labour Club,
c/o Union,
Monash University,
CLAYTON, AUSTRALIA.

Dear Mr. Harvey,

        I have received your letter and I must at once say that I really am not prepared to advise people in other countries about their methods of attacking apartheid. It is very difficult for me to judge whether the basic intentions are to institute reform inside South Africa, engage in a punitive expedition in South Africa, or dissociate, in this case, Australia from South Africa's racial policies in order to improve relations with your Asian neighbours.

        I can only assure you that of course my Party is completely against apartheid, indeed I spend my entire life fighting this system and trying to persuade White South Africans to accept changes which will result in a just society which rejects race discrimination.

        It is my firm belief that such changes must in fact be initiated inside South Africa in order to be of any lasting value. It is to these ends that the Progressive Party members devote themselves. So far, unfortunately, without a great deal of success. There is, nevertheless, a growing number of people, particularly young people, who support our views, and it would be wrong indeed for people outside South Africa to assume that there is not a considerable body of enlightened white opinion in this country.

        Yours sincerely,

Helen Suzman, M.P.

P.S. I enclose herewith one of our Party pamphlets.

*Letter to me from Mrs. Helen Suzman, anti-apartheid MP in the South African parliament.*

Surprisingly, Helen Suzman replied to me. In her letter dated 14th May 1971, which I still have, she suggested that changes 'must be initiated inside South Africa in order to be of any lasting value.'[84] Perhaps she, as well as us, was wrong about that, but this was the position that I advocated at a general meeting of students held later in the year to discuss the Springboks boycott. My only recollection of the meeting was that after I and a fellow Democrats member put our position, we were called 'fascist racist bastards' by, as I recall, a black student. It is never pleasant to be called a racist by someone of another skin colour and I later wrote to *Lot's Wife* which published my letter setting out my view on South Africa in detail.

In this letter, I described apartheid as the 'most inhumane social order ever devised' and said that the only question was how to end it. I said that to be of any lasting effect any solution would have to come from within South Africa, presumably reflecting what Helen Suzman had written to me. I described myself as a person of 'conservative politics' which is presumably how I saw myself at the time. However, I also said that if the white South Africans did not agree to political change then the black population had the right to overthrow the apartheid regime by force, likening the situation to a time of war and the efforts of the French resistance to Nazi rule. Ultimately, not a very conservative position to take.[85]

In my second or third year at Monash, I also joined the local Abschol committee. Abschol was the Aboriginal Affairs Committee of the National Union of Students [NUS] and was originally intended to help young indigenous Australians to attend university. It had wider interests as well. I recall attending a small anti-apartheid demonstration outside the offices of South African Airways during my time on the Abschol committee at Monash.

### 'FREE SPEECH'

I took over the role of Publications Officer for the Democrats midway through 1971 replacing Mark La Pirow who had handled this work for some time. The principal job of the Publications Officer was the production of *Free Speech* each week. This job involved a significant amount of time. It was necessary to decide each week what to write about, then to write the material and finally to produce the publication. I thought I could write well enough, but I could not touch type [unlike Mark] so I enlisted the help of another club member.

Tuesday or Wednesday night was spent typing the stencils which would be used to produce copies on Thursday morning in the Union building. There was no photocopying available to Clubs in those days and the method of production was to use an electric typewriter to cut a stencil to use on a Gestetner brand duplicator [that is, a mimeograph machine]. If typing mistakes were made, corrections were made with a liquid like nail polish, and the relevant part of the stencil was carefully re-typed. The stencil was then placed on the Gestetner duplicating machine, which was then inked up and the machine's handle was turned by hand to run off the required number of copies. This was done in two stages [front and back] to produce a double-sided Foolscap-size 'broadsheet.' These were then handed out by club members as students entered the Union building at lunchtime and in other ways distributed around the campus.

*Print*, the Labor Club organ, was produced off-campus in the basement of *The Bakery*, rented premises occupied by Labor Club members in Greville Street, Prahran. They also used a Gestetner duplicating machine, [86] but one they exclusively had access to, while we used one in the Union building, available to all Clubs and Societies. It was often alleged that *Free Speech* was written and produced with external aid, i.e., by the DLP or the NCC. This was not true – every word was written by us and every turn of the Gestetner handle done by a Club member on campus. It was also alleged that there was external aid because *Free Speech* had a printed letterhead similar in appearance to mastheads used by similar groups at Melbourne and La Trobe University. This much is true. Stocks of paper with the printed masthead were supplied to us: I assume by the NCC. But everything else was all our own work – and a lot of work at that.

My first *Free Speech* was Vol 6 No 17. The look and the layout were an improvement [thanks to my typist] but I cannot say that the content was particularly brilliant or insightful. My first edition dealt with a student occupation that had occurred at La Trobe University. This action provoked the attendance of police, something the Monash Labor Club had been seeking to do without success. Re-reading copies of *Free Speech*,[87] I am surprised by the moderate and relatively sober tone of all the writing, given that students produced it. There is a degree of sarcasm and weak puns and generally unfunny humour [mainly written by me] but, overall, we strove to maintain serious fact-based arguments about the issues of the day.

In the first edition of *Free Speech* for 1972 produced to introduce and attract new students to the Club, I set out the general policy positions of the Democrats.[88] These included:

- academic freedom and upholding rational debate and the free and peaceful expression of ideas – something not always the norm at

Monash at the time

- support for democratic and responsible government and opposition to revolution "for the hell of it" and in the name of totalitarianism
- aboriginal land rights and recognition that the views of aboriginal Australians should be paramount in deciding policies that affect them
- abolition of the White Australia policy [which still existed in certain aspects at the time] and greater involvement in South East Asia
- Student government to be run in the interests of the welfare of students and not as a "perpetual political campaign".

Although I did not mention it in this issue, the Monash Democrats had since 1969 been opposed to conscription for war service, at least in the form and in the circumstances in which it had been implemented by the Liberal Party but agreed that Governments might legitimately use such a power in some circumstances. Our 1972 policy statement did not specifically address the issue of the use and misuse of student funds for political purposes. This was an on-going concern for us, and I wrote extensively about it in the very next edition. In *Free Speech* Vol 7, No. 2, I drew a distinction between compulsory trade unionism – which we supported – and compulsory student unionism, which we did not. Trade unionism played an important role in improving the welfare of workers, but we could see no connection between student unionism and the general welfare of students.

These positions were developed at a time when university education was not free – the Whitlam Government was yet to be elected – and students had to pay both course fees and a compulsory student 'union' fee which was, in those days, a significant sum of money – about $250 from memory. This was a difficult sum for many students to find. Some of the 'union fee' went to maintain the facilities in the 'union building' which included dining rooms, cafes and some assistance to Clubs and Societies and other facilities, e.g., the John Medley library and general spaces to 'hang out'. However, significant funds were also passed on by the Union Board, which managed the Union building and its facilities, to the student association. This funded the activities of MAS, including the production of the student newspaper, *Lot's Wife*, and political activities. Given that the student newspaper and the political activities favoured only the vocal [and extreme] left, we felt that there was little or no reason to support them with our [or our parents'] hard-earned money.

In the MAS Public Affairs Committee [PAC] elections in 1971, the Democrats had done well. Our ticket of two, Mark La Pirow and Grant Stinear, [later, the best man at my wedding] were both elected. Mark topped the poll. The Democrats ticket polled 20% of the vote and Mark's first place should have meant that he became Chair of PAC, but the Left, who collectively had a majority, were not having any of that. In 1971, Mark also managed to get elected to the three-person Publications Committee which was designed to oversee the production of *Lot's Wife*. Mark and Grant were in largely hostile territory at PAC, with Albert Langer [now back at Monash as a student] and Jim Bacon both elected from the Labor Club ticket.[89] By this stage, the Labor Club had its rivals on the left. Mark Taft and Mike White were elected from a 'New Left' ticket. Mark Taft was then a member of the Communist Party of Australia – very old left really, but the CPA was trying to distance itself from the Soviet Union, recently responsible for crushing the 'Prague Spring' in Czechoslovakia.[90] Linda Rubenstein [standing on a Women's Liberation ticket but also CPA aligned] was also elected.[91]

In a sign of the struggle amongst the left-wing groups for appeal to students, the New Left's pitch to voters included the claim that 'New Left means – in Monash terms – that we find the politics of Albert Langer, in some aspects, only a shade better than those of Mark La Pirow.'[92] The New Left claimed to reject 'dogmatism and authoritarianism'. This claim to find Langer not much better than Mark La Pirow was not borne out in practice. The presence of two articulate and committed Democrats members on the PAC was going to be a thorn in the side of all extreme left groups at PAC meetings, so much so that there was an immediate move to try and take decisions without either Mark or Grant being present.

At the first meeting of the 1971-elected PAC, a majority resolved to support a motion proposed by Labor Club members Langer and Bacon that 'a resolution signed by at least 10 members of the PAC shall become a resolution of PAC' thereby avoiding the need for either Mark or Grant to see resolutions before they were made, and more importantly, acted upon. Thus, student funds could be spent without the knowledge of at least two [and possibly as many as five] PAC members. *Free Speech* reported at the time that MAS Treasurer Clive Porritt had said that 'The intention behind the motion is quite clear, it is to keep Grant and Mark from attending.'[93] This statement is also recorded in Paul Francis Perry's history of student politics at Monash.[94] The Labor Club also proposed that PAC initiate a series of forums on issues of interest to students, 'to be chaired in turn by all members except M La Pirow and G Stincar'.[95] As George Orwell wrote ironically in another context, 'All animals are equal, but some animals are more equal than others'.[96]

The Democrats had ongoing concerns about the use of funds by the left at Monash via the MAS. This new resolution to spend student monies without all elected student representatives being aware of decisions added to our concerns. Perry noted that the Monash University Act stated that monies could only be spent 'for the purposes of the University,' this term being undefined. Perry also wrote that Vice-Chancellor Matheson 'had never tried to stop student funds, and incurred the wrath of the DLP club by referring to the $500 given to the MAS 'Discipline Committee' (Hyde, Hadden and Kerry Langer) (that is, to be controlled by Labor Club activists) as 'an internal MAS matter', and the hundreds of dollars spent on [Viet Nam] Moratorium leaflets for High School students as "dissent on paper" and therefore legitimate.'[97] The then Chairman of the MAS Administrative Committee, Tom May, ruled that the PAC endorsed motion to dis-enfranchise the Democrats members was within the framework of MAS. The Democrats did not agree and announced that we would take legal advice and 'if necessary take more drastic action'.[98] This we did the following year.

## THE 1972 WRIT

In 1972, the Democrats decided to act. Mark La Pirow and I launched legal action against the University in the Supreme Court of Victoria. I was not legally an adult at the time being not yet 21 and thus legally only 'an infant.' As a result, I had to act through my 'next friend' Brian Ridge, a Ph.D. student in linguistics who was a member of the Democrats and over 21 years of age. Our writ was directed to certain key officers of the University, including the Vice-Chancellor, Louis Matheson and others and the University itself. It sought a declaration from the Court that the MAS was not a students' representative council for the purposes of the Monash University Act and therefore that the payment of monies by the University to the MAS was invalid and not within the lawful purposes of the University.

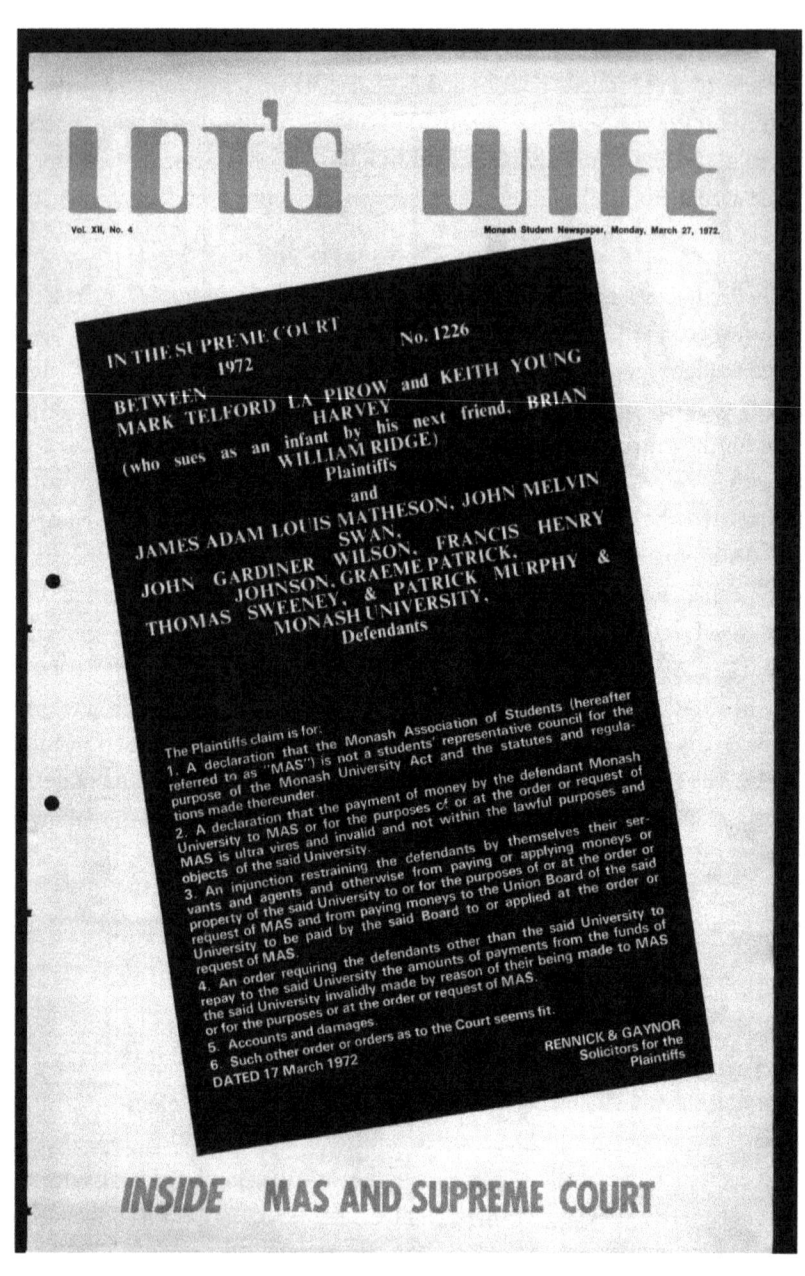

*Front Cover of Lot's Wife, Vol. XXII, No. 4, March 1972.*

*Image used under licence granted by Mark Taft, one of the editors of Lot's Wife in 1972.*

Our action sought to distinguish between funding which may be of benefit to students, that is, for the running of the Union and its facilities and those solely relating to the running of the student association. I am not sure whose idea it was to take this action initially, but I assume that it was part of a wider plan [since a similar action was taken concerning La Trobe University] and it was obvious that we needed assistance and funding to undertake this action. Our solicitors were Rennick and Gaynor, well known as the solicitors of the DLP and certain DLP-affiliated Unions, including the Federated Clerks Union. We met with our solicitor in the city offices of Rennick and Gaynor. Mark and I had the job of serving the writ on Louis Matheson. At the time, the Vice-Chancellor lived in an official residence on campus. My recollection is that we knocked on his door one Friday night at about dinner time and served him with a copy of our writ when he answered the door. I do not remember what he said to us, but I think he was more than polite.[99]

The response from the student association was swift. *Lot's Wife* [edited by Phillip Herrington and Mark Taft that year] promptly reproduced a copy of our writ on the front page of its next issue, March 27th, 1972. The same issue reported that a mass meeting of students had condemned our action. I recall that Mark LaPirow attended the meeting to defend our actions, but I did not. The outcome was as follows, according to *Lot's Wife*:

> An MAS meeting of over 1,000 students overwhelmingly passed the following motions last Thursday:
>
> 1. That this student general meeting strongly condemns Mr. La Pirow and other Monash Democratic Club members for their legalistic attack on M.A.S. and for their attempt to deny students control over their own funds, and especially for the undemocratic way in which they have carried out this attack behind our backs with no attempt at consultation with any section of the student body.
>
> 2. That this student general meeting demands that the writs be immediately withdrawn and that M.A.S. facilities be made freely available to students opposed to the writs to carry on this struggle. Further, should the writs not be withdrawn by Tuesday, 28th March, that an M.A.S. meeting be held on that day to determine further action.
>
> 3. That this student general meeting requests that M.A.S. immediately arrange stockpiling of paper supplies, money, etc., in order to have normal M.A.S. facilities available during the struggle against any injunction. The Union,

> Clubs and Societies and the Sports and Recreation Association are asked to cooperate in the supervision of any funds and facilities removed from the University accounting system on behalf of M.A.S.
>
> 4. That, in the light of the fact that our previous motion to give $500 in cash to LaTrobe SRC. has been frustrated by the Monash Administration's refusal to counter-sign the cheque, this student general meeting instructs the A.E. to organize a forum on the topic: "The growing repression in Australia (especially the present D.L.P. attacks on the Universities)", to which it will invite five (5) LaTrobe speakers (representatives of the LaTrobe S.R.C. and the expelled students) at a fee of $ 100 a speaker each.[100]

In other words, the resolution sought action by the MAS to move funds out of control of the University accounting system and authorities to get around any negative effects of the writ. The University, which determined to defend the writ if it went to trial, objected to any attempts by the student association to remove funds from proper university control understanding, in all likelihood, that this would have weakened their position in Court if this had been allowed to happen. The writ was not withdrawn by us, but neither was any further action taken. A check of the archived Supreme Court file shows that the file consists of only a couple of pages: our original writ [as reproduced on the front page of *Lot's Wife*] and a Notice of Appearance filed by the University's solicitors. Nothing further happened in the Court. The MAS was not amused by our failure to withdraw the writs. In April, *Lot's Wife* was pleased to announce our demise [a little prematurely]:

LAPIROW FALLS

At a general meeting on Tuesday April 11 the following motions were passed:

That this student general meeting, while affirming the right of Messrs. La Pirow and Harvey to criticize and try to reform M.A.S, declares that they have been guilty of a gross misperformance of duty by their recent treacherous and dishonest attacks on M.A.S. behind the backs of the students and by their refusal to abide by decisions of M.A.S. general meetings in accordance with the M.A.S. Constitution.

That this student general meeting dismisses Messrs. La Pirow and Harvey from all positions they hold under the M.A.S Constitution.

> That this student general meeting adjourn so that a brief sit-in can be held in the University Offices, to discuss with the Vice-Chancellor La Pirow & Harvey's participation in M.A.S.[101]

I do not recall that I held any elected positions at the time [I may have been on an Arts Faculty Board committee] nor do I recall any consequences arising from any discussion with the Vice-Chancellor that may or may not have happened in the course of any sit-in in the University Offices. Again, the University was unlikely to take discriminatory action against us with the possibility of legal action still present. Mark LaPirow, on the other hand, was a member of PAC, having topped the poll in 1971. I do not recall if MAS attempted to strip him of this position, but in any case, he was not prevented from re-nominating in 1972, and he was elected again with the third-highest number of votes. Evidently, a significant portion of the student body was not unhappy with him or our actions. Through the mists of time and memory, I cannot say for sure if our action had any lasting effect or produced any significant change in the funding or the operation of the student association. However, it put all parties on notice that they had to be careful how student funds were expended and accounted for if they did not want to risk the legal action being brought on for hearing and judgment.

### FUN AND GAMES, OR POSSIBLY NOT...

For the most part, student politics was carried out with considerable purpose by all parties who took themselves and the issues they supported seriously. None of us could be accused of insincerity or lack of effort. Our academic marks generally suffered because of our activity, although I do like the suggestion that a university education is what you remember when you have forgotten everything you were taught. In this respect, I had a great education at university, although my marks were mediocre. I also remember shocking a very serious student friend by suggesting that if you got 51% in an exam, you had worked too hard. As far as I was concerned at the time, 'Ps' [for passes] got degrees.

We did manage to have some fun along the way. In Volume 6, No 20 of *Free Speech*, I was able to announce that the Monash Democrats had come third in the annual billy cart race [part of 'Farm Week' activities] until we had been disqualified for a broken axle – but that we had been the first political club across the line. I suspect that the Labor Club was not a starter. On the other hand, there was a less pleasant and at times violent undercurrent at work. Two issues later I reported two assaults on club members:

> *If you can't beat them, beat them.*
>
> *Over the past three days, two assaults have been made upon members of this club. Coupled with the threat of Albert Langer's, [sic] to punch Mark La Pirow, the situation in this university is fast becoming intolerable. When you are no longer able to walk around the university in safety, this is a criminal state of affairs, that must not be allowed to continue. The assaults have been reported to the Administration and an announcement that no action will be taken is expected soon.*
>
> *We suppose that if the fascist left can't beat us on logical and rational grounds, then it is "natural" that they will fall back on this method of attack.* [102]

I do not recall now which two of our members were subject to these assaults, but this was not made up. One of them may have been an incident at a PAC meeting at which Mark La Pirow's sunglasses were broken during an attack on him.[103] In a separate matter, the threat from Albert Langer was real enough and set down by Langer himself in a letter to *Lot's Wife*. He threatened in writing to punch Mark if he [Mark] continued "to tell lies about him".

> *In view of this and of the DLP's constant crying of "wolf" about left-wing "intimidation" and "violence" directed against them. I wish to publicly announce something for Mr. La Pirow's benefit:*
>
> *The next time you publish a deliberate lie about me or anyone else in Free Speech, I will personally punch your face in. Since according to your publications it happens all the time I am sure nobody will be surprised or alarmed.* [104]

*Free Speech* also reported efforts by the left to disrupt the formation of a small club known as the Alliance for the Defence of Academic Freedom [ADAF]. The ADAF was formed by Les Goldschlager [later a Professor at Monash]. It was not associated with the Democrats but shared some values, including the core value of academic freedom and the right to free and rational discussion on campus, without the threat of violence or disruption. Elements of the left sought to disrupt meetings of the Alliance, thereby proving the need for it to exist.

In July 1972, things got less than pleasant for me because of the 'siege' of the

Union building done in the name of draft resistance. This event was planned and advertised for some time in advance and the attendance of several known draft resisters was widely advertised to try to entice a raid on the university by the Federal police so that we could all get suitably enraged about the presence of 'cops on campus'. The police wisely stayed away, apparently amusing themselves and exciting the student pickets at the entrances to the university by driving past from time to time. On the first day of the so-called siege, I recall sitting in one of the dining rooms at the rear of the Union building when a member of the 'occupying forces' came into the room and started rolling away one of the round dining tables to use as a barricade somewhere. Confronted by a staff member who asked this person [who may not have been a Monash student] what he was doing, the besieger simply looked up and replied, 'What about Viet Nam?' as if this justified any and every action that might be taken.

Later, walking through the main part of the Union building with a group of friends, I noticed another 'besieger' chaining chairs and tables into the stairwell linking the ground and first floors. We did not recognise him as a Monash student, and we were annoyed by the gall of him to barricade the building – breaking all the OHS rules that you could imagine – as if he owned the place. He was using bolt cutters to cut the metal chain he was using to create his obstacle to the entry or exit of anyone. While this interloper's back was turned, the bolt cutters were 'liberated', to use a term favoured by the left at the time. The left was furious. Apparently, some acts of resistance are less equal than others. Someone subsequently alleged that I was the culprit behind this outrage, and I became the focus of a good deal of anger although I refused to confirm or deny that I had had any part in the action. I was still driving my draft resister friend to and from University each day and this event did cause a little tension between us. He eventually publicly absolved me of responsibility in the Monash draft resisters broadsheet, known politely as *FTD*.[105]

Before this happened, one afternoon, on my way out of the Union building on my way home, I found myself surrounded by a largish group of Labor Club members and supporters of the siege demanding an admission of guilt and the return of the bolt cutters. I stood my ground in the face of this intimidation, but I did not enjoy the experience. After some time, I was rescued by an employee of the Union – Doug Ellis I think – and allowed to go on my way but this small incident removed much of the enjoyment of university life for the rest of the year, my last.

The issue of the bolt cutters was eventually 'resolved' by one club member [not me] telling a member of the left that if they went to the nearby Oakleigh police station, they might find some bolt cutters which had been handed in as lost property. This someone did and was duly given a pair of bolt cutters. Such was the end of my university experience. Not so much with either a bang or a whimper but with a slightly sour taste in the mouth. I am not certain that a university education is what you remember after you forget all you have learned, but what I did at university, the views I formed, and especially the people I met, changed the direction of my life in all its key aspects. It was now time to consider what would come next.

*Graduation Day 1973, with my parents.*

# 3

# ROPE AND CORDAGE DAYS

*'The capitalists will sell us the rope with which we hang them.'*
*Variously attributed to Marx, Lenin and Stalin, possibly erroneously.*

As the 1972 university year drew to a close and final results loomed, I now had to consider again what my future work options might be. I had postponed thinking about this by doing a degree, but a humble Arts degree did not lead directly to any particular job. Many Arts students went on to obtain a teaching qualification, but I had no interest in teaching. Looking back at my results, I am surprised to find that over the three years, my best subject was Economics, in which I managed a Credit in two out of the three years. In the subjects in which I professed some interest, that is, history and politics, I only earned Passes. I had learned quickly how to write an essay that earned a pass mark but nothing more: 'Ps get degrees.' My results were not going to get me an offer to do Honours. My only pathway was to leave university and get a job. I applied for one or two administrative positions; from memory, one of them was with the Country Roads Board, doing what I cannot recall. I was not successful.

Since I was active in student politics – and remained staunchly anti-communist – and had attended a number of meetings of student activists run by the NCC, continuing this type of activism in the trade union movement was a possibility. The struggle between left and right was still in full flight in the unions. Previously, I had not thought of working in the trade union movement, but I now knew that the NCC was also active in this field. The people I had met who were associated with the NCC through my activism in student politics were, by and large, impressive. They were decent people, with good values and committed to living out those values in the real world at some cost to themselves and their families. I shared many of their values, although at this stage I still was not religious let alone a Catholic. I was interested in continuing to be part of the struggle against communism. Since communism was strongest in Australia within the union movement, I decided that this might be a worthwhile area in which to work.

I arranged a meeting with Michael O'Sullivan, who at that time was coordinating the Victorian industrial [trade union] work for the NCC. Michael O'Sullivan was based in the NCC Victorian State Office in Elizabeth Street in central Melbourne, above a motorbike shop. The offices were basic. Michael was intelligent, friendly and very committed to his work. He was an honorary [unpaid] office holder in the Federated Clerks Union but his paid job at that time was overseeing the NCC's work in the union movement in Victoria. Michael asked if I might be interested in working for a small industrial union: the Victorian Branch of the Australian Rope and Cordage Workers Union. I considered this suggestion for a while and decided to give it a go.

Although it was not fully appreciated by me at the time, working in the trade union movement was going to be quite different from student politics at Monash, where we functioned autonomously. The NCC's work in the trade union movement was structured and organised. Activists were part of a disciplined group and acted in concert. The basic structure was democratic. Groups of activists met and decided what was to be done in each situation. Once the group had made a decision, everyone worked to carry it out. Being part of a collective that worked in a disciplined and effective manner suited me. In my case, since I was in a group of one in the Rope and Cordage Union, decisions about what I did were simply made jointly by Michael O'Sullivan and me. Michael presumably reported to others in the NCC, to John Maynes, the NCC's national manager of union work and ultimately to B. A. Santamaria.

There was another aspect to this work that should be mentioned. NCC-aligned activists did not advertise their association. This was a hangover from the environment in which activists found themselves in the post ALP split era. Being identified as NCC was considered to be an obstacle to successful work, although it must have been perfectly obvious to most people in the union movement where people lined up politically. I would have preferred a more open approach. There was, I discovered, an element of secrecy in the work of the NCC [and on the left as well]. Some of this was normal while some seemed to me to be excessive. Meetings of NCC activists began and ended with a prayer – completely in keeping with the spiritual nature of the vocation that most people in the organisation had.

These meetings also involved an acceptance of the need for confidentiality. Members agreed that they would not reveal to others the decisions that were made. This was not necessarily inappropriate: no political organisation wants its members to leak critical information to rival bodies. Company directors are required by law to keep to themselves confidential information gained in the course of business and to only act in the best interests of the corporation and its stakeholders [subject to always acting within the law, of course]. The Tolpuddle Martyrs were transported to Australia not for forming a union [which was legal at the time] but for swearing an oath of secrecy, which was designed to stop leaks of information to hostile employers and government authorities.[106]

NCC members and supporters were asked to maintain confidentiality even if they ceased to be associated with the organisation later. This notion appears to me to have been observed by few who left the NCC as a result of a falling out with another person in the organisation. Rather, many who left felt the need to tell all and make life difficult for their former colleagues. I never understood why they would do this. However, the acceptance of confidentiality had only moral force to back it up. It was otherwise completely unenforceable and had no legal meaning.

It was interesting to read later in ALP Senator John Button's memoirs that when he and others formed the group that became known as the 'Participants' seeking to reform the Victorian Branch of the ALP in the mid-1960s, that they also adopted a policy of strict secrecy and confidentiality. They knew that if their activities were exposed that the hard left then controlling the Victorian ALP Executive would seek to expel them.[107] Jim Beggs, a waterside worker and member of the Participants, makes the same point in his autobiography and notes that several ALP members were expelled from the Victorian Branch of the Party 'for making a statement about the lack of democracy in the Party.'[108]

In the NCC, confidentiality and security of communications was considered especially important, presumably because there had been breaches in the past which had caused difficulties. Letters between offices of the NCC were often cut in half vertically and mailed in separate envelopes. While my student activism at Monash was certainly discoverable by anyone who bothered to look, I followed the practice of not advertising any relationship with the NCC and attempted to 'fly under the radar', so to speak. In retrospect, this strategy was always going to have a short shelf life.

From time to time there is controversy as to whether someone is or was a 'member of the NCC'. Some documents purporting to be NCC membership records have been produced and published. However, in my experience, there was no *membership* of the NCC as such – and certainly not in my case. I never applied to join the organisation, nor paid any membership dues. I could honestly say if necessary [though it did not come up at this time] that I was not a *member*, but from what I have written above it is clear that by this time I was an NCC supporter and activist. There was probably a card with my name on it in the NCC files indicating that I was an 'M1', that is a fully-fledged Movement activist. I had not been a member of the DLP, although I had been a member of a club a Monash which was sometimes called the 'DLP Club' although it had no connection whatsoever with the DLP political party.

### WORKING FOR THE UNION

Although I did not know it at the time, the previous Secretary of the Rope and Cordage Union – Herbert J. Stackpoole – had been an anti-communist activist since the time of the ALP split in the 1950s. He had been Secretary of the Union for many years. Newspaper archives show that Stackpoole was elected to the position of Union Secretary in late 1937 and had begun his first term of office in January 1938 – about 35 years prior to my involvement. He had been an ALP Councillor in Williamstown for many years and Secretary of the Williamstown ALP Branch. Stackpoole was undoubtedly a genuine and committed ALP member and like many others found himself ousted from the Party because of the Split. He later stood as an ALP [Anti-Communist] Party candidate for parliament and although he was unsuccessful, he kept his union position for a further 18 years. Under his early leadership, the Union was active, but his best days were well behind him by the early 1970s.

Although I never met him, it would appear that he had gone a little senile or paranoid in the job. When I started working in the Union's office in the Horticultural Hall [in Victoria Street, opposite the Trades Hall] I was surprised to find that all the windows had been nailed shut. The Horticultural Hall's caretaker told me that the door to the office was always locked as Stackpoole thought he was going to be attacked. Members were not welcome to visit.

The NCC had a connection with the Rope and Cordage Union via Terry Sullivan, then the Assistant Federal Secretary of the Federated Clerks Union who was acting as the unpaid industrial adviser for the Rope and Cordage Union. Stackpoole had recently left the Union, although he did not go easily. Some of the members of the Union had organised to get him out of office since he was not servicing or visiting the members and the Union was crumbling. Not long after I started, the Union received a notice from the Industrial Registrar of an intention to deregister the Union. When the Union appeared before the Registrar to contest this decision, the Registrar said: 'I appear to have resurrected a dead body!' The Textile Workers Union had also made inroads into the Union's membership with a view to taking it over. The Rope and Cordage Union was not in great shape.

Terry Sullivan had worked with the group of rank-and-file members in the industry to help them to ease Stackpoole out. Stackpoole had now left, taking with him, by agreement, the union car. The new group now held all the elected positions on the Branch Executive Committee, but none of them wanted to be Secretary. They were willing to employ someone to do the work. There was no money for another car. Terry Sullivan put it to the Committee that I be engaged. He took me along to meet the Executive members in what was effectively a job interview. An amazing job interview since no one asked me any questions at all! They just accepted Terry's suggestion that I be employed, and I was.

In December 1972 I began work, as an ALP Government was being elected in Canberra after 23 years on the Opposition Benches. My parents did not think much of my job, although they did not say anything particularly negative. I was fast becoming the nonconformist of the family [worse was to come for them]. A cousin with whom I was close told me directly that he thought that this position 'was not much of a job' and he was right on the face of it. It was not the world's best paying job and had few apparent prospects. He did not understand my motivation.

I was employed as the Administrative Officer of the Victorian Branch of the Union since I was not able to stand for elected office at the time. I was the only employee. The office consisted of two rooms at the front of the Horticultural Hall in Victoria Street. The office was decrepit. There was no real desk. I sat at a round table on which was an old typewriter. The only other office equipment was an ancient copying machine which I never succeeded in getting to function. I later bought a Gestetner duplicating machine, a technology I was familiar with from my student days and I was able to put to work some of the skills that I had learned at university producing membership bulletins. There were about 800 members of the Union and there was some money in the bank since many members were still paying their membership dues by payroll deduction.

Horticultural Hall, Victoria Street, Melbourne. The Rope and Cordage Union office is on the left, behind the tree. Photo: K. Harvey

The rope and cordage industry had a long history in Australia and was particularly strong in Victoria. Sailing ships used a significant amount of rope but there were many other types of and uses for rope in other industries, including agriculture. There were two main centres of union membership in Melbourne: Kinnears Ropes in Footscray and Millers Ropes in Brunswick. Millers Ropes was known as a stronghold of the Melbourne Football Club. Ron Barassi's first job was at Millers. Barassi's mother was found a job there by the Club after Ron's father [a Melbourne player] was killed during the Second World War. Norm Smith also worked there. Frank 'Pop' Vine, an ex-Melbourne player, worked as a manager at Millers and was able to arrange jobs for Melbourne players.

Kinnears Ropes had taken over Donaghy's Ropes in West Geelong. Local people had not forgiven Melbourne-based Kinnears for buying the business, but it was still managed by a member of the Donaghy family, Michael Donaghy. These factories fascinated me. They were very old businesses in many respects although some new products and processes were being introduced, for example, polypropylene extruded baling yarn to replace the natural fibre yarns. The most interesting part of the factory, especially at Kinnears in Footscray and Donaghy's in Geelong, was the 'ropewalk'. This ran for about 500 meters and ropes were made by a 'traveller' running on rails for the length of the ropewalk and back again to draw out a rope that could be a kilometre or more long, as required. Downs and Son was a small manufacturer in Brunswick and Melbourne Rope Works operated a newer factory in Thomastown. Millers also had a small plant in Warragul, Gippsland, a model factory in its time set in a picturesque location on the outskirts of the rural town next to the golf course.

*Aerial photo of Donaghy's Rope Works in Pakington Street, West Geelong. Note the ropewalk running behind neighbouring houses. [Image copyright free]*

*Employee making rope with ropeway at Miller Rope, Brunswick, Victoria, 1962. Picture by Wolfgang Sievers [1913-2007]. Photo source: used with permission of the National Library of Australia. PIC WS 3148-M LOC PIC Album 1032/81.*

My starting wage at the Union was $90 per week, which I thought was reasonable at the time, although since this was my first job, I had little to compare it with. The finances of the Union were managed via a chequebook. There were three signatories and each month at the Committee meeting they would sign blank cheques in advance. I would later complete the details as needed to pay the Union's bills. This was not the best financial practice, but it worked well enough. None of the Committee members had any idea about administration or financial controls and neither did I at first. For example, I had no idea that income tax should be deducted from my pay before I paid it to myself each month. My father pointed this out to me quickly. Soon I learned to work out what tax needed to be paid on the income, deduct this amount from my wage and pay a monthly visit to the post office to buy 'tax stamps' with a union cheque to the value of the income tax. I then licked the back of these tax stamps and stuck them into a tax payments book which was mailed to the Tax Office at the end of the financial year. All very Dickensian in 1972-3.

I had no relevant training at all before beginning work for the Union. It was a near-vertical learning curve, and not just regarding office management. Michael O'Sullivan suggested that I buy a copy of the Federal Award that applied in the Rope and Cordage industry before I started work and read it. I did this, but it was not much help. Terry Sullivan was extremely helpful on a day-to-day basis for industrial assistance and I learned much from him. Terry was a quiet man and one of the unassuming achievers of the trade union movement, a veteran of the split in the ALP in Richmond. I was later to work with Terry in the Federal Office of the Clerks Union.

Over time, I came to know the members of the Union Committee very well. They were decent and genuine people; authentic working-class people with no pretensions or ego and a strong commitment to doing the right thing by their fellow workers. The President of the Union was Bob Betts, a tow motor operator at Millers Ropes in Brunswick. Bob and his wife Jean had made the move to the eastern suburbs and lived not far from where I did in Blackburn South. Maud Burns, with whom I became good friends, worked at Kinnears Ropes in Footscray as a machine operator and lived in a Housing Commission house in nearby Braybrook. We still have some baby clothes that Maud Burns knitted for our children. Edna Davies and Bonnie Turner also worked at Kinnears. As Committee members, Bob, Maud and Edna were the key people in the union. Also important were the shop stewards, especially those at Donaghy's Ropes in Geelong which was a well organised and relatively militant workplace. I have no idea what the Committee initially thought of this eastern suburbs middle-class kid – not yet 21 – they had employed to look after the interests of working-class employees in the northern and western suburbs of Melbourne and in Geelong.

By the early 1970s, these Executive members were no longer typical of the Union's membership which was then largely composed of migrant workers from Europe, mainly Italy, Greece and Yugoslavia. But they all accepted me, and I did my absolute best for them with our limited resources. We developed a great rapport. No one asked me why I wanted to work for the Rope and Cordage Union. Once, a long time after I had started, Bob Betts said to me in the pub [the Dover] 'I know what you are doing, working for us.' 'Really', I replied, 'what's that?' 'You are using us as a steppingstone to get experience to get a better job in the union movement elsewhere, later.' I was happy that this was what he thought although it was not correct. I worked hard for the union and its members and gave them 100% loyal service. There was no practical difference between the views of the Branch's elected officials and mine; later they were all happy to vote with the anti-communist, moderate ALP forces at the weekly meetings of the Trades Hall and in the bi-annual elections. They were all moderate Labor supporters interested in unionism for unionism's sake and had no other political agenda. None were ALP members to my knowledge. But they were all 100% union. While I had some other political interests, these did not get in the way of my work for the union.

*Rope and Cordage Executive Christmas Dinner, Smackas Place, North Melbourne, circa 1978. Paul Meade who succeeded me in this job is standing next to Maud Burns at the head of the table. Bob Betts is closest to the camera on the left, with his wife Jean sitting next to him. Next to her is Bonnie Turner from Kinnears. Opposite Bonnie is Edna Davies. Next to me is Paul Meade's wife. The other couple is Len Aisbett, Kinnears Personnel Officer at the time and his wife.*

For many months in my new job, I was like a fish out of water trying to survive in an alien environment. I had no experience of unionism and I was learning on the go, fumbling my way through. How on earth did I know what to think about any of the issues that arose? What was a working-class response? A traditional union view? Did I know how to go about resolving issues? I did not. I just had to start somewhere and see what happened. Slowly, I grew into the job, but it was a long time before I felt comfortable in the role. I can remember the first day [but not the date] when a particular industrial issue arose and I realised that I not only knew what to do about it, but also that I could do what was necessary with confidence. It came as quite a revelation at the time. But it took a while. However, a little dedication, honesty in my approach to my work, and mutual respect went a long way. I think that the Executive of the union came to respect me and became as loyal to me as I was to them. It was a good and genuine relationship that I hope served both parties well.

My first task was to arrest the decline in the Union and restore confidence in it. While most members had gone on paying their membership dues, some had not. Other unions had nibbled away at our membership. We no longer had members outside of Victoria; the few remaining workers in the industry in NSW having been signed up by the Textile Workers Union. Although the Rope and Cordage Union had industry-wide rules coverage, storemen and packers, cleaners and some others had been enticed away into occupation-based unions. The Textile Union had rules coverage of some of the carpet related parts of the rope business and had used this as a base to pick up some of our members who had understandably become disaffected during the final Stackpoole years.

Getting around the factories to re-establish contact with members and former members was my priority. In the larger factories, this was not difficult. In those days, most workers ate their mid-shift meals in the factory canteen. I set up a regular program of visits and, for example, at Kinnears in Footscray, Maud Burns would walk with me from table to table at lunchtime introducing me and asking employees [nearly all were members] if there were any issues that they needed addressing. There was a backlog of issues, naturally enough, but this process enabled me to get on top of them over time. In Melbourne, the employees were interested in their rights and their pay and conditions but were not militant. The employers were willing to deal with most matters by negotiation and were not confrontational. Neither was I.

The non-metropolitan factories were more challenging. Donaghy's ropes in Geelong saw itself as an active, militant workplace with a strong membership. The union's members were prepared to go on strike and did so on several occasions. When I visited, meetings were held in a large room at the rear of the factory and members were very vocal and prepared to tell me exactly what they thought of the union. But again, over time, a good relationship was established. Michael Donaghy, the Manager, had a good relationship with all his workers [he knew most if not all of them by name] and was prepared to resolve legitimate issues. We had active delegates there over the years. Ken Hunt was one of them and I stayed at his house once or twice when we had meetings of the night shift. Warragul was a smaller factory. It had been a model, purpose-built factory, advanced in design when it was built. The delegate was Jim Hunt. He was the one most doubtful about me at the beginning, but after a couple of meetings he said: 'You'll be all right'. Later, he and several others from Warragul were committed enough to drive down to Melbourne for monthly general meetings of the Union which were held in the evening.

One of the first issues I had at Warragul was an underpayment claim. It was a small workforce, but they all gathered for morning tea each day and one of the women workers was allowed time off from her other duties in the morning to bake scones for morning tea. These were enjoyed – with jam and cream - by all, including the Manager. However, the woman's husband also worked in the factory and he had read the award. It provided for a higher rate of pay for a 'Cook – Working Alone' and was a tradespersons rate [while most of the other work was semi-skilled]. Moreover, the Rope and Cordage Award had a 'higher duties' clause which provided that if a worker did any higher classified work on any day he or she was entitled to be paid at the higher rate for the whole shift! The woman's husband had figured this out and wanted me to take the claim up with the company, which I did. The manager looked at me and said: 'these are going to be the most expensive scones ever made.' I calculated a year's back pay [which was the maximum retrospectivity allowed for federal awards] but the member's husband wanted six years back pay which was the State Act provision. She did not get it and shortly afterwards no one was getting any scones, either. We had killed the morning tea goose.

James Miller's Rope Factory, Warragul, Vic.

*Millers Rope Factory, Warragul. [Image copyright free].*

Melbourne Rope Works was a challenge as well. The members there were unhappy that they had been paying their dues for a long time without seeing anyone from the Union, so they had all stopped their union fee deductions from pay. And they were not re-starting them just because I had shown up and promised to do better. Most of them re-joined the Union but insisted on paying me in cash each month in person when I visited. Consequently, I made the journey out to Thomastown on Melbourne's northern outskirts each month on a Friday, which was payday, timing my arrival to be there just after the wages had been handed out. We did not have a shop steward and the members were not stupid – they knew that I would turn up each month and listen to their concerns if they insisted on paying me in person. While collecting the cash, I wrote receipts and discussed the issues of the day in all corners of the factory.

The industry operated under a single Federal award: The Rope, Cordage, Thread, etc Industry Award, 1971. The Award had been kept up to date by Terry Sullivan although the rates of pay were low, and some rates were at times below the federal minimum wage [which applied in their place]. Earnings of employees were supplemented by shift earnings [for those workers on afternoon and night shifts] and by overtime. They could also be boosted by the operation of a bonus or incentive system which provided additional pay for beating output standards. Few workers understood how this system worked but the larger employers were wedded to it. I set out to understand the system and the time and motion study theories and practices that underpinned it.

Until writing these memoirs, I was unaware that my father, after he was de-mobilised from the Army after the war, had applied for a job in the time and motion department at Millers Ropes in Brunswick. He got an interview, but not the job. Even though award rates of pay were low, take-home earnings could be significant. I thought I was paid fairly but very often when I added up the earnings of workers including bonuses, I found that they well exceeded my modest pay. Working conditions in the industry were not good. It was all noisy factory work and while those who worked there seemed to be able to converse with one another without difficulty, I could not hear anything when the machinery was running. This made talking to workers exceedingly difficult. And it led to serious hearing loss for many workers.

Machinery at Donaghy's Ropes, Geelong. I walked past these spindles many times. [Photo used with permission].

My first appearance in the then Conciliation and Arbitration Commission was before Conciliation Commissioner John Gough early in 1973. Terry Sullivan helped me in early hearings, but I was able to do this alone before long since matters were largely agreed with employers. The employers were generally willing to flow into the rope and cordage industry award any improved conditions applying in other industries. There were regular variations to the award reflecting the outcome of national test cases on minimum wages and other terms and conditions of employment. The federal tribunal had little effective dispute settling power at the time and none in respect to unfair dismissals, so the Union did not use it for these purposes. However, I enjoyed appearing in the Commission and it gave me familiarity with advocacy at an early age.

Annually, the two unions party to the Award [the Rope and Cordage Union and the Textile Union] drew up a log of claims seeking improvements in wages and conditions. This was a frustrating process. My union was the dominant industry union in terms of members, but the Textile Union had more staff and resources. Its officials had no idea of, or interest in, properly co-ordinating negotiations. They would talk against our claims in front of the employers and refuse to caucus properly or behave in a disciplined manner. They often seemed more interested in adjourning to the pub as soon as possible and drinking away the afternoon.

## THE VICTORIAN TRADES HALL

Sometime in 1973, Michael O'Sullivan came to the Union's office in the Horticultural Hall for the first time. He took one look at the office and suggested that I move to better premises. I went to see Ken Stone, the Secretary of the Victorian Trades Hall Council and landlord of the Trades Hall. Ken Stone organised a suitable office: Room P in the old building on the first floor overlooking Victoria Street [and my old office]. This was one big room but made a reasonable office. Starting with the purchase of a decent, but second-hand, desk, I set about buying some proper office furniture and equipment. I also bought a new-fangled device – a Vocafone tape driven answering machine – to take phone messages for me while I was out and about. Gough Whitlam was reportedly an early adopter of this technology as well.

One of my first political tasks was to get the union re-affiliated to and attending the weekly meetings of the Victorian Trades Hall Council [VTHC] which met every Thursday night from 7.30 – 9.30 pm. The VTHC had been bitterly divided in the period 1967-73. Twenty-six 'rebel' left-wing unions had withheld funding from the Council. Their aim was to try and force more left-wing representation on the Council Executive and staff which was then well entrenched in the hands of the moderate ALP right led by Ken Stone. My first night as a delegate from the Rope and Cordage Union to the VTHC in 1973 was the night that this split was healed with the Council endorsing a deal that would lead to the rebel unions becoming financial again. This was good for the union movement and the Council's finances, but it also meant a new era of contest between left and right for control of the union movement in Victoria. The VTHC had a critical seat on the Australian Council of Trade Unions [ACTU] Executive which was then delicately balanced between left and right.

After moving into the Trades Hall, I became more involved in union politics there and developed contacts with moderate unions. These unions supported Ken Stone at the Trades Hall over the left-wing unions and Gough Whitlam rather than Jim Cairns in the ALP. Gradually, I became part of the Stone group of unions. None of them appeared to be aware of my student politics past or express any interest in my political affiliations. During this time, I concentrated on getting on top of my union job. I was effectively the Union's organiser as well as Secretary, although I was only an employee, not an elected official. But there was time to do other things. Early in 1973, Michael O'Sullivan had asked me to produce an *Industrial News Digest* to circulate amongst like-minded union officials in contact with the NCC. This involved me phoning up contacts in other unions, trying to get friendly but naturally reticent union officials to let me know what was going on in their sectors so this 'intelligence' could be shared with others. I produced this digest regularly for at least two years.

## NEWSWEEKLY AND SANTAMARIA

At about the same time, I was asked to join the Editorial Board of *Newsweekly*, the official publication of the NCC. This was extra-curricular work. There was a weekly editorial board meeting at the NCC's national HQ in Hawthorn. This occurred each Tuesday at lunchtime. It was at these meetings that I got to know Bob Santamaria who chaired the meetings. Each week, the Editorial Board discussed what issues should be written about and each person was given one or more articles to write. For a while, I authored the column known as '*A little bird says*' which was supposed to be witty or satirical gossip or intelligence about the goings-on in the union movement, politics generally or the ALP.

Santamaria [and therefore *Newsweekly*] had a wide range of policy interests. Santamaria had a well-developed 'world view' and was not just concerned with Communism. He took a position on many public policy issues including social issues. I disagreed with the NCC line in several areas, particularly about family and gender policies. Some of Santamaria's interests were quaint; for example, his rural policy was considered a bit eccentric. Defence policy was also an important focus, but I was not much interested in this area, although broadly supporting the approach. Part of the NCC's policy on defence was concern about the security threat to Australia from Communism in Asia. There were some in the NCC who were concerned that Australia would be attacked militarily. This was not my concern. I was, and still am, principally concerned about the human rights of those people who were forced to live under Communist rule. This was [and still is] of more concern to me than any threat to Australia itself. My position on the Viet Nam war was based on concern for the Vietnamese people, not for any flow on threat to Australia.

I was not involved in the NCC's work in social or family policy, being only interested in opposing communism. It has been said that Santamaria's wanted to impose his religious views on Australian society. However, as I understood his position on Communism, this was not true. Rather, he took a view based on human rights and personal freedom which coincided with his religious views. It is entirely valid and laudable to promote human rights and to intervene in the political process in a democratic way to achieve this outcome. Some of his other policies were based on his religious principles or personal beliefs. His views on women and the family were ones that reflected his conservative and traditional social values.

During my time on the Editorial Board, I found Bob Santamaria to be a personable and a likeable character. He was funny and often self-deprecating [although I later concluded that this latter trait was not genuine]. He seemed to take an interest in me. I may have been a bit of an oddity at the time since I was a non-Catholic, indeed a non-believer, working mainly with people who were very committed Catholics. I do not recall who else was on the Editorial Board at the time but since the meetings were held in the national office of the NCC, I met all the key figures based there.

The detail of my many conversations with Santamaria now escapes my memory, other than one which occurred later after I had decided to find out more about the Catholic faith. For a while, I attended some information sessions run regularly by a priest attached to St Francis' Church in the city.

I was not greatly impressed by this priest who I think was trying too hard to be soft and trendy in his approach. It did not appeal much to me. Santamaria must have heard of my interest and my attendance at St Francis. He expressed concern to me one day about the priest. I said, 'Yes, I don't think much of his politics.' Santamaria, very correctly, said, 'I'm not worried about his politics, it's what he is teaching you about the faith that I am worried about.' I think it was a genuine concern for my spiritual welfare. I later found another priest who gave me my final preparation for reception into the Church in 1975.

I enjoyed writing for *Newsweekly* without being brilliant at it. Churning out the required words by the deadlines was not a problem for me. Articles were often sourced from secondary material, e.g. from newspapers, etc. with our spin or political line added. This work went on for some time until I was told that the Editorial Board had been disbanded. I don't know why this occurred, but I now assume it was because Santamaria had become unhappy with the way it functioned or with one or more of its members and he wanted to be rid of them. It transpired that he was a very controlling personality and it was not hard to fall out with him, but I had no issues with him at the time. It was interesting to be working with such a major figure in Australian political life, although at the time I knew little of the history of the Movement. Since I was not then a Catholic, I had no role in any of the Church based activities nor any involvement in any of the formal structures of the NCC, other than my stint on the Editorial Board.

Meanwhile, I was continuing to be part of the Ken Stone team at the Trades Hall. In July 1974, I was elected unopposed as Secretary of the Victorian Branch of the Rope and Cordage Union. While I had never worked in the industry, the Union had a rule that if someone worked for the Union for a certain period, they could also join it. The Branch Executive supported my election as Secretary. Since I was now part of the moderate forces at the Trades Hall which supported Ken Stone, I raised with Michael O'Sullivan the idea of applying to join the ALP. Generally speaking, NCC activists or supporters did not join the Labor Party. I assume that this was so that if an end to the split in the ALP was negotiated, they would all go in together.

However, no objection was raised to me joining and I applied in mid-to-late 1974 and was accepted without question from anyone. I had no issues in signing the ALP's pledge which required me only to declare that I was not a member of any other party or organisation that stood candidates for elected office. As I had never been a member of the DLP [or any other political party] this was not an issue for me, and I signed the pledge with a clear conscience. Joining the ALP in 1974 turned out to be timely. In mid-1974, I had been elected on the Ken Stone 'Official' ticket [as it was called] to a position on the Interim Victorian Committee for Union Training. This body was set up as part of the Whitlam Government's policy to set up a government-funded Trade Union Training Authority [TUTA]. Clyde Cameron was the Minister for Industrial Relations at the time and this was one of his pet projects.

While the legislation establishing the Authority was being developed, interim Committees were set up in all States to get training started. My side of union politics thought that this was an area of work that needed to be watched carefully and appropriate people employed to run it, or it would just be a tool for the left to train future left-wing activists for the union movement. The legislation was eventually passed and TUTA properly established and funded [but the Whitlam Government lost office shortly afterward]. The new Authority decided that a purpose-built residential training college should be built in Albury-Wodonga, consistent with the Whitlam's Government's decentralisation policy. The new Fraser Government continued to fund TUTA and eventually Clyde Cameron College was built. Local residents were said to be less than happy with having a union training centre in their midst. It is said that they would have preferred a prison! They were also allegedly even more concerned when the contractor building the facility put up a sign advertising it as the CCCP: meaning the Clyde Cameron College Project, but these initials also spelt out USSR in the Cyrillic alphabet used in the Soviet Union! Other locals simply called it Red Square! I attended the opening of the College in my role as a Deputy Member of the Australian Council of Union Training.

Not long after I was elected to the Interim Victorian Committee for Union Training in 1974, I had a visit to my office from Peter Nolan, then Assistant Secretary of the VTHC. He said that the Trades Hall had had an approach from the ACTU to nominate someone to go on a study tour to the USA to examine 'labor education', as trade union training was called in the States. The trip was to take place in October/November 1974 and culminate in attending the opening of the American union movement's training college, the George Meany Centre in Washington, DC. The USA State Department had offered funding to the American equivalent of the ACTU, known as the AFL-CIO, to host a delegation of about 24 union officials from around the world to coincide with the opening. Peter Nolan asked me if I would be interested. He told me that just about everyone else involved in union education was out of the country at the time – or would be – so my name had come up. Was I interested? Of course!

Before leaving on the trip, I was at a meeting at the ACTU and Harold Souter, who was still ACTU Secretary at the time, introduced me to Bob Hawke who was President. Souter said to Hawke 'This is the young bloke that we are sending to the US on the labor education trip.' Hawke said to me: 'That's great' and added, 'The only other person who was available was Sean Kelly from Tasmania, and we're not sending that DLP bastard!'

Sean Kelly worked as the Education Officer of the Tasmanian Trades and Labor Council, where Brian Harradine was Secretary at the time. Brian Harradine was an ALP member and had been elected from Tasmania to sit on the ALP Federal Executive. A majority of the ALP Executive refused to allow him to take his place on the body because they suspected that he had NCC ties. In response, Harradine declared that 'the friends of the Communists intend to try and silence me' and was expelled from the ALP in 1975. Whitlam, who had supported Harradine, resigned his party leadership over this issue and was only narrowly re-elected in a contest against Jim Cairns.[109] Harradine went on to be elected as an Independent Senator for Tasmania and served many terms in that capacity. At the time, I merely thanked Bob Hawke for the opportunity to represent the ACTU on the trip. I enjoyed the overseas experience immensely. It ignited an interest in international unionism. One of the stops on the tour was in Boston, where we visited the Harvard Trade Union Program in session. I decided that it would be good to do this program one day.

The American trade union movement had many tough-minded activists in it with views that were both strongly pro-labor, of course, and completely anti-communist. They combined social democratic principles and policies with hostility to, and a willingness to combat, totalitarianism on the left and the right. They matched my developing views well. I never had any difficulties co-operating with the US union movement. During the 1974 trip, I met a union employee at the AFL-CIO who knew Alexander Solzhenitsyn, the Soviet dissident, who had recently been expelled from the Soviet Union and was now living in Vermont. Volume 1 of Solzhenitsyn's great account of the prison system in the USSR – *The Gulag Archipelago* - had only recently been published in English in the West. I had not yet been able to read a copy although I was later to read every word of the 1800 pages of the three-volume paperback edition. It made a significant impression on me. In June 1975, Solzhenitsyn gave two speeches to the AFL-CIO.[110] In the first of these, he outlined the repression of Russian workers by the Bolsheviks which he said began almost at once after the October 1917 revolution. He said that since the Russian revolution there had never been a free trade union in the USSR. He praised the refusal of the American unions to make and receive visits from 'trade unions' in the Soviet bloc, unlike unions in some other Western countries.

Back in Australia after this trip, life was becoming interesting on a personal level. My romantic relationship had been somewhat on and off. In one of the 'off' periods, I had finally decided to become a Catholic. For some time during 1973, I had undertaken a correspondence course in Catholicism run by the Catholic Inquiry Office in Sydney. Each week or so, an unmarked envelope would turn up with the week's lesson. My parents became suspicious, but I think they had no idea what was in the envelopes. As noted earlier, I later also took some 'instruction' at St Francis' Church in the city and later again with Fr Denis O'Brien, who was based in Braybrook. At the end of 1973, I had decided that it was time to move out of home. I had been working for a year and had saved enough money to buy a better car to replace the ancient Morris Minor I had been driving for three years. I was also able to afford to pay rent.

I moved into a flat in Wellington Road Clayton, not far from Monash University. I flatted with another member of the Monash Democrats, and later with his brother as well. Both were traditional NCC supporters and their father had been active in the NCC in the country. In this environment and with many Catholic friends I had met through my future wife I was able to consider my religious future freely. In January 1975, I was received into the Catholic Church by Fr Denis O'Brien at Braybrook. Many union colleagues came to the ceremony along with several non-Catholic friends from university. I have never regretted this decision. Despite its many flaws and flawed people, I believe that the Catholic Church offers the most authentic spiritual experience available. I decided, consciously, to join the Church that, in my opinion, God founded.

I somewhat gutlessly chose not to mention to my parents that I was planning to become a Catholic. I knew that they would not be happy. Their 'Anything But Catholic' religious strategy had not borne fruit. I told them not long afterward. We were driving home from my aunt's beach house at Rye at the time. I was driving and I figured that they would have to stay calm as I was at the wheel! I had now completed the treble: I had gone to work for a trade union, joined the ALP and become a Catholic. This just about represented everything to which my parents were opposed.

On Shrove Tuesday evening in 1975, I proposed marriage to the young woman I first met at the Monash Democrats 'O Week' stand in March 1971. Not only was it Shrove Tuesday, but it was also the second Tuesday of February and on the second Tuesday of every month, there was a meeting of the Rope and Cordage Union in the Trades Hall. I had to attend, so Mary came with me. We broke the news to our parents by phone from the Union's office and then went to the meeting. Not very romantic, but unavoidable. My now wife-to-be Mary was known by Maud Burns as 'Keith's lady friend' and the Union's committee members were happy at the news. As we had known each other for four years, we decided to waste no time in getting married and decided to tie the knot on the Saturday after Easter. This was the first available date since it was not considered acceptable to get married during Lent. This gave us just seven weeks to get the wedding organised, which was a challenge: both for us and for Mary's parents who were hosting the event. The timeline barely gave us time to make bookings, get invites out, and organise somewhere to live. Flats were in short supply at the time, but we found one in Elwood. We were married on April 5$^{th}$ in Moe at St Kieran's Church. My family all made the trek from Melbourne and beyond and of course had to witness me being married as a Catholic in a Catholic Church.

In all the circumstances, I think we could not have asked more of our parents. Others would have told us to take a deep breath and wait awhile although my mother did tell me the day before the wedding that it was not too late to change my mind! Nevertheless, she had made the wedding cake and it was decorated by one of her friends. In our minds, we had decided to get married, not engaged, and saw no point in waiting. After a brief 'overseas' honeymoon in Burnie, Tasmania it was back to work at the Rope and Cordage Union. At the end of April, the media was full of images of Saigon, the capital of South Viet Nam, falling to invading North Vietnamese tanks.

Elections for the Executive of the VTHC were held every six months: in June and December. These were keenly contested now that the 27 rebel unions were back. At their caucus before the June elections, the moderate group suggested that I should stand on the 'Official' ticket which supported Ken Stone. I was happy to do so. Ken Stone suggested that it was more appropriate for me – given my youth – to stand for the Disputes Committee, traditionally the starting point for election to Council committees. I successfully ignored this suggestion and the 'Official' ticket included me as a candidate for

Executive from the Council as a whole. Executive members were elected both from industry groups and by and from the Council delegates as a whole.

## ON THE VTHC EXECUTIVE

The 'Official' ticket was successful and in June 1975, at the age of just 23, I found myself on the Victorian Trades Hall Council Executive. I was to serve three consecutive terms as an executive member. I also represented the VTHC on a range of other committees as positions came up. As well as the Victorian Council of TUTA I found myself from time to time on various education-related bodies for which the VTHC had nominating rights. These included the Council of Coburg Teachers College and the Advisory Committee at the Education Centre at Turana, the Melbourne Youth Training Centre [a juvenile detention centre]. I also sat on several Committees at RMIT which had kept links with the VTHC since it had started life as the 'Working Man's College.' I was also involved in several Committees concerned with youth unemployment, which was an emerging problem.

I was becoming a key part of the Ken Stone team. In 1975, when Peter Nolan resigned as Assistant VTHC Secretary to go to the ACTU, the moderate caucus selected Tony Vella from the Australian Workers Union [AWU] to run as his replacement. Numbers were tight and both left and right organised hard. I was Tony's scrutineer in the ballot. The first count had Tony winning by just 150 votes to 148. The left's scrutineer naturally wanted a re-count and the second time the result was 149 to 148. At that point, the left conceded [I would have gone for another re-count myself] and Tony was declared elected by the narrowest possible margin. Tony was a genuine unionist. He was of Maltese origin and born in Egypt. I liked him and got on well with him. The AWU was traditionally fiercely anti-communist and the bearer of a great history of fighting for the genuine interests of Australian workers. At Tony's funeral many years later, his son told the story of his narrow election win and I was happy to be able to tell him afterwards that I had been in Tony's corner on the night.

The VTHC Executive normally met every Wednesday afternoon from 2 pm until about 5 PM or as necessary. One of the functions of the Executive was to decide what would go on the Agenda for the weekly meeting of the full Council each Thursday night. It was, therefore, a key committee. As Secretary,

Ken Stone had only one consistent strategy for the weekly meetings of the Executive: to talk as long as possible until everyone else gave up. Meetings ran for much longer than necessary. Ken repeated this technique on Thursday night if he felt there was a danger of any Executive recommendation being voted down.

*With Tony Vella in Noumea, New Caledonia in the 1980s*

Items for the Executive and therefore the Council agenda could be sent in by affiliated Unions or proposed by the elected Officers. I only remember a few of the debates. What sticks in my mind the most was that in those days smoking in meetings was considered to be acceptable. Ken Stone smoked as did many Executive members. Thus, I passively smoked for hours each Wednesday afternoon – at times I felt that the air could be cut into lumps with a knife it was so thick with cigarette smoke. While I was on the Executive, Ken Stone's supporters had the 'numbers' but the left often had better contributors and debaters. John Halfpenny – a rising star on the left [and later VTHC Secretary himself] – was an excellent debater. The left was not well represented on the Executive at the time, but its supporters were vocal at the Thursday night Council meetings.

Halfpenny was the lead debater for the left at Council meetings, and he was well supported by others including Jim Roulston [also AMWU], J. J. Brown from the Railways Union, and Ted Bull from the Wharfies Union. Usually, a Union's delegation at Council meetings was led by the Union's Secretary; but in other cases, other officials and organisers represented their union. The right was represented on the Executive including by the SDA's Jim Maher and Kevin Davies from the Photo-Engravers Union, a small union in the printing industry. I knew both well. I worked closely with other moderate ALP Union Secretaries at the Trades Hall, such as Bill Shaw from the Roof Slaters Union [whose office was next to mine], Alby Bonser from the Printers Operatives Union and others. On the floor of the Council, the best non-left debaters were from the right-wing unions, especially Frank Neenan and Michael O'Sullivan from the Clerks Union. Both were excellent debaters and endured much abuse as NCC and DLP 'rats'. The SDA attended the meetings but seldom spoke, preferring a low profile. Jack Waters from the Motor Transport Union was a good debater from the right.

I gradually joined in the weekly debates and from time to time went up against John Halfpenny and others. Several issues came up in which I took a particular interest. These included the proposed Newport Power Station which the left had decided to ban. They managed to get a majority of the Council delegates to support the ban against the wishes of Ken Stone. Unfortunately for the Council, the Liberal government went ahead and built the power station using non-union labor. The left also opposed the construction of the Omega Navigation Tower in Gippsland which they saw as part of the US military alliance. The tower was also built. There was much to debate and fight over between left and right. The Cold War was still in full flight and the left was still very willing to support the policy positions of the Soviet Union and its allies against those of the Western alliance.

## THE ROAD TO TASHKENT

'Reciprocal visits', as they were called in Australia, that is, visits to and exchanges with so-called unions in Communist countries were still being promoted by the left unions. Solzhenitsyn's evidence and his warnings against such visits were ignored by the left. Reciprocal visits were a major issue between left and right unions at the ACTU level as well as at the State Trades Hall level. The ACTU itself did not have completely clean hands on this issue.[iii] In 1976, the VTHC received a letter from the Uzbekistan 'trade union movement' based in Tashkent proposing the establishment of 'friendly relations' between it and the Victorian trade union movement. Uzbekistan was then one of the Soviet-controlled 'republics' in the USSR. The letter advised that:

> *The Uzbek Republican Trade Unions Council expresses sincere wish to enter*

*into friendly relations with Victorian Trades Hall Council. In this connection we invite the Victorian Trades delegation for 10 days stay in the Soviet Union to get acquainted with the life of Uzbek people and the Republican Trades-union's activity in particular. The delegation's membership would consist of 5-6 persons...*[112]

I have no idea who in the Soviet Union came up with the thought that Victorian Unions would be interested in fraternal relationships with 'unions' in Uzbekistan. Then, as now, it is one of the more remote parts of the world. It is not one of the world's top tourist spots, nor a known hotbed of unionism. However, Ken Stone was attracted to the idea of this exchange with Uzbekistan. Not only was Soviet-era Tashkent not the most attractive destination, but the union movement there was simply a Communist Party front organisation. Nevertheless, Ken Stone embraced the idea of the visit and decided to lead the delegation.

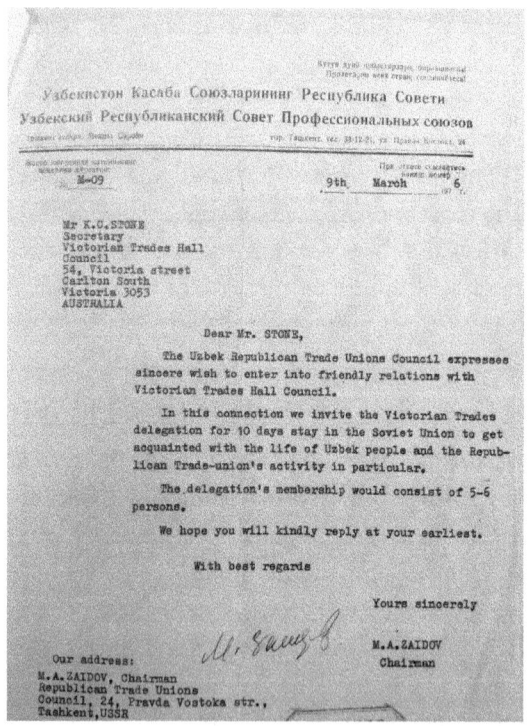

*From Uzbekistan with love...*
*Image by author, document in the Melbourne University Archives.*

The VTHC Executive, of which I was a member, recommended to Council that the delegation consist of an Officer of Council and three elected delegates. Three left-wing delegates were ultimately selected, the right refusing to take part. The Uzbek trade unions offered to pay all expenses for the trip [surprise, surprise] other than the cost of the flight to the Soviet Union. Ken got the funding commitment in writing from them but then found it hard to organise the trip. Communications with relevant people, even in the Soviet Embassy in Australia proved difficult, as this note to Ken [presumably from his PA, Cleo] shows:

> Oct 20, 1976
>
> Mr Stone
>
> *I have rang [sic] three times today the USSR consulate in Sydney and each time I keep missing on [sic] Mr Poliakof who seems to be handling visas.*
>
> *I shall try again at 9 am tomorrow morning just to ascertain the position with the passports and the visas.*
>
> *Meantime, we might as well send the enclosed self-addressed stamped envelope.*
>
> *P.S.: Mr Denisemko seems also to be unavailable each time I have asked for him.*[113]

Ken Stone decided to take decisive action to cut through the bureaucracy and go directly to what he thought was the source of the invitation. I was sitting in his office one morning when he tried to phone the headquarters of this 'fraternal' trade union body in Tashkent. Stone had engaged the help of a Russian interpreter who sat there with us. I was very amused by this. In those days, calls had to be placed and connected by an international operator, who, unfortunately for Ken Stone, was unable to find or make phone contact with our new 'sister' organisation in Tashkent. It either did not exist or had no authority to speak to Westerners phoning them up unannounced. I could imagine the consternation at the other end of the line!

I knew that Ken was ringing the wrong number. He should have called the foreign affairs office of the Communist Party of the Soviet Union. He would have been put straight through. Eventually, the travel arrangements were made, and the visit went ahead. Ken Stone had suggested that I should come on the trip, but I declined. I was not going to be part of any relationship with a bogus union organisation the sole purpose of which was to enforce

Communist party control over workers in the USSR. My recollection is that at a relatively late stage Ken Stone was unable to go on the trip. This view is supported by documents in the VTHC files. The other three delegates went on their own, without a VTHC Officer.

The final itinerary for the trip shows what a farce it was and how offensive such exchanges were for those who supported human rights in the Soviet Union. The trip consisted of dinners and sightseeing with one only visit to what might have been a workplace. In any case, it would have been a stage-managed affair. The trip was also timed to coincide with the annual celebrations of the anniversary of the Bolshevik revolution and delegates were expected to take part in these celebrations. On Sunday, November 7$^{th}$ [Western calendar], the delegation was expected to take part in the 'celebrations of the 59$^{th}$ Anniversary of the Great October socialist revolution' which was to last from 8.00 am until 1.30 pm.

Ken Stone did manage to get to the Soviet Union the next year. He attended the 16$^{th}$ Congress of the Russian Trade Union Federation in Moscow in March 1977. Ken Stone was a good note taker and his notes of this Congress meeting show the domination of the union movement by the Communist Party of the Soviet Union. A key speaker was Leonid Brezhnev, the hard-liner who was Communist Party Secretary. Ken's notes record some of Brezhnev's messages to the assembled delegates:

*Address by Leonid Brezhnev – 10.22 am*
- *Collective farmers being drawn into T.U Movement*
- *50 million women workers*
- *T.U.'s marching together with the Party-as they always have!*
- *T.U.'s must remain the school of socialist economic learning*
- *T.U.'s must remain the school of Communism (Workers of all Lands Unite!)*[114]

Brezhnev had been General Secretary of the Communist Party of the Soviet Union since 1964 and therefore the recognised and effective head of the country. His speech made it clear that the Russian trade unions had to do the will of the Party, rather than act in the interests of their members. Brezhnev was also the author and implementer of the so-called Brezhnev Doctrine which held that national sovereignty was less important than 'socialist unity':

*When forces that are hostile to socialism try to turn the development of some socialist country towards capitalism, it becomes not only a problem of the country concerned, but a common problem and concern of all socialist countries.*[115]

This Doctrine was used retrospectively to justify the Soviet invasion of Czechoslovakia in 1968 – an event still fresh in the minds of people in 1976/7. The Russian Trade Federation found nothing incompatible with union rights in having the Soviet leader responsible for crushing the Prague Spring's 'socialism with a human face' lecture them at their Congress [they had no choice, of course]. Nor, apparently, did visiting union officials from the West, of whom there were many. The VTHC's new friends from Uzbekistan were also mentioned in Ken's meeting notes, together with a record of the slogan adopted by the Congress: 'No laggards.' This is an example of 'Stakhanovism' whereby Russian workers were exhorted by the Communist Party to work harder and harder.[116]

It is almost incomprehensible that any Australian unionists would be buying this propaganda and is stark evidence of the left's double standards that applied to worker rights. The delegates who went to Uzbekistan reported on their trip in early 1977 to a weekly meeting of the Trades Hall Council. Later, there was a return visit from Uzbekistan including a formal dinner, which I was forced to sit through as an Executive member. In 1979, another invitation to visit Uzbekistan was received but I am not sure if this visit ever took place. The relationship went nowhere in the long term. In Australia, the pro-communist left in the union movement liked to portray itself as always on the progressive side of any human rights issue. But this was not true. The left was willing to ignore the mounting and extensive evidence that Communism was completely opposed to free trade unions and was anti-worker as well as anti-democratic. Human rights, including worker rights, did not exist anywhere under Communist rule.

There was plenty of evidence of this and even more was available in the West than Solzhenitsyn knew of at the time. He thought he was revealing these truths to the West, but there was already substantial evidence of it to hand, although he added very considerably to it. Did the suppression of the popular Hungarian uprising as far back as 1956, well known in the West, not tell us this? Or the suppression of the Prague Spring of 1968, still in recent memory? In 1976, as the VTHC was planning its visit to the Soviet Union, Polish workers went on strike to protest at sharp increases in the price of food.

The Polish communist regime responded by 'beating and arresting workers in the industrial towns of Ursus and Radom.'[117] Not a word was spoken about this by left-wing unions that I can recall nor was it likely to be on the agenda of any 'trade union' discussions in Tashkent or Moscow.

In January 1977, in neighbouring Czechoslovakia, several human rights activists bravely signed a document that became known as Charter 77. This document criticised their Moscow-imposed government for its failure to implement the human rights provisions of the country's own constitution, the Helsinki Accords and various United Nations human rights covenants, all of which had been formally adopted into Czech law. The Communist Government's responses were:

> *Retaliation and intimidation were deployed against the signatories, including dismissal from work, denial of schooling for their children, suspension of drivers' licenses, forced exile and loss of citizenship, detention, trial, and imprisonment.*[118]

These human and workers' rights violations were not on the agenda of the Russian Trade Union Congress in March 1977, although they would have been if these actions had occurred in a Western country. The left in Australia and other Western countries either chose to ignore all the evidence of the anti-worker nature of Communist regimes or were willing participants in this oppression. If, as Raymond Aron had suggested, it was necessary to be either for or against the Soviet 'enterprise', the left was clearly for it.[119]

It took the creation of a free and independent trade union movement in Poland just a few years later to finally destroy the left-wing myth that the Soviet Bloc was a worker-friendly regime. There was a battle of ideas going on in Western societies. I was happy to be playing a small part in this struggle. In 1978, it was time to take another step in my career in the union movement and this battle. My next move was one predicted by Bob Betts, but it did not go well.

# 4

# THIRTY DAYS THAT SHOOK THE TRADES HALL

*'Now let's define our terms. What do you mean by sacked?'*
*[Weg's Weekend, The Herald, Sat. June 17th, 1978]*

In early 1978, I had a discussion with Michael O'Sullivan. From this conversation emerged the idea that I might speak to VTHC Secretary Ken Stone about appointing me to a vacant VTHC Research Officer position. The job had not been advertised but the post had been unfilled for some time. The VTHC rules required that there be a Research Bureau and authorised the Secretary to staff it. After thinking about this for a while, I decided to give it a go. I was reluctant to leave the Rope and Cordage Union where I had been for more than five years, but the possibilities offered by the new position seemed worth it.

I made an appointment with Stone and put this idea to him. With no apparent hesitation, he agreed. I had now been a member of the VTHC Executive for nearly three years and I had worked quite closely with him and was one of his supporters on the Executive. I know that Ken Stone spoke to Assistant Secretary Tony Vella about the idea and Tony was fully in support. However, Ken mentioned it to no one else in the VTHC Office at the time.

The thinking behind seeking this job was obvious enough. The position was a potential stepping stone to other positions in the VTHC or broader union movement. Peter Marsh, the previous Research Officer, had subsequently been elected as an Industrial Officer of the Council. I have no idea whether Ken Stone did any background checks on me. He asked me no questions. My credentials as a Union Secretary, an Executive member, a university graduate with an Economics major and as a known supporter of his for several years must have been enough.

In researching these memoirs, I came across what is impolitely known in the union movement as a "shit sheet" [or more politely but less commonly as a scandal sheet] issued at the time of one of the half-yearly VTHC elections. These anonymous leaflets were produced to spread unfavourable information about individuals. I do not recall in which year this pamphlet was produced but I think it would have been in mid-1977. It sought to expose what it claimed to be my true political colours. It was headed: *Don't vote for Santamaria's agent*

As was normal for these types of publications, it was a mixture of fact, fiction and outright lies.

The first two paragraphs read:

> *The Santamaria/DLP forces are trying to worm their way back into the Trade Union Movement. This time they are being led by Keith Harvey, Secretary of the Rope and Cordage Workers Union. Harvey is a candidate in the election for the Executive.*
>
> *Harvey is trying to conceal his real Santamaria/DLP connection by pretending to be just another "moderate". However, a couple of years ago he was only too proud to show his true colours. Today, he would be rather embarrassed to be publicly reminded of his past activities.*

The sheet went on to supply a potted history of me, some of which was correct and some of which was an outright fabrication. For example, it 'revealed' that I had been a member of the Monash DLP Club and had stood for elections on the Club's ticket. It noted that I had authorised a number of issues of *Free Speech*. It also reported that in a letter to *Lot's Wife*, the student newspaper, I had described myself as a person of 'conservative politics' and that in 1972 I had taken legal action against the University which was 'part of an Australia wide National Civic Council based conspiracy to destroy democratically elected student bodies.'

> **DON'T VOTE FOR SANTAMARIA'S AGENT**
>
> The Santamaria/D.L.P. forces are trying to worm their way back into the Trade Union Movement. This time they are being led by Keith Harvey, Secretary of the Rope and Cordage Workers Union. Harvey is a candidate in the election for The Executive.
>
> Harvey is trying to conceal his real Santamaria/D.L.P. connection by pretending to be just another "moderate". However, a couple of years ago, he was only too proud to show his true colours. Today, he would be rather embarrassed to be publicly reminded of his past activities.
>
> Yet even Harvey could hardly forget that:
>
> **A BRIEF HISTORY**
>
> In 1970, 71 and 72, he was a leader of the D.L.P. club at Monash University, and stood for elections as part of its ticket.
>
> He authorised numerous publications of the D.L.P. club including "Free Speech", its weekly bulletin.
>
> He was an outspoken supporter of the Vietnam war and of General Thieu. Harvey and his D.L.P. associates even felt that the previous Liberal Government in Australia was selling out the Americans in Vietnam by not sending more Australian troops to fight.
>
> "Free Speech", in Volume 5, No. 13 came out strongly supporting Nixon's invasion of Cambodia and urged further escalation.
>
> **IN HIS OWN WORDS**
>
> In a letter in Lot's Wife, the student newspaper at Monash University, on August 5, 1971, Harvey described himself as "a person of conservative politics". This was hardly an overstatement.
>
> In 1972, Harvey and one other member of the D.L.P. club, brought writs against the university in an attempt to prevent student bodies providing funds for activities promoting peace in Indo-China.
>
> This was part of an Australia-wide National Civic Council based conspiracy to destroy democratically elected student bodies.
>
> Working with Harvey in his move to crush the independence of the student movement by using the courts, was the Santamaria inspired "Peace with Freedom" organisation. This organisation also included well known reactionaries like Knopfelmacher.
>
> Harvey's solicitors were Renwick and Gaynor, well known D.L.P. solicitors. Gaynor has stood as a D.L.P. candidate in state elections.
>
> **UNION BASHER**
>
> Harvey was well known for his union bashing attitudes. He always condemned the Trade Union Movement and the Australian Labor Party for taking actions in defence of workers and their families. He was strangely silent about the actions of large employers.
>
> **DON'T LET SANTAMARIA'S AGENTS BACK INTO THE T.H.C. EXECUTIVE.**

"Don't vote for Santamaria's agent."

The big lie was in the final paragraph which said that 'Harvey was well known for his union-bashing attitudes. He always condemned the Trade Union Movement and the Australian Labor Party for taking actions in defence of workers and their families.' This was nonsense. There was no evidence presented for this baseless charge, nor could there have ever been any such evidence. I now assume that Ken Stone must have seen a copy of this leaflet at the time it was produced, since it was released in the context of VTHC elections. It claimed that I was an agent of the 'Santamaria/DLP forces' trying to infiltrate the trade union movement and specifically the VTHC. My days of 'flying under the radar' ended with this leaflet. What is interesting in retrospect is why Ken Stone chose to ignore this information and not even ask me about it before appointing me to the position of Research Officer.

After Stone had agreed to appoint me to the position, I told the Rope and Cordage Union Committee of my decision to move to the Trades Hall. I was not leaving the Union altogether as I agreed to hold an honorary elected position in the Union. I arranged for someone to replace me in my Union role. Ken Stone and I agreed that I would start work on the 15$^{th}$ of May 1978 and I duly fronted up to the VTHC front counter at about 9 am on that day to start work. The receptionist asked what I wanted, and I had to reply weakly: 'I work here.' She knew nothing about this and neither did Cleo, Stone's Executive Assistant. It transpired that Stone had told no one other than Tony Vella that I was to start work. This became a major problem. The Council's staff was small. There were four elected officials: the Secretary and Assistant Secretary and two Industrial Officers. One of the Industrial Officers was Ron Jordan, son of former Secretary, Mick Jordan. Ron Jordan was on extended sick leave. The other Industrial Officer was Peter Marsh.

I was hurriedly seated in Ron Jordan's vacant office. Peter Marsh soon came to give me my first task, which was to write the script for that evening's radio broadcast by Ken Stone. The Trades Hall owned the license for radio station 3KZ which broadcast from studios located in the Trades Hall. At 6.55 pm every evening Ken had a five-minute slot to fill. One of the jobs of the Research Officer was to come up with a script for Ken's approval. Peter Marsh did not seem to me to be particularly happy that I had been appointed [I am still not sure why not if this was the case] but he seemed very pleased to hand over this job to me. The first few days on the job went well enough and I spent a lot of time drafting suitable five-minute talks and doing whatever else was asked of me.

In those days, the Trades Hall Council had a weekly delegates' meeting each Thursday night, which began at 7.30 pm and concluded two hours later. These meetings were considered important and newsworthy. They were generally attended by newspaper reporters who sat at a table beneath the podium on which the elected Officers sat. The newspapers regularly carried reports of Trades Hall meetings and decisions and the industrial reporters were based at the Trades Hall [unions being much more newsworthy than employer organisations]. There was also a public gallery above the main Council chamber.

On Thursday, 18th May, four days after I began work, the regular weekly Council meeting was held. At the beginning of the meeting, Ken Stone moved the reception of the Executive Report in the normal fashion. Left-wing union delegates then rose to complain noisily about my appointment as Research Officer and to oppose the reception of the Executive report for that reason. On this night, the regular Trades Hall Council President was absent and a stand-in Chair, Les Cahill, from the Printing Industry Union, was presiding over the meeting.

The left succeeded in voting down the reception of the Executive Report. The motion to receive the Report was normally a formality and simply allowed delegates to make short speeches on issues not on the formal agenda. Its reception had never been defeated. That night it was lost by a significant margin of votes. The Left had come well prepared with delegates and immediately proceeded to try and put a motion – moved by AMWU State President Jim Roulston – that I be sacked immediately from the position that I had occupied only since the previous Monday.

Les Cahill courageously ruled Roulston's motion out of order and refused to allow it to be put to a vote. He told the meeting that under the VTHC Rules, the appointment was in the power of the Secretary. The left then began a walkout from the meeting in protest, but hastily returned when they realised that because a quorum was present that the meeting would go on without them. They continued their protests. The next day *The Age* reported that 'uproar broke out in the Council chamber.' [120]

In response to these protests, the Chair closed the meeting since order could not be restored. As the Executive Report had been defeated there was no official business before the chair. Les Cahill made it clear that he was not going to allow the left to carry a motion dismissing me. It was a gutsy performance from someone who was a Past President of the Council and just filling in on the night. Politically, he was on the left, not a Stone supporter, but very principled in my possibly biased opinion.

The left complained that I had been appointed by Ken Stone without the approval of the Executive. One of their speakers went on to say that Stone 'had not even told the other Officers of the Council'. Given that Tony Vella certainly did know, and Ron Jordan was absent on leave, the only 'Officer' not told would have been Peter Marsh. However, Ken Stone had kept nearly everyone other than Tony Vella in the dark about my appointment. *The Age* reported John Halfpenny – State Secretary of the AMWU – saying that it was ridiculous that Stone's decision could not be dissented from [although what they were actually seeking was my sacking]. The Miscellaneous Workers Union Secretary Ray Hogan reportedly said that he would not tolerate my appointment by stealth and that affiliated unions on the left would not recognise my appointment. Ken Stone defended his decision to appoint me saying that the Rules empowered him to do so. He was quoted as saying:

> To my knowledge the executive report on the THC has never been rejected and has never been the cause of abandoning a THC meeting. Mr Cahill acted completely within the Rules [he said], there was no point of order for him to rule on.
>
> Mr Harvey's job would not be affected. The dissenters have had their fun. It was a political stunt. [121]

Ken Stone was wrong. His troubles, and mine, were only just beginning. On Tuesday 23$^{rd}$ May, the Melbourne *Sun's* industrial reporter wrote that 'In the heat of Thursday night's debate, one left-wing union delegate interjected that Mr. Harvey was an agent of the extreme right-wing National Civic Council.' Mr. Stone met that attack by retorting: 'He is a card-carrying member of the ALP.' This suggests that he must have made inquiries from me or others on this point.[122]

Following the aborted Council meeting, the left did not back down. Left-wing unions flooded the Executive with letters of protest seeking either that the matter be placed on the agenda for the next weekly meeting of the Council or, more directly, that I be sacked. Stories were leaked that the left-wing unions might again split from the Trades Hall [as they had done in 1967] if they did not get their way on my appointment. These letters from left unions went before the next regular Wednesday afternoon Executive meeting [which I was still entitled to attend as a member]. Ken Stone maintained that the Rules of the VTHC gave him the power to staff the Research Bureau by appointing a Research Officer and he had the numbers on the Executive to ensure that no agenda item concerning my appointment would appear on the Council's notice paper on the 25$^{th}$ May.

However, the left again came to the meeting well prepared with the numbers. They again tried to force the Council to discuss my appointment. The Thursday night meeting was described by the *Sun's* reporter the next day as 'wild.' The left tried to move that my appointment be rescinded – that is, that I be sacked – and won a series of procedural motions towards this end. But they did not get the rescission motion dismissing me put to a vote before the Council meeting had to adjourn at 9.30 pm under the VTHC Rules. The left narrowly had the 'numbers' for each of the procedural votes that night. These were 149-145, 149-147, 149-143 and 145-138 in their favour. Despite losing each vote by these narrow margins, Ken Stone and other moderate delegates successfully talked out time. However, no official business had been conducted for two consecutive meetings of the VTHC. I was the only trending topic of discussion, as it might be described today.

Ken Stone told the Melbourne *Herald* that the row over my appointment was a threat to the institution and structure of the VTHC. However, he said that he was confident that he could 'ride out' the threat to his position and the threat of a new left-wing breakaway. He also said that he did not believe that his appointment of me was the real issue:

> My appointment of Mr. Harvey is only an excuse that the Left faction, led by the Communist parties, are using as a lead-up to the June elections, which take place in a fortnight. If it wasn't for Mr. Harvey, it would be something else. [123]

Hostilities resumed the following Thursday night for the third week running. The Executive the previous day had again heard of letters from left-wing affiliates asking that the matter of my appointment be placed on the Council's business paper and Stone again rebuffed them. The left won two more procedural votes at the 1st June meeting – by increased majorities of 175 - 166 and by 180 - 152 - but again failed to get their motion to sack me dealt with by the 9.30 pm deadline.

During all this time, Ken Stone never raised with me the political allegations that were being made against me. He left me in shock one Friday night, however, when he walked into my office on his way home. He said simply: 'Be careful where you go and what meetings you are seen to be attending. That's how they got Brian'. He then abruptly left, leaving me no opportunity or need to respond. Brian was presumably Brian Harradine, who had been expelled from the ALP. This remark suggested that Ken Stone by then at least thought that I did have some connection to the NCC. He never raised it again. Perhaps he always knew and did not care.

But by the third week of disruption, the implications were now clear for the VTHC elections due to be held the following week. As can be seen from the numbers above, both sides increased their voting strength from week two to week three, but the left did better than the moderates. Normally, maximum effort to get delegates to attend only occurred at the half-yearly elections but near-maximum attendances were now being achieved each week. It was a great drama.

Delegates hardly ever seen at Council meetings were turning up to cast their votes as the whips for each side strove to maximise attendances. I remember one 'new' face in particular. Popular television actor Terry Norris came to the Council meeting as a delegate for the Amusement and Theatrical Employees Union which was on the left and which – as a union - voted against me. Terry Norris starred in ABC TV's *Bellbird* and was starring in *Cop Shop* when he took the time to come to the Trades Hall. He quit *Cop Shop* in 1982 to pursue a career in state politics by standing for a seat in the Victorian Legislative Assembly. He was the Australian Labor Party member for Noble Park from 1982 to 1985 and then for Dandenong from 1985 to 1992 after which he resumed his acting career. I remember him best for his cameo role in my demise.

Before the June elections, few observers gave the left any chance of winning enough Executive positions to claim the overall numbers on the Executive. The left had to win six out of seven contested positions. They won them all. The final margins were narrow. The left had 182 votes on the floor of the Council on election night. The highest polling moderate candidate scored 181 and two others 179 and 177, respectively. All but a handful of the total number of credentialed delegates from affiliated unions turned up to vote, the numbers attending steadily increasing over the four weeks of controversy.

These results were enough to turn Ken Stone's 14-4 majority on the Executive into a 10-8 majority for the left [when added to the uncontested positions and already elected Officer positions]. The result was a serious defeat for Ken Stone and the position he had taken in hiring me. His job was now on the line [although he was not subject to regular elections]. Stone himself was beaten in the election for a prize position on the Industrial Appeals Court of Victoria, normally a 'shoo-in' for the Secretary.

The vote was also a vote of no confidence in me. The left said that they were not gunning for Stone. It was clear that someone had to go. It was unlikely to be Ken Stone, nor would I have wished for that outcome. The left said that they would soon move to sack me, one way or another, now that they had the numbers on the Executive. One of Ken's supporters [John Melksham from the Brick Tile and Pottery Union] asked me to come and see him and said strongly that in Ken's best interest I should quit my position. He was undoubtedly right, but I did not agree to resign.

My policy throughout this time was not to talk to the press. On the Sunday night after the election results had become clear, a reporter from *The Age* rang me at home. He asked me if I was going to resign. I said 'no' to this and three other questions he asked me, breaking my rule. A short article based on my four 'no' answers appeared in the paper the following day under the headline 'No intention to quit: THC man'. On Monday morning, Ken Stone came to see me. He asked simply if what was in *The Age* was correct. I said it was. He left my office, but at 11.30 am he returned with a cheque for a month's pay in lieu of notice and sacked me on the spot. I left the VTHC office at once. Ken's parting words were: 'I'll see you on the TV'.

I went straight away to my old Rope and Cordage Union office. I phoned Michael O'Sullivan to tell him the news, but he was out. By the time he called back, I had drafted a press release. Michael seemed surprised that I was calm enough to sit down and compose a press release. In reality, the morning's event had not been a surprise, nor was I upset by it. Ever since the moderates lost the election [and even before since we could not muster a majority on the floor of Council on the issue], the likely outcome was clear. Ken Stone told the press that he had considered resigning, but this was not a sensible move. I was just small fry. If Ken had quit, there would have had to be an election for VTHC Secretary, and the numbers would not have been certain for the moderates to win back the position. This would have had serious consequences for the control of the Trades Hall and of the ACTU Interstate Executive as well.

It was obvious that I had to go. If Ken Stone had not sacked me, the Executive or the Council would have done so soon enough. I felt no ill will towards Ken Stone then, or later. I approached him for the job, and he gave it to me. He could have handled it better and possibly avoided this drama, but I doubt if he expected that the reaction would be quite as strong as it was. He had had a strong majority on the Executive to back his decision at the time he hired me. So, on the day of my dismissal, I just knuckled down and the matter entered its next phase – the media campaign. My press release said that 'my dismissal had nothing to do with my performance in the job but was a direct result of a vicious attack on me by extreme left-wing union leaders [who] have conspired to drive me from office...' I had this release typed in a friendly union office and was ready to distribute it when the Trades Hall reporters turned up having learned the news from Ken Stone.

My main recollection of their approach was that they looked at my press release and said: 'Oh, great, we can just put this in quotes' and then left. I do not recall answering many, if any, questions. The deadline for the afternoon *Herald* was approaching. That afternoon I was front-page news: '*THC Boss sacks aide*' ran the banner headline at the top of page one of the *Herald*. The full second headline read 'Left has conspired to drive me from office', quoting my press release. The accompanying photo was taken in the Rope and Cordage Union Office. I well remember going home to St Kilda on the tram that evening. In those days people bought the *Herald* on their way to the train station or tram stop and read it as they travelled home. I was standing in a sea of newspapers with my photo on the front page, but no one seemed to recognise me.

*In the Rope and Cordage Office shortly after my dismissal. This is the photo that appeared on the front page of the Melbourne Herald.*
Photo used under licence from Newspix.

The *Herald*'s cartoonist 'Weg' [Mr. W E Green] made me the subject of his 'Weg's Day' cartoon drawing me facing a bricked-up door to my office at the Trades Hall. A 'Ken Stone' figure next to me says 'I thought you'd got the message...?' I remembered a story from the time Frank Sinatra was in Melbourne in 1974 and had insulted female journalists, calling them 'hookers'. As a result, the Transport Workers Union banned him from travelling.[124] Weg did a brilliant cartoon, the caption of which read 'Ole blue eyes is black'. The *Herald later* ran a story saying that Sinatra had liked the cartoon so much that he had asked for the original and that it was given to him.

I was no Frank Sinatra but did know an official of one of the printing industry unions, Kevin Davies of the Photo Engravers Union. Through Kevin, I asked if I could have the original of the cartoon and Weg not only agreed, he added colour to it, making it a personal and original piece of political art. I had it framed. My 15 minutes of fame began. I was front-page news in *The Age* the next day as well, looking a lot like Russian madman Rasputin. I do not know how anybody could think I was a right-winger with a beard like that. My parents would have read *The Age* front-page report at breakfast, under the headline: '*Hounded from THC: Harvey*'.

*Outside the Trades Hall building on the day of my dismissal.*
*Photo used with the permission of The Age.*

On Wednesday 14th May, I issued a further press release saying that I intended to refer the matter of my dismissal to the Victorian Committee on Discrimination in Occupation and Employment. These Committees had been set up following the Whitlam Government's ratification of an ILO Convention against employment-related discrimination. They had the power to hear complaints of allegations of discrimination, to try to conciliate the issues and make recommendations to the parties. The Trades Hall had representatives on the Committee, one of whom was my wife, but she, of course, absented herself from any meetings dealing with my complaint.[125]

The next day was the next regular weekly Council meeting. Although the question of my dismissal was not on the Agenda paper, I felt compelled to speak on the matter. I decided that rather than opposing the reception of the Executive Report, as the left had done for three weeks, I would try to second its reception and use the opportunity to say a few words in my defence. In the meantime, I took myself out to Monash University to see if I could track down a copy of the letter that was being quoted at me in which I had reportedly described myself as a person of 'conservative politics'. I could not recall the letter at the time. I managed to find the relevant copy of *Lot's Wife* in the John Medley library. It was the letter I wrote about apartheid [see Chapter 2] in which I supported the right of the black population to overthrow by force the minority white regime. This part had not been mentioned by my critics.

I ate a hearty pizza at Toto's before the Council meeting and on arrival sought out the chair of the meeting [the Council Vice-President] who agreed to give me the call when the Secretary moved the motion to receive the Executive Report. I then got up and attacked the actions of the majority of Council delegates in forcing the Secretary to dismiss a worker arbitrarily for political reasons. I also read extracts from the apartheid letter that the author of the scandal sheet had chosen not to include. I was heard largely in silence.

In Ken Stone's reply, he said that the non-functioning of Council had weighed heavily in his decision to sack me. One of my supporters, Jack Waters from the Motor Transport and Chauffers Union, spoke in my support [although I had not asked him to]. One interjector said during Jack's speech 'but he's a Grouper!' Jack retorted 'A Grouper is much better than a gelded Grouper'. I did not find Jack's remark helpful.

The *Herald* story on the previous Monday said that I denied rumours that I was associated with the NCC or the DLP [although this is not in my statement]. On the 14th June, Michael Wilkinson gave me a great publicity opportunity with a big article on page 8 of the very widely read *Sun* newspaper in which he allowed me space to talk about my sacking and the effects of left-wing control of the union movement. In this article, he quoted me correctly as saying that I had never been a member of a political party other than the ALP, which was and is a true statement. However, he went on to say that some had claimed that I was a member of or had sympathies for the NCC and the DLP and then put in quotes the following statement:

> I never have had anything to do with them – absolutely nothing, Keith insisted.

If I had said that it would have been a lie. I had always been careful not to tell lies. I always told the truth, without unnecessarily revealing the whole truth. I was embarrassed that Michael Wilkinson had put these words – which I never spoke – into my mouth in quotes in the paper. Obviously, some people knew this was not true, but I could not see how I could now clarify this statement without causing great difficulty, so I let it pass.

A friend of mine was in the public gallery at the council meeting on the night I spoke about my dismissal. She overheard two young activists from the Metal Workers Union discussing my dismissal. They said that it did not matter that I had been dismissed since I had been found and given another job, which paid, they said, the great sum of $30,000 per annum. Since I was only earning $13,000 as VTHC Research Officer, this would have been a great deal of money at the time. Of course, this was not true. It was just a line being spun by the left to justify their action in dismissing a worker. I was simply out of a job. I had no place to go. *Herald* cartoonist, Weg, followed up his earlier cartoon in his 'Weg's Weekend' roundup of the week's news the following Saturday. It pictured a bearded me asking Ken Stone: 'Now, let's define our terms...what do you mean by "sacked"..?' I never quite understood what Weg was getting at in this cartoon.

The net result of the idea to get a job in the VTHC office was negative. The issue energised the left, forced my dismissal, and delivered to the left a majority on the Executive for the first time since the return of the 'rebel' unions in 1973. I was no longer on the Executive and unemployed. It might have been possible for me to undo the arrangements made regarding the Rope and Cordage Union and to return to my old position. However, in a discussion with Michael O'Sullivan, we decided that I should do something else. Michael wanted me to continue to be active amongst the moderate unions at the Trades Hall. It was important that they not fall into disarray as had happened in other State Trades and Labor Councils where the left had become dominant. The moderates had simply stopped fighting and handed the field to their opponents.

I decided to try to put together a portfolio of small union clients for which I would work on a part-time basis. This would give me an income and continuing contact with moderate unions at the Trades Hall. For a few weeks, I hawked myself around to likely small unions in need of some industrial, research or other assistance. This proved to be depressingly difficult. The problem with small unions is that they have small incomes and not much spare money for external help. In the end, I managed to find only three unions willing to hire me.

The most significant of those was the Victorian Mothercraft Nurses Association. The Association needed an organiser to visit workplaces and recruit members. The profession of mothercraft nurses was undergoing a rapid transformation. Mothercraft nurses had traditionally worked in hospitals or babies' homes, helping new mothers and their infants. By 1978, job opportunities were now to be found principally in childcare centres which existed or were being set up in the suburbs. I worked for the Association for about 12 months, two days a week, visiting day care centres across Melbourne sitting on small chairs talking to staff. I enjoyed this work and the women who ran the Association were very committed to their profession and their association.

My only other two clients of significance were the ASC&J – the Carpenters Union – which contracted me to assist mainly in writing articles for their journal and the Technical Services Guild [TSG] which paid me for about two hours a week. When I left for a permanent job the following year, I owed the TSG hours and had to pay them back as they had not asked enough of me to justify the time. I still had an honorary position with the Rope and Cordage Union and remained a delegate to the Trades Hall. This meant I could attend meetings of VTHC affiliates and keep contact with other unions. In this work, I was more successful since the moderates held together. Non-left unions launched a fight back against the left and eventually won back a majority on the Executive.[126]

Ken Stone soon regained a majority on the Executive and the left's ascendancy courtesy of the 'Harvey Affair' proved short-lived. Ken Stone's allies again held a 14-2 majority on the Executive during 1979-1981. When Ken Stone left the Trades Hall in 1985 to take up a job with the Trade Union Training Authority, he was replaced by moderate Peter Marsh. However, when Marsh resigned a couple of years later to go to the Victorian Industrial Relations Commission, he was then replaced by the AMWU's John Halfpenny. Halfpenny had left the Communist Party in 1979 and joined the ALP in 1982. The position of VTHC Secretary has been held by the left ever since.

Apart from the Mothercraft Nurses job, which provided two days a week regular pay, I had limited income. I remained politically active at the Trades Hall and attended meetings of the moderate caucus and other meetings. This activity did not attract any income and it was not possible to bill any of my clients for this work. This arrangement was not working out financially for me. I had been married for several years by this point and we wanted to buy a house and start a family. Mary had also been working for a small income. Between us, we might have scraped together one very modest income. But we were making a huge financial sacrifice with no job security and no prospects. Towards the end of 1978, a partial solution to my income problem emerged. The Fraser Government, responding to widespread concerns about the impact of emerging computer technologies on jobs and employment prospects, created the Committee of Inquiry Into Technological Change in Australia [CITCA], headed by Rupert Myers. Unions and other organisations had been expressing concern about technological change leading to redundancies, unemployment, and deskilling of existing jobs.

The Committee called for submissions from interested organisations. The Federated Clerks Union of Australia, led by Federal President John Maynes, had had a long-term interest in technological change, particularly computerisation, and especially as it affected office-based employees. The FCUA Federal Office approached me to assist them in the preparation of the Union's submission to the Inquiry. It was intended that the submission be a major piece of work and put forward a comprehensive analysis of emerging technological changes, their likely impacts, and solutions to protect the interests of current and future generations of workers. I agreed to help, and this work rapidly built up later in the year and early in 1979. Our written submission was dated June 7$^{th}$, 1979 and John Maynes and I later appeared before the Committee to give oral evidence.

This work brought me into a close working relationship with Maynes, who had been a key figure in the FCUA since the late 1940s. He was also a key figure on the anti-communist right of the labour movement, before and after the ALP Split. As a result of my work on the CITCA submission, John Maynes offered me a full-time job with the Union, as a Research Officer in the Union's Federal Office. Since this offered me a better and more secure income, I accepted the offer and began work with the Clerks Union in August 1979, quitting my part-time union jobs [although maintaining my connection with the Rope and Cordage Union]. The National Secretary of the FCUA by this time was Terry Sullivan, who had introduced me to the Executive of the Rope and Cordage Union in December 1972. Terry was a wonderful person and friend. He was nominally my boss, but in the Clerks Union, everyone danced to John Maynes's tune.

If I could have foreseen the future at the Clerks Union, I might have thought twice about accepting the job. But it sounded like a good idea at the time, especially since we were now expecting our first child and had managed to secure a home loan despite our precarious income. Working for the Federal Office of the Clerks Union put me at the very centre of anti-communist union activity in Australia. However, although this was not known at the time, the FCUA was soon to face political disintegration.

# 5

# WORKING FOR THE MAN, AT HOME AND ABROAD

*'Where's that piece of paper I had in my hand yesterday morning?'*
*'Miranda Priestly', in The Devil Wears Prada (2006)*

Working for the Clerks Union was not dull. It allowed me to be involved in significant events and gave me many experiences I would not have had otherwise. My years there often provided great satisfaction but also included some intensely difficult times. When I started at the FCUA, I joined the Union as a member. I also became for the first time a member of an Industrial Group, since I also joined the Clerical Workers Industrial Group [CWIG]. This body was a successor to the original ALP Industrial Group in the Clerks Union, formed back in 1946.

I was pleased to be a participant in the long-running fight against Communism which was still in full swing in 1979. The Clerical Workers Industrial Group consisted of members of the Clerks Union but was separate from the structures of the Union. John Maynes, who was part of the original 1946 ALP Industrial Group, was still the key figure in the Group as well as in the Union. Prior to the Split, John Maynes was a member of the ALP and was the Party's candidate in the 1952 election for the State seat of Elsternwick. He was expelled from the ALP in 1955 along with many of his other Industrial group colleagues.[127] I have written elsewhere the story of John Maynes and the Clerks Union' from the 1940s until 1993 [when it amalgamated with two other unions to form the Australian Services Union].[128]

## JOHN MAYNES

In 1979, John Maynes was at the height of his powers. Maynes led the controlling political grouping in the FCUA and was the dominant personality in the Union. It had not always been so. In earlier periods, he had been just one of several significant individuals in the Union. The original ALP Industrial Group that challenged the Communists for control of the Clerks Union had several prominent elected officials. Some of them parted ways with John Maynes and the Industrial Group at the time of the ALP split; others left later.

For example, until 1972, when he was elected to Federal parliament as an ALP member, the Federal Secretary of the Clerks Union was Joe Riordan. Riordan was a former leading member of the Clerks Industrial Group in the NSW Branch. Though he briefly let his ALP membership lapse, he was loyal to the ALP and 'the NSW line' of staying 'to fight another day' at the time of the 1950s Split [as did many such people in NSW]. While staying in his Union positions after the Split and continuing to be fiercely anti-communist, he never felt any allegiance to the NCC and its work. I am told that he personally did not like Maynes. I only met Joe Riordan once, long after he had left the Union. My understanding is that he and John Maynes did not agree on much. Both claimed to be the authors of some of the great achievements of the Union in the 1950s and 1960s. By 1979, Joe Riordan was long gone from the Union. John Grenville had become Federal Secretary after him. Grenville was politically aligned with John Maynes and the NCC at the time he became Federal Secretary but fell out with Maynes before I joined the Union.[129] I have never understood exactly what they argued about.[130]

Grenville's departure meant that Terry Sullivan, the long-standing Assistant Federal Secretary of the Union had to take on the role of Federal Secretary. I had a lot of respect for Terry Sullivan, personally and professionally, but I know he often found it difficult to work with John Maynes. Now Maynes was the undisputed master of the Federated Clerks Union, although he was not an employee of it. He worked for the NCC, directing its work in the union movement. He held only honorary [unpaid] elected positions in the FCU in 1979, including that of Federal President. Maynes was also President of the Victorian Branch of the Union, his original power base. Though only the honorary Branch President, he was the real source of authority. The full-time Branch Secretary was Duncan Cameron, also a former Industrial Group member and NCC supporter who had fallen out with both John Maynes and the NCC.

Maynes and Cameron now disliked each other with a great passion. In April 1982, I became a member of the Clerks Union Victorian Branch Executive at the regular triennial elections, when Deputy President Frank Neenan retired. Michael O'Sullivan moved up to the Deputy Branch President position and I became Vice-President at age 29. Harry Darroch was Assistant Secretary and politically loyal to Maynes, but he was also Assistant Secretary to Duncan Cameron. Harry Darroch was not in an easy position. In 1982 our election as Executive members was unopposed, the last uncontested election for a long time. I attended many meetings of the Victorian Branch Executive. They were generally awful. I was largely a spectator. The two old bulls – Maynes and Cameron – fought each other to the death at every meeting. Michael and Harry tried to be constructive. Duncan Cameron resisted John Maynes who gave him an extremely hard time in return.

To be fair to Maynes, I imagine that he could have dropped Cameron from the Group's election ticket at any time, but he chose not to do so. Duncan Cameron kept his position until he decided to retire in early 1985, just before the 1985 election. Executive meetings were rarely productive or enjoyable. I recall one meeting when John and Duncan were arguing about a decision to be made on a particular matter. Duncan's method of keeping the minutes was to record decisions on a handheld tape recorder when each agenda item was concluded with a decision made. No agreement was being reached on this issue. Eventually, Duncan surrendered. He said to John: 'OK, you win, just tell me what words to put on the tape.' In response to this abject capitulation, John Maynes simply said: 'If I had wanted the position of Branch Secretary, I would have stood for it at the last election.' In other words, even in victory, I am not going to help you out. Executive meetings in this period were a terrible experience.

My role as Research Officer in the Federal Office was a new one and largely undefined. It meant I did anything and everything and I was largely directed by John Maynes in his role as National President, although often through Terry Sullivan. Being Research Officer meant that I did not have a specific industrial portfolio to look after, but I did do some industrial work and limited advocacy in the Arbitration Commission from time to time if no one else was available. John Maynes largely drove the research and policy agenda of the union and he had a wide range of policy interests. John was a difficult personality to deal with [though he could be generous]. He gave me the impression that he thought that he was surrounded by fools a lot of the time. He appeared to think that people working for other organisations were always better than his employees. Because of his sometimes abrasive manner, many people found it difficult to give him personal loyalty. John Maynes did have a sense of humour which he revealed from time to time. In July 1985, our third child was born. In early August, I received a letter at home from John. It read:

> Dear Keith,
>
> Tess and I would like to convey our congratulations to you and Mary on the birth of your new daughter.
>
> I raised with Tess that a suitable gift would be for her to volunteer to babysit in the first couple of months, but she has turned this down.
>
> Yours faithfully
>
> John Maynes

Some people find it strange that one of my favourite movies is *The Devil Wears Prada*, in which Meryl Streep plays Miranda Priestly, a women's magazine editor. Priestly is an impossible boss. In the movie, Anne Hathaway plays Andrea/Emily [Priestly can't bother to recall her actual name], an assistant to the editor who is forever trying to satisfy her boss's unrealistic demands: 'Where is that piece of paper I had in my hand yesterday?' No one calls Priestly out on her unreasonable behaviour. I viewed the movie as a documentary. I understood what the Anne Hathaway character was going through! Working for John Maynes was regularly unpredictable and unreasonable. 'Can you get me the newspaper article about the new President of Singapore that I was reading at home three days ago?' I might have asked in response: 'In which newspaper?' John did not recall. In the movie, Priestly asks Andrea/Emily for an article in 'The Post', not telling her that it was in the Washington, not the New York, *Post*. I understood.[131] I knew never to throw away anything John had ever asked for, because he would ask for it again and usually more than once, and because he would lose it – where is that piece of paper you gave me yesterday?' The staff in the Federal Office never gave John the original of anything if they could help it.

John always wanted more and better information on which to make a decision, often when that information was unobtainable. Perhaps he found it hard to make decisions and justified a delay by waiting for 'further and better particulars.' Since complete information was generally not available [this was before the internet and Google], decisions sometimes did not get made in a timely way. John's regular demands for information did propel me into being a rapid response researcher. John also seemed reluctant to give precise instructions. At times, working for John felt like feeling your way down a narrow pathway with electrified fences on either side. John was not a 'light on the hill' type of leader who pointed to the goal and let people get there on their abilities and methods.

In 1979, though, despite his sometimes difficult personality, John was in almost complete control of the FCUA. His supporters controlled all Branches of the Clerks Union, except the small South Australian Branch and the Taxation Officers Branch. In the large Central and Southern Queensland Branch, he had seen off a challenge in 1976 from another NCC defector, John Forrester, who had split from the NCC in the mid-1970s. Maynes asked his supporter Joan Riordan to stand against Forrester for the position of Branch Secretary and she did, winning handsomely.

John's influence in the wider trade union movement was reasonably strong in 1979. He had a good relationship with Jim Maher, the Victorian Secretary and Federal President of the SDA, the Shop Assistants Union. The two men were long-standing friends and colleagues. The two Unions had jointly bought a building at 53 Queen Street in Melbourne via a trust company known as FEDSDA. The SDA had benefited even more than the FCUA from the Retail union membership agreement with the major retailers and was well on its way to becoming the biggest union in Australia. Through joint campaigns with the SDA, John was able to put many of his ideas and plans into effect, in a way which would not have been possible for the Clerks Union on its own. John was an ideas man, as well as a numbers man, although Michael O'Sullivan did much of the detailed leg work on the numbers.

All of John Maynes's ideas may not have been original, but he read widely and identified trends and useful ideas from many sources. These he turned into policy which he pushed through the Clerks Union and for which he sought support from the wider union movement. The Clerks Union took a wide range of policy issues seriously although in the Branches the emphasis was always generally on the more mundane 'bread and butter' industrial issues facing members. John Maynes was largely immune from most of the day-to-day pressures of unionism, despite being Victorian President. He focused on the big picture and the big policy ideas. On more than one occasion, after a National Executive Committee meeting in the Federal Office, I can recall Branch officials saying quietly to me 'Oh well, now back to the real world!' Maynes was in many ways at the forefront of ideas but at the same time living in the past. He had been the driving force behind wresting the Clerks Union from the hands of the left. But his organising solutions often belonged to a bygone era. His social policy was 1950s conservative Catholicism. He was a man of contradictions.

*At an FCUA Victorian Branch Dinner. Standing are the author [left] and Duncan Cameron. Seated [from the left] are John Maynes, Keith Marshall, then President of the Industrial Relations Commission of Victoria, and Harry Darroch.*

Despite these challenges, the FCUA under John's leadership had managed some important and leading-edge industrial gains. Unionising white-collar workers through the application of the 'preference to unionists' provisions of the Conciliation and Arbitration Act was one such achievement [although several other FCUA officials, including Joe Riordan, played key roles as well].[132] John's interest in technological change and its effects on workers was translated into work to secure important employment protections for workers. In the early 1980s, the Victorian Branch of the Clerks Union applied to vary the Victorian Commercial Clerks Award [the main State clerical award] to provide new rights to employees facing technological change. The clause sought to be inserted into the award provided that if employers were even contemplating technological changes that might impact their employees, they had to notify those employees and the Union Secretary and discuss the effects of any possible changes. The Chairman of the Clerks Wages Board refused to grant the provision claimed by the Union.

The Branch appealed this decision and was successful in convincing the Victorian Industrial Relations Commission to insert this clause. The employers were strongly opposed to this measure. They, in turn, appealed the Commission's decision to the Victorian Supreme Court which upheld their appeal, quashing the clause. The Victorian Branch had to consider whether it was worth the risk of further appealing this decision to the High Court of Australia, the ultimate arbiter. The Branch decided to appeal again, and in 1984, while I was in my first term as a member of the Branch Executive, the High Court ruled in our favour. Key to the High Court's decision was a consideration of whether notification about contemplated technological change was an 'industrial matter' and the Court concluded that it was.[133] This was a major win for employees facing the effects of technological changes then sweeping through white-collar employment as a result of computerisation. The FCUA sought to flow this decision to other clerical awards in other States.

The Clause that the Victorian Branch of the Clerks Union won was significantly stronger with respect to notification rights than any other award provision later obtained in other awards. In 1984, the ACTU was successful in its Termination, Change and Redundancy Test [TCR] Case. The ACTU's claim and the outcomes were more extensive than the Clerks' decision, but under the Federal clause employers only had to notify employees and their unions after they had decided to make changes that would affect employees.[134] The Victorian clause required notification before decisions were made. The federal TCR clause ultimately became both the standard federal award clause and *Fair Work Act* provision and the additional benefits of the Victorian clause have been lost.

One of the effects of technological change and the computerisation of office work was the widespread incidence of injuries to office workers, particularly women doing keyboard work, and especially through Repetition Strain Injury [RSI]. John Maynes took a keen interest in this issue and he and I worked closely on this matter, assembling a group of occupational health and safety experts to advise the Union on ways to combat this occupational epidemic. Maynes had a range of interests and ideas that he pursued. He was particularly interested in promoting the idea of 'phased-in' retirement, so that older workers could gradually exit the workforce and create job opportunities for young people.[135]

The Union, and especially John Maynes, campaigned hard against a consumption tax when it was proposed by the incoming Hawke/Keating Government at the Economic Summit in 1983. This action, supported by the ACTU leadership, kept this issue off the national political agenda until the Howard Government reintroduced the idea and eventually legislated for a Goods and Services Tax [GST] in the late 1990s. Under the leadership of Maynes, the Clerks Union played a prominent role in policy debates about family income support, supplying part of the support which enabled the Hawke government to boost family income support payments.

The Clerks Union prided itself on its support for equal pay for 'work of equal value' not just for equal work. In 1969, the ACTU took a test case to the Federal tribunal seeking equal pay for equal work. The FCUA did not support a claim in this form - and said so - believing that only a relatively small number of women would benefit. Only about 18% of women workers did receive better pay from the 1969 decision because the rest could not demonstrate that they performed 'equal work' due to gender segmentation in the Australian workforce. In 1972, the ACTU pursued another case based on equal worth and this was successful.[136] This claim was the correct policy approach that had long been advocated by the Clerks Union. John Maynes was ahead of his time on this question. The principle of 'equal pay for work of equal value' is the basis for the current 'comparable worth' provisions in the current *Fair Work Act*. But even these provisions struggle to produce results for women workers who are still paid on average significantly less than men, despite equal award wages.

John Maynes was also concerned about the impact of multinational companies on employment opportunities and working conditions and wages in Australia and other countries. He was at the forefront of thinking about this issue, addressing an international union conference on this subject in Malaysia as early as 1974[137]. Maynes was a genuine trade union internationalist. He believed that it was important that all workers in every country should be organised into unions so that labor standards could be raised and protected everywhere. He worked well with unionists from South East Asia and the Pacific [especially Fiji] and in particular with those from Japan. I was told that John Maynes had been a guard in a prisoner of war camp during World War Two. He had a limp which kept him from more active service. But he had no trouble relating very well to Japanese unionists.

John Maynes loved international travel. He was of the view that you did not just go to a meeting overseas and come straight back. It was important to get the most value possible from airfares and add other relevant activities to any trip. He encouraged many within the Clerks Union to broaden their horizons and travel overseas to interact with unionists in other countries and cultures. He encouraged me to do so. He was generous in this respect. John Maynes was also an entrepreneur at heart, as one of his sons said at his funeral. But, Doncaster Travel, the one business that he got the two Unions involved in via FEDSDA, produced no useful financial return to the two Unions.

Given his often difficult personality and style, two questions can be reasonably asked: 'Why did anyone listen to John? Why did you keep working for him?' For me, the answer lay in the importance and relevance of the work I was doing, both industrially and politically. John's supporters were all committed to the same vocation, to the same cause. We put up with John Maynes, probably when we should not have done so, because we saw real value in the work we were doing. Maynes had his talents, despite not being the best leader of people. Maynes was a hard worker and many of his policies were appropriate to the needs of workers. He read voraciously including newspapers, magazines, court transcripts, everything. He was interested and inquisitive about the world around him. John Maynes could fit things into a world view. He did not write particularly well however and one of my jobs was to try and put John's thoughts into a more coherent and more elegantly expressed way. I was not the only one who had this challenge. I was secretly pleased when a newspaper report of the FCUA's submission to the Committee of Inquiry into Technological Change in Australia [the CITCA inquiry] – which I had drafted under John's direction – described the submission as 'lucid.' I was not quite sure what that word meant at the time but when I looked up the definition, I found that it meant a period of clarity in between bouts of insanity. I took that as a compliment. I spent a lot of time re-working John's many ideas into clear English, whether it be the Minutes of Union meetings or articles and pamphlets for publication, of which there were many.

John Maynes did not have the eloquence of his colleague Bob Santamaria nor the public persona. But he tackled the issues as he saw them. He was prepared to stand up in a hostile union meeting and advance his ideas. Despite his faults, he fought the good fight to the end. Many others fell by the wayside. I worked very closely with John and became his biographer [in a minor way] after he died. He was bitterly disappointed that his life's work was undone at the end. He stayed too long at the helm of the Clerks Union and became absorbed with protecting his legacy. I developed a good working relationship with him and survived to tell the tale. I can well understand those who found him too difficult to work with over the longer term.

## THE SPLIT IN THE NCC AND THE ROLE OF SANTAMARIA

Although I did not know it then, when I began working for the Clerks Union a serious problem was developing inside the NCC. Within two years this led to a permanent rupture in the organisation and the exodus of nearly all the people associated with the NCC who were working in the trade union movement. The internal operations of the NCC were a mystery to me. I knew people who had certain roles in the Movement, but not how the organisation's rules and processes worked. The NCC, it seemed to me, was focused on its work, not its internal structures. My assumption was that there would not be internal politics within the NCC because of the nature of its work and the motivation of the people involved. This view turned out to be completely wrong.

If I had known anything of the NCC's history, I would have known that it had been through many difficult times and several incarnations. This was largely due to differences within the Catholic Church in Australia about the role of the Movement as a Catholic organisation. There was a major rift on this issue between the Sydney and Melbourne Archdioceses which was referred to and resolved by the Vatican. But I had not even been a Catholic all that long and these matters were unknown to me at the time. I was only interested in the anti-communist cause in which the NCC was a major force.

In retrospect, I should have known that something was amiss in 1980 when certain NCC officials stopped returning my phone calls. I had reason to ring some of them from time to time. John Maynes had an office in the NCC National Headquarters which was now in Queen Street in Melbourne. I went there from time to time. Depending on the issue of the day, I might need to talk to other people who worked there. During 1980, not long after I began working at the Clerks Union, John Maynes, Michael O'Sullivan and Gerald Mercer, then National Secretary of the NCC, convened a meeting of industrial and certain other supporters of the NCC. They jointly briefed us on a dispute that had emerged in the NCC. Many of us at this meeting were surprised and disappointed by these developments. The protagonists in this dispute were Maynes, O'Sullivan and Mercer on the one hand and B. A. Santamaria and his supporters in the Queen Street office on the other hand. It was not clear to me in the beginning what Santamaria's real views were, but his supporters appeared to be waging some sort of battle either on his behalf or with his consent. The reason for the conflict was obscure but the reason for the non-returned phone calls was now obvious. Factions were forming.

This dispute has been documented elsewhere, particularly by Patrick Morgan, Mark Considine and Gerard Henderson.[138] I have no reason to disagree with the accuracy of their accounts which agree with each other in key respects. Having no formal role in the NCC, I was not directly involved in this dispute. But I, and I suspect most NCC supporters, saw B. A. Santamaria as a great talent and formidable leader and were extremely disappointed to learn that there was an internal dispute going on. Moreover, we were shocked to learn that the leader of the Movement appeared to be tolerating, supporting, or even encouraging certain behaviour that was reported to us at the briefing.

Patrick Morgan, who had access to Santamaria's files in the State Library of Victoria, published two volumes of documents dealing with Santamaria's life and work, including this internal split. Despite having access to relevant documents, Morgan concluded that the reasons for the NCC split 'remain something of a mystery'.[139] Morgan also says, however, that 'Once the dispute developed Santamaria was the instigator and driver of these events'[140] but this fact was not clear to me at the time. The industrial wing of the NCC backed its leaders John Maynes and Michael O'Sullivan. After the first phase of the NCC's internal troubles, a trial separation of the disputing parties was agreed to in August 1980. Those full-time NCC officials in the industrial camp were situated at the NCC's Victorian State offices in Queensberry Street, Carlton. Certain divisions of labour and income were agreed to on an interim basis.

This arrangement lasted for two years. At the end of this period, despite proposals to work towards full re-integration put forward by John Maynes, relationships between the two groups broke down completely. On the 5th September 1982, Santamaria sacked five NCC officials associated with John

Maynes. Those five officials legally challenged the validity of this action by the NCC President and a date was set for a court hearing. On the 2nd November, Melbourne Cup Day, Santamaria moved to occupy the Queensberry Street offices, changing the locks, and putting security guards inside. Morgan records that 'all files and personal belongings were removed.'[141] This was disturbing behaviour but there was worse to come. These actions are documented in Gerard Henderson's book.[142] Some of Santamaria's former friends, colleagues and supporters went to their graves with the threat of personal legal action against them started by Santamaria still unresolved.[143]

Immediately after the occupation of the Queensberry Street offices, a roster of industrial wing supporters was arranged to mount a watch over the premises to prevent the Santamaria forces from removing files. This activity went on for some time. I took part in this roster, standing in Queensberry Street at night, on one occasion fielding questions from an inquisitive journalist.

Before the final split, I decided that I should go and see Santamaria and hear from him his version of events. I made an appointment to see him in his Queen Street office. I must have told Michael O'Sullivan I was doing so. Just before I left for the appointment, I saw a message on my desk to call Michael. I knew instinctively what he would say to me if I returned his call. John Maynes would have spoken to Michael and asked him to ask me not to go to the meeting with Santamaria.

I did not call Michael back. I kept my appointment with Santamaria. The meeting did not go well. Santamaria was patronising in the extreme. He made it sound like it was my fault and my error that I had not been to see him earlier 'given our relationship,' as he put it. Even without having been brought up Catholic, I knew an attempted 'guilt trip' when I heard one. I resented Santamaria's tone at once. If this was going to be his approach to this matter and to me, given our good past relationship, only one conclusion was possible: truth and fairness were not on his side. Today, I do not recall in detail the arguments that Santamaria put to me. But my feeling at the time was that they were neither convincing nor genuine.

It is always disappointing when someone held in high esteem turns out to be a god with feet of clay. This was not the last time this would happen to me. I returned to my office and returned Michael's call. I told him that he did not need to worry about where my loyalties lay. Sometime after the NCC split, John Maynes - with the consent of his colleagues - gave me several files relating to this rupture and asked me to look at them with a fresh eye. Maynes wanted me to see if I could work out what was the underlying basis for the dispute since it was never clear to him either. Because of this request, I had an opportunity to look at these documents and issues in some detail. As was the case with other researchers, I could find no substantive reason for the emergence of the dispute. The 'reasons' advanced by Santamaria in the documents were all minor matters which did not warrant any action against any individual let alone splitting the organisation. None of them were touched on by Santamaria in our meeting, I recalled. Patrick Morgan is correct in concluding that the origins of this dispute are a mystery.

I did not keep any of these files given to me by John Maynes or make copies. The conclusion that I put to Maynes was that these events perhaps could be likened to the so-called 'Cultural Revolution' in China, which I had studied at Monash University. In the Cultural Revolution, Mao unleashed his cadres [the Red Guards] on the Communist Party itself as well as on society. Mao remained slightly aloof while his acolytes wreaked havoc. This reminded me somewhat of what Santamaria appeared to have been doing [without the bloodshed], although it still does not explain it. Patrick Morgan's view that Santamaria must have been driving this dispute appears correct to me, given what I had read. John Maynes is quoted in the Considine paper saying that it appeared that the organisation had a 'death wish' visited upon it.[144] This also appeared to be true. While I, like others, cannot be certain of Santamaria's reasons for starting this dispute, there are two or three likely explanations for his actions.

Santamaria may have wanted the NCC to end then and there. His intent may have been to preserve his legacy and reputation. Perhaps he wanted to find an excuse to wind it up and looked to manufacture some allegedly bad behaviour by others to justify this outcome. Someone other than him would be to blame for the premature end to the work which he had started in the 1930s. A second explanation may simply be that Santamaria wanted to end the industrial work. He had once seen the work in the unions as the solution to Australia's communist problem. Now he seemed to think that unions themselves were the problem and he no longer wanted to be associated with people who supported unionism. Perhaps Santamaria was now too close to the Liberal Party and was possibly embarrassed by his union connection.

Patrick Morgan says that:

> Santamaria was moving to the position that unions were in some ways an impediment to the development of a properly functioning nation. He had increasing contacts with the business world, from which some of his funds came, and was advising the Sir Charles Court Government in Western Australia on how to control union activities in that state. Some said that Santamaria had changed sides... [145]

By the time these events took place, I had been working in the trade union movement for more than eight years. I had represented poorly paid blue-collar and migrant workers [and now clerks]. My initial motivation in entering the union movement may have been political anti-communism but I had now seen firsthand the value of unionism. If Santamaria did have the view suggested by Morgan, I certainly would not have supported him. Another third possibility was that Santamaria now simply thought that social and moral issues were more important than communism and that he wanted to concentrate on those matters. If so, he needed an excuse to shut down the industrial work.

In 1997, the year before he died, Santamaria was interviewed as a part of Film Australia's Australian Biography series.[146] In this lengthy interview, now freely available, he was asked, amongst many other things, about the reasons for the internal dispute and split in the NCC. The interviewer asked Santamaria when he thought there was a need to change the focus of the Movement away from work in the Unions to a more 'cultural sociological focus'. That is to say, to focus the Movement on social issues, such as those concerning the family, the role of women, the 'sexual revolution' and changing attitudes to religion. Santamaria said that his concerns about these issues had been emerging from the 1960s and that he was aware of these significant social issues from the very beginning. He told the interviewer:

> So it was something big and different. And again, the question was, is this our business or not? And ... because it seemed to be nobody else's business.

He was then asked: 'Did everybody agree with you?' Santamaria replied:

> No. There were people in the NCC and they were friends - they'd been close friends and collaborators of mine for thirty years - who felt very strongly that I was leading the thing along the wrong lines. That it was still important to concentrate absolutely on the unions and on the Labor Party. My argument was that the unions were going to cease to be critical to anything that we were interested in. As long as we could ... had enough strength to hold Communism,

> or a revival of Communism, at bay, I thought that the union movement would decline in importance, and it has in fact. When today you've only got - what is it? - about twenty-five per cent of the workforce who are members. And I think that that will inevitably happen, although I'm opposed to it happening. I believe in the union movement. So that was ... and they left us. And it was a very bad blow to me. That was about 1978 to 1980.[147]

Santamaria's explanation for the NCC split – according to this answer – boils down to the suggestion that he thought there should be a pivot in the organisation's work towards social issues and that those working in the trade union rejected this move. This was 'a bad blow' to him. This explanation has no basis, for at least two reasons. Firstly, the NCC - as a whole - had been engaged in work promoting the NCC's social policies for many years. There is no evidence that those in the NCC leadership who ended up being opposed to Santamaria had different views to him on these questions. Rather, they fully supported those policies and saw the trade union movement as a way to influence social policies as well as strictly industrial ones. To give just one example, the FCUA fully supported policies to improve family income support in Australia and were successful in gaining ACTU and ultimately Hawke Government support for such measures.[148]

Trade union activists associated with the NCC were also engaged in contesting the field of women's policy against what they saw as 'radical feminists' on issues such as abortion. To give another example, during the International Year of Women in 1975, the FCUA and the SDA [as I recall] sponsored a visit to Australia by Helga Cammell, a senior official of the international white-collar union federation to which both Unions were affiliated. The visit was intended to be a counterfoil to some of the more radical feminist policy positions that were being promoted by left-wing activists at the time.[149] Helga Cammell was to be the voice of a more moderate feminism [although I doubt that she would have supported any of the NCC's views on women and family issues]. I was not part of this endeavour and did not support many of the NCC's policies on the role of women and the family. But for Santamaria to suggest that there was a lack of support for activities on social issues from the NCC's trade union leaders and activists is disingenuous, to say the least. It appears to have been a post-event concoction.

Secondly, in the papers relating to the NCC split that John Maynes gave me to read there was no suggestion at all that the issues at stake involved the policy directions of the NCC. They all related to internal administrative matters or to the 'authority' of Santamaria as the National President of the NCC.

Thus, at its most fundamental level, and based on the documents that I saw, Santamaria seems to have seen the dispute as him asserting his personal authority and leadership over the whole organisation. This came out clearly in the documents that I read. But there was no actual threat to his position as National President. It seemed to me that any threats to his authority existed only in his mind. Patrick Morgan reproduces in his book a Confidential Briefing Note written by Santamaria in August 1980 as the first division of the NCC was being implemented. In the very first paragraph he says:

> 1. *The organisation has always been bound together by fundamentally religious bonds, and the trust deriving from them. Among other things, this meant that the use of "political" methods for serious purposes relating to the control of the organisation itself, e.g. winning positions, changing the constitutional structure by deception, while understandable in political bodies, were excluded. ...* [150]

But this is exactly the sin Santamaria had now committed. He treated his 'opponents', some of whom did not even know they were opponents, in a political and deceptive manner. Some of Santamaria's long-time colleagues were devastated by his actions and by his breach of their trust. Some of them would have originally joined the NCC because of his leadership. They had often given up much to do work which they saw as a spiritual vocation. There are many good organisations which have split, including religious organisations proper, and the impact is often severe. Many people will lose faith not just in the organisation and its leaders but in the inherent value of the work itself.

Pressed by his Australian Biography interviewer to 'sum up in a few sentences what was really the heart of the thing that made this [NCC] division occur', Santamaria replied:

> *Well, as far ... I really can't understand, even today. I can't understand why what eventuated did eventuate...* [151]

This answer is neither candid nor sincere and yet may be the last words that he spoke publicly on this matter. As far as I can tell, Santamaria is the only person who knows why this split occurred. He never acknowledged his role in it nor his responsibility for it. According to him, it was the fault of others and he was the victim. His reasons for the split have gone to the grave with him, but they are not the ones he has given. The split in the NCC did not disturb my commitment to the cause of anti-communism. I came to my ideological position independently, long before I had heard of B. A. Santamaria and the NCC. If others had let the anti-communist fight down by their actions, for me the struggle was still important and not yet over.

As a result of this split, the NCC's former industrial activists formed a new body. It was initially known as the Industrial Action Fund [IAF] - which was at once proscribed by the Victorian ALP - and later simply as Social Action. A new structure was created for this new body by John Maynes and others, but I refused to play a formal role in it since in my judgment it repeated the problem of central control that had rendered the councils of the NCC undemocratic. However, I did actively support the work of Social Action. It tried to keep its union activists together, but the nascent group had little funding and little ability to influence events. John Maynes now became a full-time Federal President of the FCUA – since he no longer had his NCC position – and was now based in the Federal Office of the Union.

Social Action supplied a meeting place for activists. It was the location of meetings of 'Full Time Officers' [FTOs]. Social Action also published a monthly magazine, initially known as *Solidarity* or *Solidarnosc* after the Polish trade union but later simply as *Social Action*. The magazine was edited by Gerald Mercer who was one of a handful of staff of the new body. There was a three-person editorial board of which I was a member and together we wrote virtually all its articles from April 1981 until December 2005 when the magazine ceased publication. Working with Gerald Mercer was a pleasure. He was one of the few people I have ever met in politics or the union movement without a blistering ego. John Maynes and Michael O'Sullivan drifted away from Social Action and the Editorial Board became the key body. Eventually, it was decided to wind up the organisation in December 2005.

## POLISH SOLIDARITY

If B. A. Santamaria, or anyone else, needed evidence of the ongoing importance and value of free and independent trade unions, both in their own right and for their importance in the fight against communism, it was about to be provided in Eastern Europe. In August/September 1980 as the NCC began its trial separation period, the Polish trade union Solidarnosc [Solidarity in

English] erupted onto the world stage. A strike had begun in the Gdansk shipyards on Poland's Baltic coast and Lech Walesa climbed the walls of the shipyard not only to lead the strike but to form a country-wide movement.

Within a short period, Solidarnosc had 10 million members and the Communist regime in Warsaw had been forced to recognise it and to negotiate with it. Solidarnosc was the first free and independent union movement in the Soviet bloc and its emergence was given moral support and encouragement by the Polish-born Pope John Paul II. Here was what anti-communists had been waiting for: a crack in the monolithic Soviet empire. There had been popular uprisings against Soviet-imposed regimes before, including in Hungary in 1956 and Czechoslovakia in 1968, but both had been put down by Soviet tanks. The world waited to see what the Soviet Union would do in Poland. Solidarnosc was a live demonstration of the importance of real trade unionism, both in the struggle for workers' rights and improved living standards and in the struggle against totalitarianism. These were exciting times, full of hope.[152]

While the NCC bickered internally, concrete action for social justice and freedom was occurring in Eastern Europe. The NCC should have been focused on the opportunities presented by this development, but it was self-destructing. In December 1981, the Polish government cracked down on the new union movement. The Communist regime declared martial law, banned Solidarnosc and detained its leaders. Lech Walesa vanished from sight. Two Solidarnosc officials were abroad when martial law was declared and avoided detention: Jerzy Milewski and Magda Wojcik who were based in Solidarnosc's Brussels office. In 1982, the FCUA and the SDA jointly decided to invite these two officials to Australia for a speaking and publicity tour to highlight the plight of the suppressed union. This was practical action in defence of free trade unionism.

The tour was organised for the second half of 1982. It included media interviews, public meetings, and meetings with union bodies. The trip was successful in raising funds to support Solidarnosc's work in exile and clandestine work in Poland. I was not directly involved in organising this visit but did have the opportunity to meet the visitors when they were in Melbourne. They presented the FCUA with a framed Solidarnosc print which ASU National Secretary Paul Slape later gave me when I retired from the ASU. It proudly hangs on the wall in my home. Re-reading the media surrounding this visit, it is interesting to note that the Polish visitors came under attack from elements of the pro-communist left during their visit and in some meetings with union bodies.[153] Solidarnosc was attacked as a 'counter-revolutionary' and reactionary body even though it genuinely represented millions of Polish workers in a way that the bogus communist-run unions in the Soviet bloc never did. Sections of the left continued to defend anti-worker actions by the Soviet Union and their satellite states.[154]

In its report of the Solidarnosc visit to Victoria, the FCUA's Victorian Branch journal *The Clerk* reported the welcoming words spoken by Victorian Trades Hall Council Secretary Ken Stone, my former employer.[155] Stone said that he had been present at a meeting of the International Labour Organisation conference in Geneva in June 1981 at which Solidarnosc had represented Polish workers. This was a huge development since this was the first time a free and independent union had been able to represent workers from any Communist country.[156] I recalled that it was only a few years previously that Stone had been happy to visit bogus unions in the Soviet Union and to host visits in return. Stone had also attended the Russian 'trade union' Congress in Moscow in 1977 just four years earlier which had been addressed by the Secretary-General of the Communist Party, the person and organisation now suppressing free trade unionism in Poland.

In September 1982, just as the visit from the two Polish trade union activists was ending, B.A. Santamaria sacked John Maynes and his colleagues from their positions in the NCC. The timing could not have been more astounding. However, the FCU and the SDA continued to support the work of Solidarnosc throughout the dark years of the 1980s. The *Australian Solidarity with Poland Fund* was set up to supply ongoing assistance through fund-raising and donations. Jim Maher was President and John Maynes the Organising Secretary of this fund and it had an extensive list of patrons and honorary members. The Fund raised hundreds of thousands of dollars to support Solidarnosc and its underground work in Poland.

Both FCUA National President John Maynes and SDA National President Jim Maher were later recognised by Solidarnosc for their help in the Union's darkest hours. Both met Lech Walesa in Gdansk in 1990.[157] In 1990, Jim Maher was awarded the Commander's Cross of the Order of Merit of the Republic of Poland. In 2010, both Maynes and Maher [amongst others] were posthumously awarded Medals of Gratitude by the Polish Government on the 30th anniversary of the formation of Solidarnosc. The medal is awarded to those of non-Polish descent who supported Poland in its battle for freedom and democracy.[158] In 1990, I had the small job of organising a reception at the Union's office for a visiting Solidarnosc MP, Andrzej Lapicki. He was one of the new members of the Polish parliament elected in a clean sweep of available positions won by Solidarnosc in the first free elections in a Soviet bloc country in 1989. It was immensely satisfying to play even a small part in these historic events which were, in part, the fulfillment of political hopes I had had since I was at school in the 1960s. But this was still in the future in 1981-2, and the outcome was not at all certain.

## INTERNATIONAL AFFAIRS

Working for the Federal office of the Clerks Union and John Maynes meant the opportunity to travel overseas. John Maynes was genuinely interested in the international trade union movement and encouraged this interest in others. In January 1981, I represented the ACTU at a meeting of an International Labour Organisation [ILO] Committee discussing industrial issues facing salaried employees and professional workers. This was my first overseas trip connected to the FCUA, which had nominated me to attend on behalf of the ACTU and Australia. The ILO, formed by the Treaty of Versailles in 1919, brought together countries with the aim of setting basic minimum standards for employment. Its remit included a range of employment-related issues, including occupational health and safety, education and training, technological change, and the like. Countries could become members of the ILO and were obliged to send tripartite delegations to meetings: government representatives [Ministers and/or public servants as the status of the meeting required], employers and unions. Government bore the cost.

The salaried employees and professional workers committee meeting in Geneva in early 1981 was a private sector committee and there were not many other unions interested in such employees in Australia. Since the meeting was in the middle of the northern winter, there was no other interest from within the FCUA. The ACTU chose two worker representatives to attend. Before leaving Australia, the whole delegation [including the employers] had a briefing from the Federal Department on how the ILO worked. We were told that if this were our first meeting of the ILO, we simply would not understand what was going on and would have to wait for a further meeting to be able to take part effectively. This was completely wrong.

The meeting in Geneva lasted two weeks. The ILO processes were very bureaucratic. It was amazing to watch the system in action. Prior to the meeting, the ILO distributed a background discussion paper on the themes of the meeting. It was a serious and well-written document. For the first week, the meeting broke up into sub-committees to consider the various themes in the discussion paper. In 1981, one of these was technological change in which the FCUA had a significant interest. I had some knowledge of this subject because of the work I had done on the Union's CITCA inquiry submission. I was allocated to this sub-committee by the workers' group. The ILO had a secretariat which helped the workers' group to function in the byzantine world of the ILO. There was similar help for the employers.

In addition, international union federations had the right to attend ILO meetings as observers and supplied leadership to the union delegates. At this meeting, the union federation was the white-collar international union federation known as FIET, its acronym in French. The FCUA was an active affiliate of FIET. John Maynes was an Executive Member of the international body and President from time to time of its Asian regional grouping. The FIET briefings and assistance were excellent and there was never any difficulty in understanding the ILO processes. It was possible to be fully involved from day one. Before each session of any committee or sub-committee, the workers' group would meet. FIET, through Heribert Maier, the General Secretary, or one of his staff, discussed with the group the significant points likely to come up in the day's discussions and suggested approaches that we should take. Participants were asked to address certain points so that the union position was on the record and would be considered in the outcomes of the meeting.

*Attending my first ILO meeting in January 1981.*
*Image used with permission of Studio L. Bianco, Geneva.*

At major meetings of the ILO, the outcomes are often Conventions or Recommendations dealing with particular workplace issues. Conventions, if ratified by member States, are binding and countries are obliged to give effect to them in national laws. Several of Australia's industrial relations laws benefiting employees have been based on ratified ILO Conventions. These include those on Discrimination in Employment and on Termination of Employment – the unfair dismissal laws. In the case of the meeting in 1981, the outcome was more modest: a report and some non-binding recommendations for countries to consider. Nevertheless, the workers' group wanted the best possible report and recommendations as these could help in negotiations with governments and employers. The employers' group generally wanted the ILO to say as little as possible and certainly nothing that could be used against them in their home countries.

The ILO process was that for the first week, delegates commented on the draft report, highlighting and supporting those parts they liked, and downplaying those they did not. The goal was to influence the draft Conclusions document that was prepared by the ILO Secretariat over the intervening weekend for consideration in the second week. All discussions were conducted in diplomatic and nuanced language. 'It's a very good report, but...' usually meant that the speaker disagreed with the report! Participants could speak in any of the ILO's working languages and their words were simultaneously interpreted by a bank of interpreters in booths at the rear of the room. Delegates had earphones and could listen in the working language of their choice.

Language was important at these meetings. I remember the English-speaking chair of a working session imploring delegates to speak clearly in standard, non-colloquial language to help the interpreters. He then called for speakers saying, 'Now, who wants to open the batting?' ignoring his own plea. The official written languages of the ILO were English and French. That meant that the text of all meeting outcomes had to be agreed in both languages. The French government delegate liked to tell everybody that the French language version was not correctly worded.

I was fascinated by this process and by language differences. Coming from Australia and tolerably literate in English I was impressed by the working ability of many people in two or three languages. Heribert Maier, who was Austrian, would turn up one day and do his briefing in English, the next day in French, then German. I understand that he could get by in Spanish as well. The hotel maids I met could speak more than one language. Geneva is in a French-speaking part of Switzerland and some people went there just to learn another language. I was embarrassed that I could only speak one language [as was the case with most other English speakers]. I resolved two things as a result of my trip to the ILO: firstly, that I would like to work for an international union body and secondly that I would learn another language before I died. I never achieved the first goal [I only ever applied once, unsuccessfully]. I am still working on the second. When I returned to Australia, I took some French lessons but could not keep it up for long. I returned to this task later in life.

When I flew to Geneva in January 1981, I booked myself an economy class ticket. The FCUA's travel policy allowed me to arrive two days before the meeting so that I was not jetlagged at the start of the meeting. I was somewhat annoyed to learn later that the rest of the Australian delegation had flown

First Class, as allowed by the policy of the Australian Government which was paying the bill. In my spare time over the two weeks in Geneva, I worked hard to ensure that I had a first-class seat on the way home! This was not easy in the days before email and mobile phones. Approval was obtained and bookings made just before I left Geneva.

John Maynes insisted that I could not just go to Geneva and come straight back home. He wanted me to return via London and meet with a union official or two. At one of these meetings in London, I recall discussing the approach of unions in the UK to British membership of the European Union. Left-wing unions were opposed to Britain's membership. Why was this? Because the Soviet Union was opposed to a strong Europe [as is Putin's Russia today]. This was yet another example of the maxim that every policy was seen through the prism of support or opposition to the Soviet 'experiment', that is in practice, the Soviet Union's policy objectives.[159] In London, I also met with an organisation known as the Industrial Research and Information Service [IRIS] and its Executive Officer Andy McKeon. IRIS, I believed, was a body somewhat similar to the NCC and the ALP Industrial Groups in orientation and, to a lesser extent, in action.

Before making this trip, I had thought that the NCC and the Industrial Groups were unique to Australia and, to a certain extent, this was true. However, IRIS had a similar concern, that is, penetration of the UK trade union movement by the Communist Party of Great Britain. IRIS may not have had the same level of participation by rank and file workers as the ALP Industrial Groups, but it was opposed to the activities of British communists and supported moderate candidates in union elections. IRIS was run by a board of anti-communist unionists and British Labor Party members.

After a day or two in London, I went out to Heathrow to catch my flight home. This is when my first-class seat became useful. Unfortunately, it was a foggy night in London and while other airlines were taking off, Qantas would not fly. The 16 of us in first class were taken off the plane first, bused to an airport hotel, given the key to a room, and pointed in the direction of the restaurant. In the morning we were taken back to the plane. I do not recall going through customs and immigration when getting off or back onto the plane. I flew to Singapore where John Maynes had arranged for me to visit the Asia Pacific office of FIET and meet its Regional Director, Christopher Ng.[160] The plan was for me to spend the night in a hotel in Singapore and then meet

Christopher but due to the delayed flight, I arrived the following morning. I went straight to his office and spent the day with him trying - not always successfully - to stay awake. Christopher Ng took me back out to the airport to catch the night flight to Melbourne.

I was exhausted and slept most of the way [not getting much value for the Government's first-class ticket!]. When I woke in the morning, I looked at the passenger sitting next to me. He was filling in his arrival card, writing the name 'Keith Harvey' on it. Still waking up, I was thinking 'hang on, that's me', when the Pursuer arrived to sort out this apparent mistake of two people with the same name sitting next to each other in the 16-seat first-class section. What are the chances? My companion's name was also Keith Harvey [but with a different middle name] but was not at all talkative. He was a courier for 'The Department of Transport' [he said] and had a briefcase chained to his wrist, looking very official and serious. He was not one for small talk. I returned to Australia and promptly came down with a stomach bug which laid me low for several days.

At the time of my visit to Geneva, London and Singapore, I was 29 and had been employed by the FCUA for about 18 months. It is to the credit of John Maynes that he supported me in undertaking this trip and arranging for me to meet some of his union contacts abroad. Exposure to the work of the ILO added a new dimension in my understanding of the need for a collective, worldwide approach to the fight to secure and keep decent conditions of employment for all workers. The strength of the ILO lies in its tripartite nature. The involvement of both employer and worker representatives ensures that its outcomes are firmly based on the realities of work, although getting tripartite agreement on issues is a challenge. The work of the ILO is important and useful, particularly in emerging economies.

Countries that are members of the ILO are invited to ratify its Conventions especially the key ones of freedom of association and the right to organise and bargain collectively. These form the basis of an international labor code. If member states ratify ILO Conventions and then do not abide by them, complaints can be made to the ILO. Even the Australian Government has had complaints successfully taken against it and been forced to change legislation as a result. International pressure through the ILO and other international agencies can be helpful in trying to eliminate abuses of worker rights, such as forced labour. Much later in my time at the FCUA and again at the ASU, I was able to attend several more ILO meetings both in the Asia Pacific Region and, in 2000, the International Labour Conference itself in Geneva. This Conference is the ILO's centrepiece meeting and lasts three weeks, although junior ranked delegates were only allowed to stay for the first two weeks – when the detailed work was done.

My trip in 1981 to snowy Geneva was my first as an employee of the Clerks Union. It would not be the last. Throughout the 1980s, I found myself traveling abroad regularly and often to much warmer places.

# 6

# MY COLD WAR IN THE WARM PACIFIC

*'The battle of ideas in the international arena is going on without respite. We will continue to wage it vigorously...our entire system of ideological work should operate as a well-arranged orchestra...'.*

Konstantin Chernenko, Address to the Central Committee of the Communist Party of the Soviet Union, June 1983 [161]

In the early 1980s, the Cold War was still raging and the participants in this struggle had discovered the Pacific as a new theatre of activity. While Cold War action was at its most intense in developed economies, the big power blocs and their allies were always on the lookout for ways to cultivate new alliances and friendly relationships in the Third World. Mainly this activity occurred in Asia, Africa and Central America but by the 1980s there were several newly independent nations in the Pacific. Population numbers were tiny in nearly all these countries and this meant that their Governments' financial resources were limited. A small amount of aid or assistance could buy a lot of influence. This is still true today.

There was concern that the Soviet Union was taking an interest in the Pacific [previously regarded as an American 'lake'].[162] As usual, left-wing organisations were involved, including unions. Australian and New Zealand left-wing unions created the Pacific Trade Union Forum [PTUF] to engage with emerging regional union groups and through them with the broader body politic in this region. The origin of the decision by left-wing unions to take an interest in the Pacific has been traced to a meeting of the World Federation of Trade Unions [WFTU] in Prague in 1978.[163] The WFTU consisted of pro-communist unions from Western countries together with communist controlled 'unions' in the Soviet bloc and other Communist countries. It was, in effect, an arm of Soviet foreign policy. Western union federations, including the ACTU, had broken away from the WFTU as soon as its true nature had become known in the post WW2 period.[164] Western unions formed the International Confederation of Free Trade Unions [ICFTU].

The ACTU and the NZ Federation of Labour [NZ FOL - as it was then known] were both affiliates of the ICFTU but this did not stop some individual unions in Australia or New Zealand from affiliating with the WFTU. The NZ FOL had elected a new left-wing leadership in 1979: Jim Knox was President and Ken Douglas - a member of the pro-Moscow Socialist Unity Party - was Secretary.[165] Even though the NZ FOL was an ICFTU affiliate, Jim Knox appeared to have no difficulty in also attending WFTU conferences, visiting the Soviet Union and undertaking other activities for the WFTU, including in the Pacific.[166] Knox was not a member of the Communist party, but left-wing and anti-American. At the WFTU meeting in Prague in 1978, it was determined that the WFTU and its affiliates should take an interest in the South Pacific, through the union and broader labour movements. Present at the Prague meeting from Australia and New Zealand were Jim Knox, ex-Communist Party of Australia member John Halfpenny, Bill Richardson [from the Australian white-collar union federation ACSPA – shortly to merge with the ACTU] as well as Pat Clancy, Secretary of the Building Workers Industrial Union [BWIU], a key WFTU affiliate in Australia. Clancy was President of the Socialist Party of Australia [SPA], a hard-line pro-Soviet break away from the more 'moderate' CPA. Knox, Halfpenny and Richardson would soon turn up in the Pacific.[167]

At the third meeting of the Nuclear Free Pacific Conference in Hawaii in 1980, it was agreed to form the Pacific Trade Union Forum.[168] Representatives of the WFTU and its affiliates attended PTUF meetings despite having little real presence in the region.[169] The PTUF organised itself around an anti-nuclear stance and in particular in opposition to the testing of nuclear weapons in the Pacific. This was an excellent issue for the left to campaign on. It was a popular policy with Pacific nations and particularly so in New Zealand where, in 1984, a new Labour Government was to ban visits of US nuclear powered and/or armed naval vessels.

The Pacific had indeed borne the brunt of the nuclear age. The two nuclear bombs dropped in WW2 had fallen on Japan, a Pacific Rim nation. The Americans had tested their weapons in the atmosphere over Bikini Atoll in Micronesia [although they were no longer doing so]. The French had conducted atmospheric tests and were still conducting underground tests in the Mururoa Atoll in French Polynesia in the early 1980s. As an issue, nuclear testing fitted well with the foreign policy objectives of the USSR. A Pacific Nuclear Free Zone would have the benefit of making it more difficult for the Americans to deploy their naval forces there especially if more Pacific countries were to follow NZ's later lead and ban visits by nuclear-capable warships.

The first PTUF conference was held in the new Pacific nation of Vanuatu in 1981. Initially, the non-left trade unions in Australia ignored these conferences but later decided that it was unwise to leave this field uncontested. When the PTUF, of which John Halfpenny was now Secretary, announced that it was holding its second conference in Noumea in New Caledonia in 1982, moderate unions decided to attend. I was asked to go as a representative of the FCUA. Several senior union figures from the right turned up, including Simon Crean, then Vice President of the ACTU and later Leader of the Federal ALP, and John MacBean, NSW Labor Council Secretary. Tony Vella also went from the VTHC. The left did not quite know what to make of this.

The conference took place over three days. Because of the limited air services between Australia and Noumea, the capital of the French overseas territory, we had to stay for a week! The meeting ran on French time; that is, it started at about 8.00 am and met until 11.00 am. Then there was a long lunch break until 2.00 pm and an afternoon session. The Australian delegates were briefed before the first session by Bill Richardson, now ACTU Assistant Secretary due to the recent amalgamation with the white-collar peak council ACSPA. Richardson, with Halfpenny, was the key Australian organiser of the PTUF. Bill Richardson briefed us about the 'Pacific way' of making decisions. Unlike the 'brutal' Anglo-Saxon means of resolving matters through majority decision making [the raw use of numbers – which we were all used to], Richardson said that Pacific islanders liked to talk issues out and reach agreed positions by consensus.

*Hard at work in Noumea with from left, Margaret Halfpenny [wife of John at the time], Tony Vella, me, John MacBean, Simon Crean and Bill Richardson.*

This sounded very impressive until the first session began. The big local issue at the time was the question of independence for New Caledonia from France. The local indigenous population, known as Kanaks, supported independence which was strongly opposed by the white French settlers and some other inhabitants of mixed origins.[170] The Kanak people were well represented at the conference by *the Union Syndicale des Travailleurs Kanaks et des Exploités* [USTKE] - the Union of Kanak and Exploited Workers – which had been founded the previous year. Before the conference began its first session, however, the representatives of USTKE demanded that the conference must first agree to its position on independence before any other business could be discussed.

This flew in the face of any notion of proceeding in a consensual 'Pacific way'. Rather, it was a very left-wing and European tactic and a confrontational approach. This demand caused Simon Crean some serious difficulties in his position as ACTU Vice President. The meeting was forced to adjourn before it even got underway to allow for some form of compromise to be worked out which would allow the conference to continue. Eventually, a compromise was negotiated, and the conference went on to make decisions on a range of issues. After the conference, the Australian delegation had about four days to see the sights of New Caledonia before returning home. The Pacific Trade Union Forum met again in October 1984 in Nadi, Fiji. I again attended on behalf of the FCUA.

## LABOR COMMITTEE FOR PACIFIC AFFAIRS

Non-left unions in Australia and the US decided to form a rival body to the PTUF to counteract the influence of the left in the Pacific. Thus was created the Labor Committee for Pacific Affairs [LCPA] modelled on the Labor Committee for Transatlantic Understanding which brought together American and European unions in opposition to the left in Europe. The LCPA was organised via the Asian American Free Labour Institute [AAFLI], an arm of the AFL-CIO, and funded (presumably) with the help of United States government grants. These developments led me to further travel in the Pacific and to become more familiar with the region. Because South Pacific populations and economies were not large, and many workers were still engaged in primary production, conditions for the development of trade unions were not favourable. Few sizeable unions existed. The most developed unions were in Fiji, where a very well organised union movement existed, and in Papua New Guinea. But smaller union federations were emerging in Vanuatu and elsewhere.

The LCPA did not do a great deal. It met initially in Australia and determined that its first major activity would be to invite a group of unionists from the Pacific region to take part in a study tour of the United States. This tour took place in October-November 1983 and I again attended on behalf of the Clerks Union. The USA, through a variety of non-government organisations, hosted a range of overseas visitors, especially during the Cold War. Other countries had similar programs. There was nothing particularly unusual about these types of study programs which were intended to create a favourable impression of the host nation.

The LCPA gathered unionists from PNG, Fiji, Australia and New Zealand to take part in this first tour. It was not hard to get union officials [or anyone else, for that matter] from the region to take part in such a trip. Australians and New Zealanders were always happy to travel overseas to the USA or Europe, particularly if someone else was paying. The same applied to Pacific Islanders. Australians might think of the Pacific as a paradise, but the Pacific islands are some of the most remote places on Earth. An opportunity to get off their island and go to the 'big smoke' of Los Angeles or New York, for example, was always going to be popular. Accepting such a trip was not a reliable indicator of political orientation, however. Some of the Pacific unionists also accepted trips to the Soviet Union or one of its satellite states [as Australian unionists had also done].

There are two Pacific islanders that I met on this trip who are worth mentioning. The first is Joseph Kabui, at the time an Industrial Advocate for the Bougainville Mining Workers Union. I got on very well with Joe. He was a Catholic, an ex-seminarian in fact, highly moral and very committed to social justice. Some of his colleagues from Papua New Guinea [PNG] did not have the same standards as Joe. The PNG delegation arrived in Los Angeles to start the exchange program earlier than the others from Fiji, Australia and NZ. All delegates were provided with a modest *per diem* to cover meals and other expenses. Some of the New Guineans had spent their whole allowance in the first few days before the rest of us had even arrived, much of it in bars and some of it with women. This caused real issues for the tour organisers.

*With Joe Kabui on the train from New York to Washington.*

Joe Kabui was completely different. When we were in Washington as part of the tour, the study group was taken to a 'restaurant' for an evening meal. The venue turned out to be a table-top dancing joint [all the delegates on the trip were males]. Our American union host found nothing inappropriate about this venue. Joe Kabui and I left together in disgust. I can still hear our tour leader's words in my ear as we walked out: 'But the food is great!' All the others stayed but Joe and I found somewhere more suitable to eat, regardless of the quality of the food. Joe Kabui returned to PNG to make a huge impact on his country and on Bougainville. He was working for the Mine Workers Union and the big issue on Bougainville was the copper mine owned and operated by the Australian company Conzinc Rio Tinto at Panguna. The local landowners did not like the mine and its effects on Bougainville society. This led to conflict and demands for independence from PNG.

Not long after he returned home, Joe Kabui went into politics and became President of the Regional Government of North Solomons, which included Bougainville. He then threw in his lot with the secessionist movement and became a commander in the Bougainville Revolutionary Army. This bitter conflict cut Bougainville off from the rest of PNG and the world. The conflict raged for some years but, eventually, a settlement was reached resulting in an Autonomous Bougainville Government. Joseph Kabui was elected its first President in 2005 but died suddenly in office in 2008.[171]

Of similar significance in the future affairs of his country was Mahendra Chaudhry, Assistant Secretary of the Fiji Trades Union Congress. I cannot say that I got to know Mahendra well. He ran a tight ship and kept his delegates under close control. They did not socialise much. The Fiji trade union movement was probably the strongest in the region other than in Australia and New Zealand. Not long after this trip – in 1985 – the Fiji Labour Party was formed and in 1987 surprised everyone with an election victory. Mahendra Chaudhry – a Fijian of Indian origin - was Minister of Finance in this Government which was shortly afterward deposed in a coup by the native Fijian dominated army. Labour party leaders were detained. Chaudhry later became leader of the Labour party and in 1999 the Party again won an election and Chaudhry became Prime Minister. The following year he was deposed in yet another coup. However, he remains the leader of the Labor Party to this day [2021] and continues to campaign for worker and democratic rights in Fiji.

The LCPA study tour to the USA was of mixed quality and relevance. Since there was government funding involved, as well as meeting union officials, the tour included several sessions at the US State Department for discussions on regional policy issues. My notes show that at one session the New Zealand delegates spent a lot of time complaining about the visits of nuclear-powered warships to New Zealand. The State Department might have concluded that they had wasted their money bringing these four 'right-wing' unionists from New Zealand to Washington. One session discussed arms control with a Director for Arms Control from the National Security Council. The New Zealanders were horrified. While arms control was one of the big political issues of the day, these sessions with government officials gave the wrong message to participants in what they thought was a union study program. Other sessions were much more useful. We met with the *Social Democrats, USA* whose political positions largely matched my own. They were pro-labour and anti-communist but came from a strictly secular point of reference. There was no Catholic Action element identifiable in the US as far as I could see.[172] The religious affiliation of many Social Democrats appeared to be Jewish [and they were pro-Israel, of course]. Their written materials and analysis of world affairs were of a high standard.

The number of Pacific countries involved in this initial study program was small. It was decided that in preparation for a further study tour that the LCPA would seek to involve more countries. Thus, in July 1984, it was decided that Larry Specht, the American Director of the LCPA, and I should visit Vanuatu and Western Samoa. Our purpose was to gauge interest from unions in those countries in taking part in a second study tour. When Larry Specht arrived in Australia in mid-year, he found that political support for the Committee's activities was waning. NSW Labor Council Secretary John MacBean expressed this view to Specht. Later, one of the New Zealand unions also rang expressing doubts about the future of the work. Consequently, it was decided that Specht and I would still both go to Vanuatu but that after this part of the trip, he would return to Brisbane to talk to Errol Hodder of the Australian Workers Union to build support for the LCPA. I would go on to Western Samoa alone.

At the airport at Port Vila [the capital of Vanuatu], Larry and I were met by Kenneth Satungia, the Secretary of the Vanuatu Trade Union Congress, the VTUC President, and about six other unionists. It was a warm greeting. Vanuatu was fascinating. Formerly known as the New Hebrides, it had become independent only in 1980. Before independence, it had not one but two ruling colonial powers: the United Kingdom and France - in what was known as a 'condominium' government. The English and French settlers [and the ni-Vanuatu, the indigenous people] could choose to live under either English or French laws. There were two sets of everything – courts, police forces, jails, etc. It was a bizarre arrangement, sometimes called the 'pandemonium'! English and French were spoken and used in Government. The national language was a pigeon tongue called Bislama. This name was derived from the original product for which traders came to these islands - Bêche-la-Mer - a sea cumber used in Asian cuisine. The British government had been happy to move to independence but the French government, and, more particularly, some French settlers, resisted. When independence occurred in July 1980, a settler rebellion broke out on the northern island of Espiritu Santo.[173]

The new government of Prime Minister Father Walter Lini - an Anglican priest - was showing signs of being influenced by left-leaning nations. His Government would later seek exchanges with the Libyan regime of Col. Gaddafi, establish diplomatic relationships with Cuba and sign a fishing treaty with the Soviet Union which included port access for their fishing vessels. These were worrying developments for the Australian government, amongst others.[174] There was no sign of any difficulties when Larry Specht and I met with Kenneth Satungia and his colleagues in 1984. Specht invited the VTUC to take part in a second LCPA exchange visit to the US later that year and Kenneth at once volunteered himself for the trip. His ready willingness to take part in the trip was not surprising. I am certain that locals were not naive; they knew what was going on in international affairs. They were understandably prepared to take aid and assistance from anyone who was offering it, if they thought it would help develop their countries and institutions. Kenneth Satungia did express some disappointment with the Pacific Trade Union Forum. He argued - correctly in my view - that it concentrated on policy issues when what organisations such as his needed was help in union organising. At the time Larry and I visited, the VTUC had only two 'full time' officials – but both were unpaid. Kenneth Satungia indicated that his union federation had little interest in foreign policy issues. They were - along with most others in the region - opposed to French nuclear testing in the Pacific but not, he told us, to nuclear energy as such.

After our formal meetings, Larry Specht and I had time to have a look around. Vanuatu is an archipelago of about 80 islands. Specht was a frustrated travel writer who liked seeing exotic places and we made the most of our time. Firstly, we flew north to Luganville, the main 'town' on the island of Espiritu Santo. I at once thought of it as the last town on the road to nowhere, an example of how remote, isolated and small some Pacific island locations can be. By chance, we arrived on the island on the fourth anniversary of independence [and of the local rebellion]. There were Independence Day celebrations and a parade. It was the first time since the conflict four years earlier that Vanuatu Government representatives had felt comfortable turning up to celebrate independence on the island. The parade was a modest affair, starting with some soldiers from the Vanuatu Army, followed by an army band and concluded with contingents from the local Scouts and Guides. After some official speeches in a park, the band played a few tunes, including *It's a long way from Tipperary*. It certainly is, I thought. We stayed less than a day, met a local union official [a shop steward] and generally looked around. I ran out of film for my camera and could not find anywhere to buy more. It was a remote spot with extremely limited facilities.

Early the next day, we flew down to the island of Tanna to the south of the capital. The main interest on Tanna is Mt Yasur, an active volcano, claimed to be the most accessible in the world. Our light plane landed on a grass airstrip. The 'terminal' was a tin hut. We arranged a trip to the volcano with a local tour operator. Mt Yasur is an ash volcano located on the opposite side of the island to the airstrip. On the leeward side of the volcano, the landscape resembled the Moon. It was an ash-covered desert. We drove across this moonscape and up the mountain on the windward side. It was possible to drive almost to the rock-strewn summit. A short walk took us to the edge of the crater. Ash billowed upwards but away from us. Every few minutes there was great thumping sound, and rock flew up into the air and then fell back into the crater. Now we knew where the rocks lying at our feet came from. There were no safety arrangements: visitors could walk to the rim of the volcano and peer in. 'You should come in the evening', our guide said, 'you can see the molten lava glowing in the dark'. It did not seem an attractive proposition.

I spent the weekend in Port Vila by myself. Larry Specht returned to Australia. After a further brief meeting with Kenneth Satungia, I flew to Apia, the capital of Western Samoa. Western Samoa is an independent country. A German colony before WW1, it had become a New Zealand trust territory under the Treaty of Versailles in 1919. I stayed in Aggie Grey's hotel. Until then, I had not heard of Aggie Grey. She was a pioneering hotel owner in Western Samoa, knew James A Mitchener and was popularly believed to be the inspiration for the character Bloody Mary in Mitchener's book *Tales of the South Pacific* on which the musical *South Pacific* was based. Western Samoa was also an interesting place. On the long bus ride at night from the airport to downtown Apia, it was difficult not to notice that the local houses did not have external walls. Families could be seen inside their homes as we drove past. I later discovered that privacy was 'protected' simply by the fact that it was considered impolite to look in. I doubt that this policy worked well on the road from the international airport.

There was only one union in Western Samoa - the WS Public Service Association. I met and had lunch with several of their officials - their President, Secretary and Treasurer - at various times over two days. The WS PSA was a strong union with financial and physical assets and a solid membership. It had been involved in one major strike in 1981 lasting 13 weeks which had rocked the conservative country. I extended an invitation to the Union from the LCPA to nominate a representative for the next US study tour.

Like many Australians, I knew little about Samoa. What I did know was largely based on Margaret Mead's *Coming of Age in Samoa* published in 1928 which suggested, among other things, that the Samoans had a very liberal approach to sex. I discussed this idea with at least one of the PSA Executive members. He said he definitely had no experience as a youth of free and easy sex! Other writers have claimed later that Margaret Mead was duped by the locals or at least that she was the victim of an elaborate joke. In 1984 Western Samoa was a deeply religious and conservative society. The Western Samoa PSA appeared to be a well-run union which needed little outside help. It was also unhappy with French nuclear testing, but its main emphasis was on union development.

At the October 1984 PTUF meeting in Nadi, Fiji [which I attended], Jim Knox from the NZ FOL attacked the activities of the LCPA in the Pacific and launched an anti-US and anti-French tirade.[175] In a letter to Larry Specht after this conference, I noted that this attack did not appear to have any impact on the VTUC or WS PSA representatives who were present. There was, I believe, a second LCPA study tour to the US, but I did not go on it. A further meeting of the PTUF took place in Auckland in 1986, but I was not a delegate. By this stage, the ACTU and the ICFTU were seeking to bring the Pacific unions inside their tent in a formal sense. In 1988, the ICFTU and the ACTU created SPOCTU - the South Pacific and Oceania Council of Trade Unions – to bring all the national trade union centres together in a structured, ICFTU-oriented body. The ACTU officers, under pressure from moderate unions, decided to appoint Michael McLeod from the Labor Council of NSW as ACTU International Affairs Officer. Involvement in the PTUF ceased. SPOCTU existed until 1998. As the Cold War ended in 1989-1991, the political interest of both left and moderate unions in the Pacific waned, leaving the field to more regular union activity which concentrated on union organising and development.

## THE HARVARD TRADE UNION PROGRAM

My final overseas trip whilst at the FCUA was to attend the 1987 session of the Harvard Trade Union Program [HTUP] in Boston. I had been interested in attending this program since my first trip to the States in 1974 when our study group had observed a session of the Program. The HTUP was run by the Kennedy School of Government at Harvard University and was a serious and prestigious training course. Some of the best union and academic minds interested in labour relations in the US taught the course [and still do]. One night after work at the FCUA I was having a drink in the Old London Inn around the corner from the Union's Queen Street office with John Maynes and others. The subject of the Churchill Fellowship which offered fellowships to study in the UK came up. One of the National Industrial Officers for the Union did this program in 1977 before he joined the FCUA. John Maynes said to me 'You should do that program'. I replied, 'I'd rather do the Harvard program'. John Maynes said, 'Fine, I'll arrange it'. And to his credit, he set this process in motion and strongly supported my application.

In 1986, I applied to attend the 1987 program. Undertaking the HTUP is not cheap. American Unions pay for their officials to go but for Australian unionists, there was a scholarship made available for up to four union officials each year. The Scholarship was funded by the American/Australian Chamber of Commerce, but the selection process was largely controlled by the NSW Labor Council of which John MacBean was then Secretary. The scholarship paid both the significant tuition fees plus a reasonably generous living allowance. Accommodation for each student was also provided in apartments in Soldiers Field Park on the Harvard Business School campus in Boston. I went to Sydney to be interviewed by the selection committee which consisted of John MacBean and two others from the Chamber of Commerce. There was one stumbling block. I had decided that, as the course was 10 weeks long to which 30 days of travel around the US was added, I would only go if my family could accompany me. The Americans on the interviewing panel thought this was unwise believing that the presence of my family would be a distraction from my studies. However, John MacBean strongly supported my request and the others eventually agreed.

Several practical obstacles nearly prevented me from attending. One was accommodation. Students were normally given a room in a two-bedroom apartment shared with another program participant. I could not do this. It was suggested that my family and I rent privately off campus, but this proved prohibitively expensive and almost impossible to arrange.[176] After several international phone calls to the program Director in Boston – and with the assistance of Wendy Edwards, the local Harvard Foundation Secretary – a compromise was reached in December 1986, just before we were due to leave. My family would have the use of an apartment, but we would have to pay the cost of the other 'half' of the apartment. This amount roughly equalled my living allowance, so I received a sum of money from the scholarship as a living allowance and promptly paid it all back.

We lived on my salary during our time away. The exchange rate was very unfavourable at the time. My sister and brother-in-law fortuitously rented our house from us in Melbourne while we were away, and this helped. All the single HTUP participants ate out every night and had their apartments cleaned. We shopped, cooked and cleaned for ourselves. Shopping was the most difficult task as we had no transport. The Americans on the interviewing panel in Australia need not have worried. I was back in the apartment each evening straight after class. Having my family with me meant I never once went to the HTUP 'common room' on campus. Some students spent many nights there drinking and occasionally getting into arguments with other participants.

When I arrived in Boston with my family, we were pleasantly surprised to find that one American had also brought his wife and daughter. They had been given the apartment next to us. It was the first time that any families had accompanied students. Our neighbour was a Teachers' union official from Portland, Oregon, who had driven across America to attend. His daughter and our son were of school age and he and I often walked them to the local elementary school on our way to class.

Winter in America is cold, as the song goes. It is not an exaggeration. Boston was having a very cold winter in 1987. We arrived on January 2$^{nd}$ as Boston had its first big snowstorm of the season [our plane was lucky to be able to land]. Getting around without a car in the snow and ice was difficult. Walking was even a problem on the black ice that seemed to form and re-form every night. Temperatures were at or below freezing most of the time. Keeping three young children warm when outside was a serious job.

Our time in America was a great family adventure, but extremely hard work, even for simple activities like doing the shopping and getting clothes for five washed and dried. There was a phone in the apartment, but we only used it for local calls. We did not phone home the entire time. I wrote to the Union in Melbourne twice with information about the program. This experience was quite different from today's instant communication around the world.

The formal HTUP program was extremely stimulating. It was wonderful to be able to take time off to learn, discuss and debate labor unionism and later to meet with both 'international'[177] and local union officials. The program ran each day from 8, 8.30 or 9.00 am to 5 or 6 pm each evening, Monday to Friday. Amongst other things, I learned how to use a spreadsheet for the first time in the computer lab [Lotus 1-2-3]. The class studied strategic planning for unions and discussed union organising methods. There was also a joint class with second-year Harvard Business School MBA students. Harvard is one of the most prestigious business schools in the United States. In the 1987 class, one of the students was the young Australian Warwick Fairfax who went home after completing his MBA and launched a 'leveraged buyout' of the family media business. This ended badly for young Warwick and for the Fairfax company, proof perhaps that not everything they teach you at the Harvard Business School can be relied upon.[178]

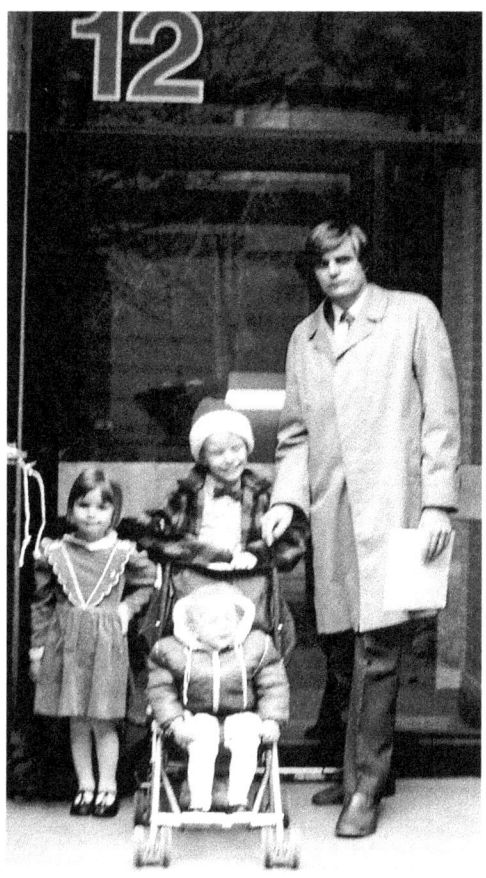

*With my children on graduation day at Harvard. Note: the beard has gone during my time at the HTUP. Photo: M. Lambert*

The joint HTUP-Harvard MBA class was run by Associate Professor Janice McCormack. One of the most interesting parts of her class was a mock negotiation for a new labor contract [enterprise agreement]. I have participated in and conducted myself a number of these over the years, but Janice McCormack ran the best exercise I have experienced. Two teams were formed – union and management – and given some common and some different case materials about the business concerned to read in advance. Both sides had to formulate their bargaining claims in advance. Each team was required to specify in writing what they thought they could win in the negotiation and, more importantly, the minimum outcome they would accept. These were placed in a sealed envelope and given to the lecturer. The participants knew that at the end of the negotiation [which ran for several weeks], the outcomes reached were going to be compared to what the teams had said they wanted or would be prepared to accept as a negotiated outcome. This measure injected realism into both the claims and the performance of the teams. Negotiators did not want to come up short of what they had said they would achieve. This meant that the mock negotiations became serious. If agreement could not be reached by the given deadline, the union was automatically considered to be on strike. This was how the American system worked. I was on a union team. The leader of my 'union' team was Warwick Fairfax, but he wisely delegated the actual negotiating to an experienced American union official.

Harvard University uses the 'Case Study' method of learning extensively and especially in the Business School. Instead of formal lectures, students are given a case study to read in advance and to discuss in class. This can result in a 'bull pit' - especially in the MBA program - as students vie with each other to be heard and to impress the lecturer. The Harvard MBA program is highly competitive, and students competed hard with each other to get the best marks and the best job afterward. Many of the other classes in the HTUP also used case studies. This teaching method means that students often walk out of the class with nothing but their notes and the case study, not the wisdom of the lecturers. It is harder to say precisely what has been 'learned' compared to the normal lecture format that I was used to in Australia. Some other HTUP classes taught in the Kennedy School of Government and the Law School utilised more traditional teaching methods but also occasionally used case studies. HTUP students were required to buy textbooks and with these, my notes and other materials collected during the program, I brought back to Australia a considerable amount of information on union issues.

While I was at Harvard, I managed to find time to write an article for *Social Action* magazine. Australia was popular in the USA in early 1987. The America's Cup was being sailed off Fremantle. This was the first time for many years that the race had been held outside the United States as Alan Bond's team had won it in 1983. Paul Hogan's movie *Crocodile Dundee* was doing good business in the USA and Robert Hughes's book *The Fatal Shore* had been released to critical acclaim and good sales. Hughes was the Art critic for *Time Magazine* and well known in the US. My article reported this interest in Australia but also on the American relationship with the Soviet Union. While I was at Harvard, a 14-hour mini-series *Amerika* was aired on US television. It was set in a future USA ten years after it had been occupied by the Soviet Union [and UN Peacekeeping Forces]. Both the USSR and the UN protested the airing of the show. So did some Americans who were concerned about the damage it might do to US-Soviet relations. It is amazing to think now that as late as 1987 it was felt that the USSR could either be a military threat to the US or that anyone was interested in maintaining relationships with this disintegrating empire. My *Social Action* article was published under the inaccurate by-line 'From our correspondent in New York'.

During my time at Harvard, I received an invitation to a conference in Washington. It was provocatively called *The Red Orchestra, the case of the Southwest Pacific*. It was organised by the Hoover Institution of Stanford University to discuss the activities of the Soviet Union and its surrogates in the South Pacific. I was invited because of my involvement with the Labor Committee for Pacific Affairs. I initially declined the invitation, thinking that it was inappropriate to take time off from the HTUP. However, I later discovered that this was acceptable to the HTUP team and I flew down to Washington, DC for the two-day conference. The conference was attended by a few Australians, including Michael Easson from the NSW Labor Council, Michael Danby from Australia-Israel Publications [later an ALP MHR], and others.

It was at the *Red Orchestra* conference that I met my first [and only, to my knowledge] CIA agent. Sitting at the conference table before the first session began, I introduced myself to my neighbour. 'Hi, I'm Keith Harvey from Australia'. He replied, 'I'm [name forgotten, not withheld] from the CIA'. I asked him for his business card, but he said CIA employees were not allowed to have them. He gave me his personal card instead – no CIA logo disappointingly. He explained that he was an 'overt' employee of the CIA. His job was to do research, attend conferences and the like. The conference itself was forgettable and little came from it except a book,[179] but the story of meeting someone from the CIA is an opportune lead into the question of CIA involvement in and funding of anti-communist activities.

Sometime after returning to Australia, I turned on the radio to hear former CIA employee Phillip Agee saying that anyone who had accepted a US-funded trip to the United States was, prima facie, in the pay of, and an agent of, the CIA. This claim is, in my experience, nonsense. By this time, I had been on three funded trips to the States: in 1974, 1983 and 1987. Although the American Government was facilitating and funding these trips to some extent this was not particularly remarkable. Other foreign Governments did and do the same. Governments like to expose their countries to people they think might be up and coming or current leaders. This was particularly true during the Cold War. At no time on any trip was I ever approached by anyone seeking to either recruit me or to compromise and thus blackmail me into working for the CIA. Phillip Agee's statement was wrong. The trips that I have been on have also been undertaken by people from the left of the ALP. None of them have, to my knowledge, ever mentioned any approach from the CIA.

The American trade union movement I saw was militant at home but anti-communist abroad [at least at the level of the international unions: some local unions were more left wing]. American unions did not seek revolution at home or overseas. Their position was that unions should be fiercely independent of any outside control, whether by employers or governments of any persuasion. American unionism was what they called 'business unionism'. This meant that they saw their only job as getting the best possible deal at work for their members. They neither wanted to run the companies their members worked for nor overthrow the capitalist system.

The Harvard Trade Union Program itself had been accused in the past of running a US government or CIA line. This was certainly not true when I was there. The issue of the CIA came up in the labor history course taught by James [Jim] Green. I enjoyed Jim's course immensely. I disagreed with him when he said that the first eight-hour day was won in Boston in the late 1800s. Being from Melbourne, where stonemasons achieved the first eight-hour day in 1856, it was necessary to correct him. The last session of Jim's 10-week course dealt with the foreign policy positions and programs of the AFL-CIO. I was surprised to see in the readings for this session much criticism of the role of the AFL-CIO in Latin America and elsewhere in support, it was suggested, of US foreign policy. It included a discussion of the role of the CIA in funding this work.

I expressed my concern about the tenor of these readings to Jim. He seemed surprised that I was concerned. He thought this information was not controversial. He knew more about these matters than I did, and the readings may well have been correct. However, what they did show was that neither the CIA nor the US government was directing the curriculum of the HTUP. If either of them had been, Jim Green would not have been on the faculty. Not long after I completed the program, I noticed that Noam Chomsky, a fully-fledged member of the American left-wing intelligentsia had also joined the HTUP faculty.[180] Not a likely faculty member for a CIA funded program. I can only say that in all my time and all my trips to the US, I never saw or experienced anything which suggested interference or involvement by any intelligence agency. Various people and institutions were working for common goals and outcomes - which included support for the development of free and independent trade unions. I was happy to be part of that work.

## AROUND THE STATES IN 30 DAYS

At the end of the HTUP program, the Americans went home but the foreigners undertook a 30-day study tour in the US, again funded by 'Uncle Sam'. This posed a few issues for me, as I was accompanied by my family and we had to pay all the additional travel costs ourselves. We decided on a modest program involving the minimum number of flights and which would leave us on the West Coast and able to pick up our flight home. The last day of the HTUP was a nightmare for us. We had to attend the graduation ceremony and lunch, finish packing, clean the apartment and get to the airport for a flight to New York. It was one of the most difficult days of the trip. Boston may have been a progressive city in an advanced industrial civilisation, but it did not have a reliable taxi service.

Several local people had offered to drive us to the airport, but I naïvely declined their offers. I found out why they had offered too late. When we thought we were close to being ready, I phoned the taxi company to book a cab. 'Sorry, we have no taxis available'. 'What do you mean, no taxis?' 'We are not taking bookings today'. 'How are we supposed to get to the airport?' 'Go out onto the street and hail a taxi'. We did not live on the street but in an off-street apartment complex. The street was some distance away. We had five people, including three young children, and lots of suitcases. It was snowing and very cold. But hailing a taxi on the street is what we eventually had to do. It was a dreadful experience. We eventually arrived in our New York hotel at about 10 pm, exhausted, to find that there was no bed for our youngest child and staff who did not appear to care.

We spent the weekend in New York. On Monday, I had two meetings. The first was with a New York retail sector union. In the second meeting at the Labor Institute, I discussed vocational training particularly for women workers facing new technologies. The next day the family flew to Washington where fortunately we were able to stay for about two weeks in one place. Travel with three young children was difficult at the best of times. In Washington, I had a range of meetings. Looking back over my notes now they make interesting reading. I met with officials from several international unions and discussed union specific issues including union education, comparable worth, new technology, occupational health and safety and membership organising. In addition, I had several discussions about unions in South Africa, Central America, and the Pacific, including the Philippines.

Why would I be discussing unionism in these countries? Simply because in the context of the Cold War there was little that was a strictly local issue without any global implications. Each week at the Victorian Trades Hall Council or at one or more ACTU committees or forums, the left would be promoting positions favourable to them and their allies around the world. For example, the left was then promoting a rival trade union federation [the KMU] in the Philippines and trying to undermine the ICFTU affiliate, the TUCP.[181] In El Salvador, a civil war was raging between the Sandinistas and the contras, covertly assisted by the US government. These struggles were fought not just on the home fronts but around the world. It was necessary to understand the issues to be able to take the debate up to the left. There was debate about all these issues.

Some American unions that I spoke to did not support the work of the American Institute for Free Labor Development [AIFLD] in Central America. However, AIFLD had two of its workers killed by right-wing death squads so it was not just those on the left who disliked their work. During the Cold War, the world was somehow a smaller and more binary place. The battle lines were clearly defined. Everyone knew what side they were on and was prepared to engage with the opposition on each front that opened up. Few issues seemed to be dealt with on their strict merits. They were all seen in the context of a larger struggle.

After two weeks in Washington, the family and I flew west. We went to Albuquerque where I spent time with a United Food and Commercial Workers Union [UFCW] local.[182] This was an interesting visit because I was able to discuss first-hand the incredible difficulties of union organising in the American south-west. Later, the family and I hired a car and drove to Las Vegas spending a night at the Grand Canyon before flying on to Los Angeles. I had several meetings in Los Angeles, including with Ann Imparato from an AFSCME local[183] who had been on the HTUP and with whom we had become friends.[184]

One of the most enjoyable days was with United Food and Commercial Workers [UFCW] Local Union 905 based in a small ten square mile part of the suburban sprawl of Los Angeles [near Long Beach/Harbor City]. This was a truly local Local, intimately connected to its members and almost as far from the concerns of Washington DC as it is possible to be in mainland USA. The local union officials I met here were only interested in their members and in winning the best possible labor contract [workplace agreement]. The officials of Local 905 knew I had my family with me and invited us all for the day. We had a hire car and somehow navigated the LA freeways down to their office at Long Beach.[185] After discussions about union organising and labour contract negotiations, we all went out for lunch. Later I received a copy of their union newsletter with an article about our visit.

*Visiting UFCW Local 905 at Long Beach, California.*

The officials from UFCW Local 905 were committed and genuine union officials of whom the union movement needs more. After a short holiday in Hawaii with my family on the way home, I returned to Australia to find the Victorian Branch of the FCUA in turmoil.

# 7

# WINNING THE COLD WAR AND LOSING THE CLERKS UNION

*'Things fall apart; the centre cannot hold...'*
W. B. Yeats, *The Second Coming*

This chapter requires a word of explanation. It is not a history of the Clerks Union. I have previously written a brief account of the 'rise and fall of the Clerks Union' by reflecting on the life and times of John Maynes.[186] Nor is it a full account of how the Victorian Branch was lost to the left. Rather, this chapter principally concerns my involvement in events in the Branch in the tempestuous years of 1987 to 1991. Some explanations and opinions are offered as to why 'things fell apart'. Lindsay Tanner has also written a frank account of his successful campaign to change control of the Victorian Branch of the Union.[187]

These years were equally tumultuous in world events. To put these local events into a global political context, included within the chapter are 'text boxes' briefly noting what was happening internationally. In the Soviet Union and Eastern Europe, the Cold War came to a dramatic and unexpected end. The text in these boxes is written by me but is based on two accounts of events in Eastern Europe: that of Catholic historian Warren H Carroll's *The Rise and Fall of the Communist Revolution*[188] and Tony Judt's *Postwar – a history of Europe since 1945*.[189] Carroll writes from a Catholic perspective and is interested in examining the role of individuals in making history. Judt initially came from a Marxist background but his reading of events in 1989-91 in Eastern Europe is remarkably like Carroll's.

Before leaving the west coast of the US in 1987, I was aware that political disaster had struck the Victorian Branch of the Clerks Union. Terry Sullivan, National Secretary of the Union, had written a letter that found its way to me in Los Angeles. It gave me the news that Lindsay Tanner had been elected Assistant Branch Secretary. In the 1982 Victorian Branch elections, the Clerical Workers Industrial Group [CWIG][190] team had been elected unopposed. By 1985, at the regular triennial Branch elections, the Branch had become a target for the left, following our re-admission to the ALP. Now there were some ALP Conference delegate positions at stake, a valuable prize. There was a political cost to re-affiliation with the Labor Party.

Lindsay Tanner, then a member of the Socialist Left faction of the ALP, had formed a team to challenge for control of the Branch. In 1985 the CWIG's candidates, running under the Clerks Ranks and File Team [CRAFT] banner, swept this challenge aside, winning all positions by a 4-1 margin. No one, including Tanner, would have expected to beat the incumbents in that election and the winning margin was comfortable [and perhaps too comfortable]. Tanner kept on with his campaign to win control of the Branch in the years that followed the 1985 election. While Tanner and his team campaigned well and hard, I doubt they ever expected to win control of the Branch. The incumbent Executive had a reputation as an experienced and successful election winning machine; totally undeserved when put to the test.

After the 1985 election was declared, the Tanner 'Reform Group' team challenged the result in the Federal Court. They argued that a ballot 'irregularity' had occurred which had affected the result. To mount this challenge, the Reform Group was using provisions in the law which were the modern version of the 'clean ballots' legislation of the 1940s. These laws were first used by the ALP Industrial Groups in the late 1940 and 1950s to challenge Communist control of unions, including in the Victorian Branch of the Clerks Union. The Reform Group's alleged 'irregularity' concerned the eligibility of one of the CRAFT team to stand for election. Hugh Armstrong, formerly an Industrial Officer in the National Office of the Union, was the CRAFT candidate for the post of Assistant Branch Secretary. He won the position in the 1985 ballot by 5,023 votes to 1,302, about the same margin as all other candidates on the ticket.

Hugh Armstrong was an excellent Industrial Officer; tough, courageous, hard-working and principled. He came to the National Office from South Australia in late June 1980. Hugh had been an office-bearer of another union in South Australia and had a skilled blue-collar background. When Hugh Armstrong accepted the job with the Clerks Union, he also joined the Victorian Branch. He listed his occupation as 'Ind/Officer' or Industrial Officer when he filled out his membership application form. The Reform Group challenged his right to be a member of the Union since the Union's Rules said that a person had to be engaged in 'a clerical capacity' to be a member. It could be argued that the job of an Industrial Officer was not a clerical occupation. If so, Hugh Armstrong was ineligible to be a member and unable to stand for election.

Realising this possible problem, Hugh Armstrong had [after the 1985 election] obtained a part-time clerical job with a law firm. He qualified anew as a union member and the Federal Court ultimately ruled that he was entitled to be considered as a member of the Union dating back to June 1980. This did not resolve the problem, however. As the case progressed and based on evidence given during the inquiry into the election, it emerged that there was a further argument that Hugh Armstrong was an 'unfinancial' member of the union. Unfinancial members could not stand for election.

The administrative practice of the Branch was not to charge pro-rata membership fees to new members who joined late in any quarter for that quarter. They were just asked to pay a joining fee and began paying full quarterly dues from the beginning of the next quarter. Hugh Armstrong had done this and had bought an 'annual ticket' [12 months membership up front] each year from 1st July 1980. All of CRAFT's likely election candidates bought annual tickets each year to try and avoid eligibility problems. Hugh Armstrong always believed himself to be fully financial, as did the Branch itself.

Unfortunately, the Branch's administrative practice did not conform to the letter of the Rules of the Union. By its administrative error, the Branch itself had made Hugh Armstrong technically unfinancial [for just a short period in June 1980, five years before the 1985 ballot] and the Federal Court so found. None of this was Hugh's responsibility. But from small errors, great events may flow. The devil really is in the detail. On the 24th October 1986, the Court ordered a fresh election for the position of Assistant Branch Secretary. This election was held in March 1987 while I was in the US and the result was declared on the 31st March. Tanner won by 3645 votes to 2163, a winning margin of 1500 votes. This was a massive voting turnaround in just two years. No one was more surprised than Lindsay Tanner himself: 'I almost fell off my chair' he wrote in his account.[191]

As soon as I read the news from Terry Sullivan I wrote to Hugh Armstrong, offering him some words of condolence and encouragement. When I got back to my office, I found that neither the Victorian Branch nor the National Office was in a happy place. Recriminations were flowing back and forth about why the election had been lost. Only a modest campaign was waged by CRAFT. Expecting to win, the CRAFT team did not want to do a full mail out of 'how-to-vote' leaflets to all members. Postage was expensive and another ballot was due in 1988. For this election, CRAFT only mailed out election leaflets to country members and tried to get city delegates to distribute 'how-to-vote' advice on the job. This method appears to have failed and was a major mistake. A view was expressed to me that John Maynes had left the running of the election campaign to others in the CRAFT team, to see how they could perform. Sadly, relationships that had endured for many years were now strained. The 'positive' out of the election was that CRAFT had lost only one position, not control of the Branch Executive. The unexpected result should have served as a warning of what might happen in 1988. The election outcome made Executive meetings even more unpleasant. The rest of us tried to send Lindsay Tanner 'to Coventry' but we were not good at it. The plan certainly was to keep him away from contact with the union's members so Tanner could not use his new position to campaign against us in the run-up to the 1988 triennial election.

In my possession there is a file full of memos from experienced Branch organisers who with great goodwill expressed their concern about the way the 1987 campaign had been run. Numerous suggestions were made about what should be done in the lead up to the 1988 ballot. Now that the Socialist Left had tasted unexpected victory, they would be expected to throw everything into the 1988 campaign, believing that they could win. Some had the view that the 1987 result was an aberration, a 'mistake' by the members or a 'by-election' type result handed out to keep the incumbents on their toes. In this hopeful view, all would be rectified in the 1988 'general election'. CRAFT was not likely to repeat the mistake of not mailing a 'how to vote' to all members on the roll. These matters were to concern us for the rest of 1987 and the early part of 1988. This turn of events also troubled our new friends in the Labor Unity faction of the Victorian ALP. They did not want to see their strategy of boosting the anti-left numbers in the Party undone by the loss of the Clerks Union to Socialist Left control.

In Australia, there was little time to contemplate events in Eastern Europe and the Soviet Union. The CRAFT team worked hard to maximise its chances

> **THE SOVIET UNION**
>
> *On the other side of the world, in the Soviet Union, portents of great change could be observed if only there was time to look closely. In November 1987, on the 70<sup>th</sup> anniversary of the Bolshevik Revolution, Soviet Communist Party Secretary Mikhail Gorbachev denounced Stalin's crimes against the people of the USSR. While he did not go much further than Khrushchev had many years before, there was now a faint hope that real change might be possible in the Soviet Union and Eastern Europe.*

in the 1988 election. Neither side left anything in reserve. Tanner's team campaigned well, enlisting the media and even Ministers in the Victorian ALP Government in seeking to allege scandal and cause embarrassment for the incumbents. There were some openings for the Reform Group to do this. For example, there was the decision to allow Social Action rent-free accommodation in premises leased by FEDSDA Pty Ltd in South Melbourne. The split in the NCC had left the Industrial Action Fund/Social Action without premises. FEDSDA was a trust company jointly set up by the FCU and the SDA to buy and manage a building owned by the two Unions at 53 Queen Street, Melbourne. FEDSDA had rented a small building in South Melbourne and used it to store archived files there, but also allowed Social Action to occupy part of the building without charge. The Reform Group used a media and a political strategy to paint this decision in a poor light. In his book *Sideshow – dumbing down democracy*, written after his departure from Federal politics, Tanner revealed how he went about this:

> *Politicians and journalists often collude to shape a viable story through selective manipulation of available facts. I had my first real taste of this process in the late 1980s, when I was trying to get media publicity about corruption in my union, the Federated Clerks Union. After failing to get television coverage because of the lack of good pictures..., I approached the Melbourne Herald. They were interested, but they needed an event to trigger a story. So I dreamed one up.*
>
> *I discovered that whenever the state attorney-general received a complaint regarding irregularities within a company, the matter would be automatically referred to the corporate regulator for consideration. As the issues in play involved a union-owned company, I duly made the complaint, and was able*

> to create a story around the attorney-general referring my complaint to the regulator for investigation. The fact that this was a routine move, and that it implied no wrongdoing on the part of the company, was conveniently overlooked.[192]

In May 1988, shortly before the Clerks Union ballot was due to open, the SDA's State Secretary Jim Maher was reported in the press complaining to the ALP Premier John Cain about the Corporate Affairs Commission inquiry and the Minister's role in it. He was reported as saying that the inquiry had cleared FEDSDA of any wrongdoing.[193] Of course, the damage had already been done.

The act of FEDSDA in buying an interest in Doncaster Travel, a suburban travel agency, was another poor decision, especially since John Maynes had personally invested in it as well. Doncaster Travel was a flight of fancy that delivered little or no return to FEDSDA or the two unions. John Maynes's personal involvement simply meant that there was an obvious conflict of interest that could not easily be explained and was well exploited by our opponents. It was poor corporate governance. John Maynes derived no personal financial benefit from his investment because the business did not deliver a return on his [or the two unions'] investment. At best, the business broke even.

Tanner campaigned effectively on several fronts. He tried, partially successfully as it turned out, to win over employees of the Union and succeeded in two cases: one in the Victorian Branch and an employee of the National Office, Lance Betros. Tanner's methods were open and transparent – he sent copies of his letters to the Branch's organisers to Branch Executive members. We were unaware that Tanner had managed to recruit a supporter in the National Office until he published his account of the campaign – *The Last battle*.[194] Of the two defectors, the Branch employee was the most significant, although it is fair to say that this person approached Tanner, anonymously at first. Tanner tells this story fully in his book.

Both sides produced an enormous amount of election propaganda and campaigned on the job, on the phone and by door knocking members at their homes during the voting period. The election was delayed for a couple of weeks by the Government-appointed Returning Officer. Elections in the important NSW Branch thus took place earlier than in Victoria and the incumbent team in NSW led by Branch Secretary Vince Higgins was re-elected reasonably comfortably [a margin of about 1800 votes on a modest 28% return].

The incumbent all-male Executive team in Victoria was looking decidedly old-fashioned by 1988. It was decided to enlarge the Executive by adding a second Assistant Secretary and pre-selecting a woman – Linda Salameh, an existing Organiser – as the CRAFT candidate for this position. Linda Salameh had only been an Organiser for a short time, but everyone saw the need for a woman as a candidate for a full-time position. A female candidate, Rosemary Carter, was also pre-selected for one of two additional honorary Vice-Presidential positions.

> **POLAND AND THE SOVIET UNION**
>
> *In May 1988, Polish workers again re-occupied the Gdansk shipyards where Solidarnosc had been born some eight years earlier.*
>
> *In the Soviet Union in the same month, Communist Party Secretary Mikhail Gorbachev renounced the Brezhnev Doctrine which asserted the 'right' of the Soviet Union to intervene in other countries to preserve communist control [as it had done in Hungary in 1956 and Czechoslovakia in 1968]. Gorbachev also took the first steps to assert the rule of law in the Soviet Union – separating the 'leading' role of the Communist party from that of the State for the first time since the Revolution. In June, the first Catholic Mass was said in the Kremlin since the Bolshevik Revolution.*

CRAFT decided to nominate Michael O'Sullivan for the position of Branch Secretary, relegating Harry Darroch to the position of First Assistant Secretary. Hugh Armstrong was not a candidate for any of the full-time positions in the Branch but nominated as a National Council delegate representing the Branch. John Maynes decided not to run again as Branch President. Since Michael O'Sullivan – his logical successor as President – was now running for Secretary, I agreed to be the candidate for Branch President to succeed John Maynes. Long-serving senior Organiser Mike Cashman was to stand for Deputy President. John Maynes nominated for a position on Branch Council. He was still National President but had also announced that he would not re-nominate for this position when it fell due later that year. Lindsay Tanner presciently described all these moves as 're-arranging the deck chairs on the Titanic'. Since he had been so successfully shackled to his desk, he resigned his position as Assistant Branch Secretary in May, a month or so before the election, so that he could campaign full-time without limitation.

*The 'Official Rank and File [CRAFT] tram ticket for the 1988 election.*

The Victorian Branch ballot closed on Tuesday 21st June 1988 at 9 am. Counting began at once. The Branch Executive was meeting at the same time in the National Office Board room. Scrutineers were present at the ballot count and phoned in regular reports.[195] About 40% of eligible members had voted – not a bad return, but not exceptional. A high return was thought to favour the incumbent team. The first phone report from scrutineer Tony Medlicott came at 11.00 am. The position of Branch President – the one for which I was the CRAFT candidate – was being counted first. Tony Medlicott reported that the voting appeared to be going about 55%-45% in our favour, although the first actual numbers reported had me trailing slightly. John Maynes said, 'that's about what I expected'. He claimed to have thought all along that we would be returned to office, but narrowly.

Tony Medlicott phoned again at 11.35 am – out of 678 votes counted I was leading narrowly: 345 to 333 for my opponent, Reform Group candidate Barbara Lewis. This was too close for comfort for me, but John Maynes went on with the Executive meeting in the usual manner. Of all the matters the Executive discussed that morning, I can only remember one: arrangements for a Victorian Branch retirement function for John Maynes. It was never held. The midday tally had Lewis ahead by 50 votes out of nearly 1000 counted. John Maynes did not seem perturbed, the 55-45 margin 'which he had expected' seemed to have stuck in his head. Branch Secretary Harry Darroch was carefully recording decisions being made. Michael O'Sullivan and I exchanged looks – we instinctively felt that any decisions being made at this meeting would have a short shelf life.

By the end of the day, Lewis was leading me by 350 votes out of 4450 counted. It was clear that I could not win from this far behind. There was some speculation amongst our supporters that Lewis's vote was a 'women's vote' and that CRAFT's other candidates would do better if the contest was not a male against a female. That evening the team had a morose wake at Mike Cashman's home. It was becoming clear that we had lost the election and control of the Branch. The final margin for President was 3635 for Lewis and 3153 for me – a 500 vote losing margin. Some of CRAFT's other candidates did do significantly better than I did. In the best result for the Executive, our candidate for Senior Vice President, Rosemary Carter, was beaten by only 160 votes. Even smaller margins occurred for some other positions, including for State Council members where the lowest margin was just 35 votes. These margins would become important later. But the CRAFT ticket lost every Branch Executive position - the key positions which determined control of the Branch. Michael O'Sullivan lost to Lindsay Tanner for the key post of Branch Secretary by a slightly smaller losing margin than mine. CRAFT lost all the Victorian Branch National Council positions, cutting off the supply of fresh talent for elected national officer positions. At that time, National Officials were elected by and from the National Council. To be elected as National Secretary, for example, the candidate must first also be a member of the National Council representing a Branch.

In the 1988 elections, as was normal, there were votes within sections of the union as well as for positions elected by the whole Branch membership. In the Airline section, where 50% of eligible voters had returned their ballot papers, CRAFT candidates lost by a huge margin of about 800 votes to 200. The voting differential in this one section alone was enough to lose us the whole election. This result could have been offset by strong wins by CRAFT candidates in other sections. Unbelievably, [to the CRAFT team, that is] the two competing tickets were tied in the conservative Retail section, which should have strongly favoured the incumbents.

Losing in the airlines' section was not so surprising. Airline members were very active and informed and sometimes hard to please. The Airlines section was allocated to one of our very best organisers and members were well serviced by him, the Branch and the national Union. The pay and conditions of airline members were better than those of any other members of the Union.[196] However, there were many issues in the industry and the Union was perceived as being too timid in dealing with them. But how the vote could have been tied the Retail section seemed to be beyond belief.[197] CRAFT did win several Branch Council positions in other sections, especially in the large Commercial section where experienced members like Jim Hewat, Jim Lanigan [who was employed at the Ironworkers Union] and other excellent unionists were re-elected. But they were now in a minority on the Council and faced a hostile Executive. CRAFT probably still held a majority of delegates to the annual State Conference, but this would be of little consequence and use over time. The Reform Group had not been able to put together a full ticket to contest all positions, so CRAFT won some positions by default.

The ballot was declared on Friday the 24th of June at 1 pm. Of all the incumbent office bearers, only Harry Darroch, who was Branch Secretary, lost his paid job on that day. I was employed by the National Office of the Union, so my employment was not affected. Michael O'Sullivan was employed by FEDSDA Pty Ltd, the trust company which owned the building at 53 Queen Street. Linda Salameh and Mike Cashman were branch organisers. Harry Darroch had the difficult job of handing over control of the Branch to incoming Secretary Lindsay Tanner. He did this very professionally. Harry did not have to do this on his own. All outgoing Executive members, that is, Michael O'Sullivan, John Maynes, Harry Darroch and I, attended this tense handover meeting with Tanner and his new Executive team.

The next week, however, Linda Salameh and Mike Cashman were sacked by the new Executive, along with all the other Branch organising staff. This was the decision of the new Executive at its first meeting which took place the weekend after the declaration of the ballot. New Branch Secretary Lindsay Tanner went to the Organisers' room on the 7th Floor of 53 Queen Street at 9.00 am on Monday the 27th June and terminated the employment of all the organisers. They were given 30 minutes to hand over union property and to quit the building. The organisers refused to accept this decision and immediately occupied the seventh-floor room that was their office. The clerical staff of the Branch went on strike in support of the Organisers and formed a picket line outside the Union's main office on the sixth floor.

> ### POLAND AND THE SOVIET UNION
>
> *In the Soviet Union, the Communist party met from the 28th June to the 1st July 1988 to endorse Gorbachev's reforms. Boris Yeltsin, who was to play a key role in the demise of both the Communist Party of the Soviet Union and the USSR itself, re-emerged as a key figure at this conference.*
>
> *In August 1988, the Polish Communist regime entered into its first negotiations with the independent Polish trade union Solidarnosc since the imposition of martial law in December 1981.*

The sacked organisers lodged claims asserting that they had been unfairly dismissed in the Victorian Industrial Relations Commission. The National Office of the Union supported and funded this action, which was ultimately unsuccessful. John Maynes re-engaged those organisers who wanted to keep working for the union as National Office employees.

The strike by the clerical staff was eventually resolved and they returned to work. To my mind, these employees are the unsung heroes of this story. Mainly women, they continued to work 'behind enemy lines' as it were, for some years, in a very unfriendly work environment. The clerical staff was a group of dedicated and courageous people. This was particularly true after the new Executive moved the Branch office out of the Union's building in Queen Street and into offices owned by the left-wing BWIU. This was hostile territory. Tanner might have imagined that the clerical staff would quit rather than work in a building where a portrait of pro-Soviet Communist Party boss Pat Clancy still hung on the wall, but they did not. In 2021, more than 30 years after these events took place a group of them continue to meet regularly for lunch. I join them from time to time. I admire them as people with steadfast faith and commitment to their values. Not one of these women cracked under pressure.

## WHY WAS THE 1988 ELECTION LOST?

Everyone had a theory about why the CRAFT team lost the 1988 election. The first of these was that the election had been stolen by some old-fashioned ballot-rigging. This idea was suggested while the count was still underway. Organiser Tony O'Brien raised this possibility, noticing that a significant number of the crosses marking ballot papers for the opposition ticket had a similar and distinctive look. Without being able to see the ballot papers, those not present at the counting of the ballot papers found this hard to imagine. After all, a cross is a cross, it seemed. Tony O'Brien was able to show us later what he meant. The distinctive cross he identified did have features that made it possible to believe that one person had filled in a large number of ballot papers.

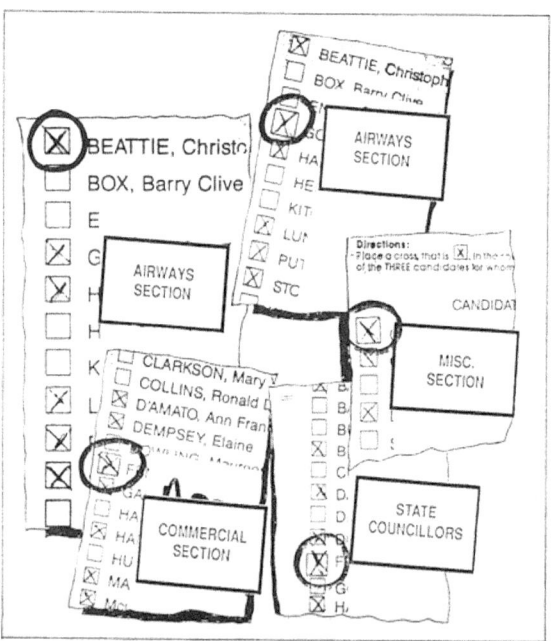

The three-legged cross on the above ballot papers is a distinctive aspect of ballot rigging evidence now affirmed by three handwriting experts.

*A photo collage showing the distinctive 'three-legged' crosses on several ballot papers.*
*Photo and accompanying text: Social Action*

After the ballot had been declared, the defeated CRAFT candidates sought expert advice from a handwriting expert. He also thought that the ballot papers in question had been completed by one person. It was now the turn of the defeated candidates to seek an inquiry into the election. Our application alleged that an irregularity had occurred which had affected the outcome of the election as there were more suspect ballot papers than the lowest winning margin for the Reform Group team. The election inquiry dragged on for some time, but ultimately the Federal Court found that the result of the election had not been affected by multiple voting by any individual or individuals unknown. I cannot say for certain that there was, or was not, any ballot rigging. The Court's decision stands. In the 30 years since the election, no one has produced any further evidence to suggest that there was interference in the ballot.[198] In any event, even if it had occurred, limited alleged malfeasance at the ballot box does not explain the massive swing against the old Executive over three years.

There were other theories advanced as to why the election was lost. Everyone who expressed a view was probably correct to some degree since there were undoubtedly many factors involved. The Victorian Branch of the FCUA was not the only union in Victoria to change hands in 1988. The Victorian Branch of the TWU did the same. There was a view that the so-called 'two-tier' wage system then in vogue played a major role. Under this arrangement, to obtain wage increases employees had to give up terms and conditions of employment. In white-collar and clerical areas where there were few or no restrictive work practices, this was difficult, and members strongly resented this system.

In his account of the election, Lindsay Tanner draws attention to what he says was a lack of membership servicing by the Branch. This was a big factor. Between 1985 and 1988 the Branch was well below proper organising strength and service levels suffered. Several new organisers were appointed in late 1987 and early 1988 but it was too little, too late. There were several discussions about this problem at Branch Executive meetings prior to Tanner being elected as Assistant Secretary. John Maynes's position was that new staff could not be introduced into an organising team that was, in his view, 'dysfunctional'. This was a mistake. Having too few organisers was demoralising for those who were working hard because their workload was excessive. Members found it difficult to get answers to their questions quickly. The Branch struggled to find suitable candidates for organiser positions and the failure to fill the gaps in a timely way was costly. The Reform Group tagged the incumbents as the 'Old Guard' and this label stuck. I was the newcomer on the Executive, but John Maynes, at the other end of the scale, had been in office since 1949.

However, despite all the theories, I do not think that anybody knows why the incumbents lost or why the Reform Group team won. Undoubtedly, there was a combination of factors in play, but which were most important to the members who voted remained a mystery. This is because no attempt was made to find out. When I returned from Harvard in mid-1987, after Tanner had won the Assistant Secretary position, I suggested that we do some market research to find out why people had voted for the Reform Group. My idea was to get 20 supporters to phone 20 members at random and simply ask them what was in their minds when they voted. This suggestion was ignored and having made it, I did not press it further. The CRAFT team never sought to find out what was going on in the minds of the members when they voted in 1987 or 1988. The Branch Executive advertised itself relentlessly through the Union journal *The Clerk* and election propaganda and in other ways. Negative campaigning was conducted against the Reform Group. At no time, however, was there follow up after elections to see what resonated with members and what did not.

This is not to say that no market research was done at all. The Branch had spent tens of thousands of dollars researching member attitudes in 1984 and 1987. John Maynes came up with this idea and asked me to find an independent academic who would be able to conduct an extensive survey of our membership. The intention was to gain a picture of the Union's membership demographics and attitudes on a range of questions, including what they thought of the Union, service levels and even what they thought about their organiser. I found an academic at La Trobe University who would do this work properly and professionally. Through him, the Branch carried out very large-scale opinion research built on large sample sizes, big enough to give meaningful results in some individual workplaces. The survey was confidential and did not reveal who had completed it. But enough questionnaires were mailed out [and returned] to get statistically significant results from individual workplaces with as few as 50 members. In 1987, more than 3,000 questionnaires were returned, about 45% of those mailed out, so the response rate was high. Members were willing and eager to say what they thought.

These surveys were conducted in both Victoria and NSW in both years.

Apart from the academic involved and his assistant, only John Maynes and I saw the mass of raw data. I had the job of trying to make sense of it. Some of the demographic data was not a surprise. For example, the average length of membership across both Branches was about three years. In the well paid and career-oriented industries such as airlines, breweries, oil and the Australian Public Service, average membership duration was as high as 7-9 years. In retail, it was just two years. Members were asked a range of questions about whether the union was too militant or not militant enough and whether they thought the union was generally a good, fair or poor union.

The range of responses to these questions was fascinating. Overall, members thought our level of militancy was about right - about 60% had that view. But in the critical airline industry, only 37% of members thought so. In the airlines' section, members were more knowledgeable, engaged and aware, but also more polarised in their attitudes. Some of the survey results may explain our poor showing in airlines. Members did not think that the Union as a whole was strong, militant or active enough on the job. The airlines industry was regulated by national awards and agreements and industrial outcomes were beyond the control of a single Branch, elected official or organiser.

However, the findings of these surveys do not explain the election outcome in 1988. The survey results in 1984 and 1987 were essentially the same in both years and in NSW and Victoria. In Victoria, the Executive thought it was running a good Branch [until it started losing elections]. The Victorians probably looked down on their NSW colleagues. This attitude was wrong, and this error jumped off the page when John Maynes and I looked at the comparative results across Branches. In 1985 the Victorian Branch Executive won with a 4:1 result. In 1988, it lost 54-46%. NSW won both elections. The 'two-tier' wage system operated in both States. Members in the airline, breweries, oil and similar industries operated on national awards and agreements. Retail relied on State awards in the main. These extensive surveys, while interesting, did not explain the different election outcomes in the two states in the two different elections.

Part of the losing result must be put down to leadership: that of the Union in the two Branches and of the Reform Group teams challenging the incumbents. John Maynes dominated the Victorian Branch in an unhealthy way. Mistakes were made. In NSW Vince Higgins ran a much tighter and more cohesive team. Tanner's campaign in Victoria was very well run, imaginative and effective; the

Reform Group in NSW could not mount the same quality campaign. In politics, as in football, a team plays as well as the opposition lets it.

## THE UNFINANCIAL IRREGULARITY, AGAIN

While the defeated candidates failed with the claim of ballot rigging, we did have success in forcing a partial new election. The Federal Court found that 148 voters had been wrongly removed from the voters' roll.[199] Ironically, this was done by the Branch following its standard practice but the Court again ruled that it was not in strict accordance with the Union's Rules. There were not enough incorrect deletions from the roll to have possibly affected the outcome of the election for the key Branch Executive positions. CRAFT's closest losing margin was 160 votes for an Executive position. But there were much smaller margins in some of the other positions contested – as low as 35 votes in the case of Branch Councillors elected by the whole membership. The Federal Court ordered a new ballot to elect two Branch Councillors.

---

### EASTERN EUROPE

*The year 1989 was another eventful time in the Soviet Union and especially in Eastern Europe – the 'Year of Miracles'. In March, there were semi-free elections at the federal level of the USSR. Boris Yeltsin topped the poll. A strike by miners [no less] demanded the removal of the central role of the Communist Party in the USSR!*

*Elections were held in Poland on the 4th and 18th of June. While some of the lower house seats were reserved for the Communist party, all 100 Senate seats were freely contested. Solidarnosc won 99 of them. By August, Poland had a non-communist government for the first time since the Second World War.*

*The USSR did not intervene in Poland and by the end of the year nearly every Soviet satellite had collapsed, and power was in the hands of non-communists. On November 9th, the Berlin Wall fell and was systematically torn down by protestors. Thousands of East Germans fled to the West and the Communist Party dissolved itself.*

*The triumph of freedom in Eastern Europe did not extend to China. Tens of thousands of Chinese citizens who protested in Tiananmen Square in May/June were crushed by Red Army tanks on the 4th June [as Poles went to vote].*

In addition, two of the candidates on the Reform Group's Branch Executive ticket were found not to have been continuously financial for the 12 months immediately prior to the election. This was required by the rules to be eligible to stand for election. Both were declared ineligible to stand at the 1988 election. This included my direct opponent, Barbara Lewis. For a while, I thought that I might be declared elected President unopposed. This would have been difficult, as I would be presiding over an otherwise hostile Executive. However, the Court ordered a re-run for the two Executive positions as well as for the two Branch Council members.[200]

This re-election was held in September 1989. It was the third Branch election in three years and was held 15 months after the 1988 ballot. Michael O'Sullivan and I were the two candidates for the Executive positions which were being re-contested. As our senior candidate, Michael ran for the President's position this time around, while I stood for Deputy President. I took leave from my job in the National Office to campaign amongst the membership. This proved to be quite difficult without any help from the Union officially. Some leads were given to me as to places to go to try to talk to the members, but it proved almost impossible to get past the reception desk in most cases. Unsurprisingly, our team lost the re-election for the two Executive positions but managed to pick up one of the State Councillor positions. The Branch remained in the hands of the Reform Group.

In Australia, my colleagues and I could hardly take in the full impact of the momentous events in Eastern Europe. Our hopes for the defeat of totalitarian Communism were being realised far faster than we could have hoped. Better still, there was virtually no bloodshed – truly, a year of miracles. One of the members of CRAFT in Victoria – Irma Steinkulher – was of German ancestry. A relative of hers still living in Germany at this time managed to obtain some fragments of the Berlin Wall, one of which Irma gave to me. This is a great treasure of mine. It was a potent reminder that Soviet bloc was falling apart – its centre could not hold, either.

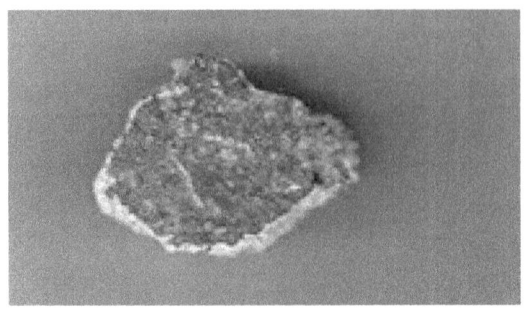

*A fragment of the Berlin Wall*

## DEAL OR NO DEAL?

During 1989-90, an uneasy peace broke out in the Clerks Union. John Maynes did not like to give in easily. He fought the dissident Branches – in particular the Central & Southern Queensland, South Australian and now the Victorian Branch – on every conceivable front. However, the cost of this to the Union in legal fees was considerable and there was no end in sight. Members were not benefitting. In Tanner's account of this period, he says the initial approach for a settlement of matters in dispute came from the National Office, that is, from John Maynes. The Reform Group Branches were, according to Tanner, suspicious but eventually entered negotiations with Maynes that successfully resolved all the outstanding legal issues between the National Union and its Reform Group led Branches.

I was not primarily involved in these negotiations – they were mainly conducted by John Maynes himself as well as by Michael O'Sullivan and the Union's legal officer. I did attend several meetings to determine a group position and went to some of the negotiation sessions with the Reform Group if they coincided with meetings of the National Executive or National Council. Of these negotiations, Tanner wrote:

> *Negotiating with Maynes was a nightmare, not because of his innate skills, which were considerable, but because of his totally idiosyncratic approach. It took ten times as long as equivalent negotiations would have taken with anyone else. We had to put up with hours and hours of little homilies about all sorts of extraneous matters. Maynes was an expert on everything...*[201]

Welcome to our world! I still smile when I read Tanner's words. He and his colleagues did not appreciate the full extent of the difficulties anyone had in dealing with John Maynes. Tanner refers to some final negotiations held during the National Executive meeting at Opal Cove near Coffs Harbour in late 1989. I remember these discussions well. There were four matters still in dispute. Our group caucused in advance and decided quite quickly that we could agree with the Reform Group's position on all four matters. It was agreed to meet their representatives that evening at about 7.30 pm. All John Maynes had to say on our behalf was 'yes' four times, but he could not readily

---

### THE BALTIC STATES AND RUSSIA

*Following the year of miracles in Eastern Europe, the Soviet Union itself began to disintegrate in 1990. In March, two of the Baltic States, Lithuania and Estonia declared their independence from the USSR. Gorbachev tried, brutally at times, to stop the breakaways.*

*In May, Boris Yeltsin became President of the Russian Republic, still part of the USSR. In July, Yeltsin resigned his membership of the Communist Party.*

*In February, the left-wing Sandinistas were defeated in Nicaragua, a Central American hotspot in the Cold War.*

---

do so. We discussed these issues until after midnight without reaching the agreement which had been possible at 7.35 pm. Because the hour was late, the discussions were adjourned until the next day to again discuss these matters which we had already agreed to concede! I am still not sure why John Maynes took this approach. Was it that he did not want the other side to think that they had had an easy win? Did he think that if he talked and talked that a better position might emerge? I am not sure, but Tanner is right in one respect. Dealing with John Maynes always took much longer than expected. Nevertheless, an agreement was eventually reached between the disputing parties that settled all outstanding legal issues.

Not resolved, however, was the question of political control of the Union and its Branches. During 1990 our team prepared itself for the next round of Branch elections, due in 1991. During the year, several meetings were held to prepare a national campaign and ticket as well as strategies in key Branches. Early in 1990, our team had its first break for years, although it came at a cost to the Union. The elected officials of the Taxation Officers Branch [TOB] of the Union – supporters of the National Reform Group – suddenly defected to the Public Sector Union, taking with them most of the Branch's members.

This was a significant blow to the Union and an unexpected one. The TOB had offices in the Union's building at 53 Queen Street which they abandoned overnight. This was an unwelcome surprise to the National Union but a disaster for the Reform Group, which was also taken unawares. The defection of this Branch took away the possibility of a Reform Group majority on National Council. The Reform Group was outraged. John Maynes could count on support from the large NSW Branch, as well as the smaller ones in Tasmania, West Australia and North Queensland. The Reform Group controlled the small SA Branch as well as the much bigger Victorian and Central and Southern Queensland Branches. A political stalemate within the Union was emerging.

The CRAFT team met regularly to plan our 1991 election campaign and to select candidates for National Officer positions. In 1988, John Maynes had said that he was not standing again for election. However, there was no one to replace him at the national level because of the loss of the Victorian Branch National Council delegates and he was still in office. National Secretary Terry Sullivan was retiring at the 1991 election. Assistant National Secretary Dick Wasson was terminally ill with cancer. These planning meetings took place without John Maynes. My notes from these meetings show that they were attended by all our Branches and key national office figures, other than John Maynes. NSW Branch Secretary Vince Higgins was the senior figure in the Union after John Maynes. Terry Sullivan, Dick Wasson and Vince Higgins were all involved in these meetings.

The plan that developed was to pre-select Hugh Armstrong as National Secretary, Peter Abrams as Assistant National Secretary and Michael O'Sullivan as National President. All of them were involved in these discussions. To achieve this outcome, it was necessary to win back the Victorian Branch and its crucial National Council delegates. This is what the team planned to do. I was at one of these planning meetings held interstate [in conjunction with a National Council or Executive meeting] when John Maynes unexpectedly walked into the room. He sensed that this was an election planning meeting. For some reason, he took it badly, presuming it was a conspiracy against him. It was not. People were only doing what was necessary to take the Union forward into a post-John Maynes era. I do not remember the precise words Maynes used, but he glared at us all saying something to the effect 'I know what this is all about'. He left in a huff.

This stance did not change my view of what needed to be done. It was necessary to plan for the future. But there was life left in the old bull. The 'Emperor' struck back. In the first half of 1991, it was suddenly announced by John Maynes that he and all the Branch Secretaries who supported him had made a pact with the Reform Group-aligned Branches for a 'no contest' outcome at that year's Branch elections. A deal had also been done for the elected National Officer positions. This pact involved each side agreeing not to run candidates against existing officeholders in any Branch. This would mean that the Reform Group would keep control of the Victorian Branch. The status quo would apply in every other Branch as well. The Reform Group had agreed that the four National Elected Officers would be Ralph Clarke [Reform Group] as National President; Michael O'Sullivan, Deputy National President; Hugh Armstrong, National Secretary; and Peter Abrams, Assistant National Secretary.

This outcome naturally came as a shock and a surprise to me and to CRAFT supporters in the Victorian Branch who were keen to take on Tanner's Reform Group again. In all the other Branches held by our allies, the Branch Secretary had agreed to this pact with the left-wing Reform Group. Their elected Branch officers and staff naturally fell into line with their Secretary. It was obvious why the other Branches had agreed to this arrangement. It preserved their positions and control without facing a vote of the membership. The immediate 'victims' of this deal were CRAFT's activists in Victoria. They had not been consulted about it and had no say in this arrangement despite years of struggle and personal sacrifice.

All the key professional staff of the National Office agreed to support this deal except two: Hugh Armstrong and myself. We met with our rank-and-file supporters to discuss this deal. Naturally enough, they were adamantly opposed to not contesting the Victorian Branch election. Hugh Armstrong and I supported them. This made our life difficult in the National Office. One by one everyone else in the office came to see us seeking to pressure us into accepting the deal. Vince Higgins, Secretary of the NSW Branch went further. To our faces, he suggested that if we did anything that threatened the control of his Branch, we would be well advised not to walk down any dark lanes in Sydney at night! We did not really think that he would have done us any physical harm, but we got the message that he was not happy with us.

Our relationship was later restored, and he and I became and remained good friends.[202]

The whole of the Union seemed to be arrayed against Hugh Armstrong and I, other than our very loyal supporters in Victoria. The base of our support in Victoria was Social Action and Gerald Mercer and Jim Hewat. Jim Hewat was a State Councillor who had been taking the fight up to the Reform Group ever since our 1988 debacle. Together, these two people could put a decent campaign in place. For some time, John Maynes and Michael O'Sullivan had been distancing themselves from Social Action, the organisation they, with Gerald Mercer and others, had created in the aftermath of the split in the NCC in the early 1980s. Their decision to do a deal with the Reform Group cemented this drift. It became a new rift.

## BEING SUED

By this stage, I had another problem. In late 1990 and early 1991, the group in Victoria was still in campaigning mode. It was issuing regular editions of the *Clerical Worker*, the publicity organ of the Clerks Rank and File Team [CRAFT]. Frank Lee, whose day job was editor of the FCUA's national journal *The Clerk* was largely responsible for writing our propaganda, under John Maynes's overall control. The *Clerical Worker* was a registered publication with Australia Post. However, my name was shown on each issue as the responsible person. In early 1991, Frank Lee came to me with some draft copy for a new issue. The headline on the front page was '$6 million Cover-up'. It told a story about financial losses at the Victorian Branch since the Reform Group had taken over. As well as the words 'cover-up' in the heading, the text also used the words 'missing' and 'disappeared' with respect to union funds. The substance of the article's text was correct. The Branch had spent all its income and much of the financial reserves it had when the Reform group was elected to office in 1988. But the article could give the impression that there was something untoward about what had happened to the money.

I told Frank Lee that I did not want my name attached to the publication with this article in it. He argued that it was all justifiable and I reluctantly agreed to let it be printed and distributed. This was a mistake and I knew it was a mistake when I did it. I should have trusted my instincts and been more resolute. Frank Lee sent the article to the *Sunday Herald-Sun* and journalist

David Wilson printed an article based on it, which also 'quoted' me. I did not like the look of the newspaper article either. Shortly afterward, on a Sunday afternoon at home, there was a knock on the door and a process server served me with a writ for libel filed by Lindsay Tanner and Barbara Lewis against both the Herald and Weekly Times as publishers of the *Sunday Herald-Sun* and against me personally.

This was not a pleasant experience. I imagined in my mind the family home being sold to pay the punitive damages. Tanner told me personally that the focus of the action was against the Herald and Weekly Times and not me but that was hardly the issue. They had served and named me as a co-defendant. The newspaper was big enough to look after itself. My circumstances were much different. I might not have minded so much if I had written the article and had been happy with it. But I knew I would find it difficult to justify all the words used if the matter went to trial because I had not liked them when I first read them. [By this stage Frank Lee was supporting the proposed deal, leaving me high and dry. He was not being sued.] Personal concern about the writ and the financial implications for my family existed until the matter was finally settled in 1992 with an apology from me and a statement that I had not meant nor intended to imply that either Tanner or Lewis had corruptly or otherwise misappropriated any Union money. I certainly did not think this to be the case at any time and was genuinely very willing to say so.

Hugh Armstrong and I fought the proposed 'no contest' pact for some time but eventually our colleagues in Victoria released us from our opposition to the deal, given our positions in the National Office. We both told John Maynes that we would not oppose the deal. Hugh Armstrong became a party to it, as he had to since under it, he was to become FCUA National Secretary. I am happy to say that I was never formally a party to it and did not feel bound by it, although I could not say so publicly. The CRAFT activists in the Victorian Branch were not a party to the deal and not bound by it in any way. They held a further meeting of the group which endorsed the idea of running a ticket in the Victorian Branch. At this time, I was normally chairing these meetings, but I deliberately chose not to attend this one. John Launder, an old friend and a former Branch organiser, chaired this meeting.

I was one of two signatories to the bank accounts which held what was left of CRAFT's campaign funds. These were monies privately raised by the group to fund election campaigns. Union funds could not be used for this purpose.

By 1991 only about $8000 was left in the CWIG/CRAFT account. There had been three elections in three years, but this sum was still a significant amount of money at the time. Without it, it would have been difficult to run an effective campaign. The other signatory was Michael Cashman, a former Branch organiser still employed by the National Office. Michael was part of the group that wanted to fight on in Victoria. Since I could not be seen to be breaking the deal, I wrote to the bank advising that there was a dispute over the funds and asking that the account be frozen until further notice. I later wrote again saying that no withdrawals should be made unless both signatories signed a withdrawal slip. The bank accepted this instruction.

In this way, John Maynes and Michael O'Sullivan were able tell Tanner that the deal was being honoured and that we [that is, me] had frozen the bank account to stop any 'friends' in Victoria accessing any money to run against him. After the meeting chaired by John Launder, which decided to contest the election in Victoria, I received a visit at home from him. John came at about teatime and we offered him a meal, which he accepted. The purpose of his visit, though, was to put pressure on me to release the CRAFT funds. Those people at the CRAFT meeting would have thought that John Launder was in the best position to influence me. He handed me a letter:

*20/9/1991*

*Dear Keith,*

*I understand that you have at this time refused to countersign withdrawal forms for the use of the two CRAFT account monies, the use of which has been endorsed by a well attended meeting last Tuesday 17/9/1991 of CRAFT supporters who had contributed to those election fighting funds. I would anticipate that you have seen a copy of the motion that was carried with one abstention.*

*As the person who was elected Chairman at that meeting, I would ask you to acquiesce to the freely expressed wish of that meeting which included many whose active support for CRAFT goes back as much as forty years. You must be aware of the people who attended that meeting and where they are coming from. They are the union members who have been the salt of the earth, loyal, never been in it for themselves, but who have steadfastly stuck to their principles of <u>what they believe is right and just.</u>*

*Keith, it would be anthesis of all that we believe if the wishes of those people* were not upheld. The fact that certain individuals who either were not able to attend that meeting or who wished not to be there, does not destroy its validity to act the way it did. The presence of some of those individuals also would not have changed the course of the meeting's decision either.

Remember the decision to take the path of collaboration with Tanner for whatever motive, was made without reference to these people. It does not matter that even in the eyes of those who have chosen to collaborate that those who don't wish to, are all wrong, misguided, 'drop-kicks' or whatever other adjective that might have been applied, it is their democratic right to choose what every path of action they desire. Further as a group they have clearly and indisputably chosen.

They want to use those funds, as qualified in the resolution, to fight an election and that is their right, both as CRAFT supporters and more importantly as union members!

Keith, no one regrets the current differences more than I, too many travails have been commonly shared, the good times and the bad, we do not want to exacerbate the differences, none of this has been our choice.

We also appreciate the difficulties you may see yourself in, but once again you cannot ignore the right of those members who have democratically chosen to go a different path at a meeting which others who were invited to attend did not appear.

Yours sincerely

John Launder

The letter was very well argued, and the points made were valid. The funds in CRAFT's bank accounts had been raised to advance the group's cause. The people who had personally contributed the money had neither been consulted about the deal and nor agreed to it. While I was not able to agree with John Launder on the night, I thought about what he said, and the points raised by the letter. My options seemed limited. If I had released the funds, I would have had little choice but to resign my position in the National Office of the Union. If I refused, I would be breaking faith with some good, honest and committed friends with whom I agreed.

## A BROWN PAPER BAG

The more I thought about this, the more I felt that I should release the funds. I decided to tell John Maynes of my decision. I did not expect this to be an easy conversation but was surprised by the outcome. When I told John of my decision to make the funds available to CRAFT, he asked me not to do so. This did not surprise me, but what came next did. He offered an alternative source of funding for the CRAFT campaign – himself! John Maynes said that if I kept the CRAFT funds locked up in the bank, he would supply an equivalent sum of money to me to pass on to those who wanted to stand against Tanner. I did not expect this outcome, but I agreed at once. John Maynes was breaking his own deal with Tanner, the one he had just signed. He told no one else in his group [naturally]. I only told Mike Cashman what the source of the funds was. Thus, on a regular basis, I would go into John Maynes's office and he would hand me a brown paper bag [yes, literally] with cash in it. This was meted out to me in instalments. Often, I would have to chase him for the cash.

---

### THE USSR: 'THINGS FALL APART, THE CENTRE CANNOT HOLD'

Those who had dared to struggle in the USSR, won. In June 1991, ex-Communist Boris Yeltsin won election as President of Russia in a popular vote of the people. However, during August 19-21, Communist Party hardliners staged an attempted coup against Gorbachev and his reforms as well as against Yeltsin. Gorbachev was isolated in the Crimea.

Tanks surrounded the Russian parliament building and threatened to attack. In his finest hour, Yeltsin stared them down, literally, personally persuading the tank commanders to turn the tanks around so that they would defend, not threaten, the Russian Parliament.

In response to this failed coup, Yeltsin forced the suspension of the Communist Party of the Soviet Union in Russia on August 23rd.

On the 21st December, the Commonwealth of Independent States [CIS] was created to replace the USSR. Gorbachev resigned his Soviet positions on the 25th December – Christmas Day in the West – and the Soviet Union ceased to exist. Bolshevism ceased to rule Russia.

In Australia, the Communist Party of Australia dissolved itself.

---

I did not know [or ask] where he got it from, whether it was his own money, or whether he got it from right-wing sources within the ALP who were happy to see Tanner challenged. This latter source seems most likely. When handed the money, I would walk upstairs to where Michael Cashman worked and hand the paper bag to him. It all found its way into the campaign. I did not keep any records of the cash and I suspect that while it did not quite add up to the sum in the CRAFT accounts at the time it came close. After the election was over, the campaign was in debt. I again spoke to John and he agreed to me releasing additional CRAFT funds to the campaign. In total, more money was spent on the campaign than CRAFT had in the bank when the election was called. One thing I did like about John Maynes: he did not believe his own propaganda. He saw no issue at all in undermining the deal that he had entered into! He would have been pleased to see the Reform Group lose and was happy someone was having a go.

Michael O'Sullivan would never have done this. He would have found it abhorrent to break a deal that he had made. He fully honoured the deal with the Reform Group. Tanner notes in his book that when the 'Old Guard' made a deal they stuck to it. Well, not everybody. He also recorded that 'a renegade element' within the 'Old Guard' refused to accept the deal and contested the Branch elections. Tanner wrote:

> Much to our dismay, the challenge gradually turned into a very serious one. Quite a lot of resources were poured into it, and our opponents' propaganda was a lot smarter than we had faced from the Old Guard. They attacked the deal as an undemocratic device designed to deprive members of a vote...[203]

It is interesting to note Tanner's comments that the election material from this new group was better, which was a great credit to them. Although the 'renegades' could not field a full team, they put a credible list of candidates into the ballot. The result was extremely close: The Reform Group just scraped back with as little as 51% of the vote. Tanner won his position as Secretary against the relatively unknown Pauline Taylor by just 226 votes. Tanner said:

> I felt that the election results vindicated the deal completely. It is always dangerous to talk about 'ifs' but if we had faced a full contest from the Old Guard, with much more "credible" candidates and money, I find it hard to believe that we would have done any better than our narrow win. If anything, we might have lost. [204]

Tanner's comments say it all. The new scratch team campaigned more effectively than CRAFT had done previously and achieved a better result. Moreover, what Tanner says is undoubtedly true. If a united effort had been made, victory was possible. The deal was not necessary. The best course would have been to fight. As the Maoists at Monash University might have said many years earlier: 'Dare to struggle, dare to win.' Since the election was a 'keep what you had' deal, the Maynes team could nominate enough people to keep their numbers on the State Council. I was nominated by the Maynes group [and therefore was on the Tanner ticket as well]. The 'renegade' ticket also supported me since I was in reasonable favour with them. I and a few others in this position effectively topped the poll and were elected almost unanimously.

After the 'no contest' election, [205] serious moves were made to amalgamate the FCU with two other unions as part of the ACTU's union merger push. In 1993, the FCU became part of the Australian Services Union and the National Office left 53 Queen Street for the ASU's premises in Carlton South. This did not eliminate politics from the Union. Michael O'Sullivan later faced a challenge for the position of ASU National Executive President from his former deal partners in the Victorian Clerical Branch [Lindsay Tanner having moved into Parliament by then]. I had been working for the Clerks Union for 14 years by 1993. Despite the Clerks Union trauma of the second half of this period, the outside world had changed for the better. What had seemed impossible to imagine in 1979 when I started with the FCUA and in 1984-5 when the split in the ALP ended, had become a reality in Eastern Europe and Russia at least. Despite our home-grown problems in the Clerks Union, the larger battle for freedom was being won. With the Cold War in Europe won and the FCUA now part of a bigger union, my world of work was changing as well.

# 8

# FOR TWO ARE BETTER THAN ONE: SOCIAL JUSTICE AT WORK

*Extract from the Treaty of Versailles 1919:*
'WHEREAS *the League of Nations has for its object the establishment of universal peace, and such a peace can be established only if it is based upon social justice...*'

The amalgamation of the three unions to form the Australian Services Union in 1993 changed the industrial/political world in which I operated. Unlike the FCU, the ASU had a limited political persona. The merger brought together a politically disparate group of Unions. The Branches of the pre-existing unions operated in different factions within the ALP: the Socialist Left, Centre-Left, Labor Unity and Centre Unity. It was difficult for the Union to have a united political view on anything much and, as a result, the early National ASU was not a political influencer of great significance. The former Clerks Union Branches from the NCC/Industrial Group background had always been interested in social, industrial and political policies. On the other hand, the former white-collar Municipal Officers Association [MOA] Branches saw themselves largely as non-political professional industrial technicians, mainly concerned with industrial awards. The blue-collar Municipal Employees Union Branches were politically divided, and little interested in policy.

The staff of the new National Office numbered about 50 at the time of amalgamation but had dwindled to about 13 when I retired in 2011. The National Office focused on trying to run and grow this new organisation, but, sadly, many of the growth strategies struggled to succeed. The clerical membership of the new Union was about 80,000 at the time of the merger in 1993. It steadily declined in the face of technological and industrial change and, perhaps, a lack of experience in some merged State Branches about how to unionise clerical and administrative employees. The ACTU's 'union rationalisation' policies did not help either, favouring 'industry' unions at the expense of occupation-based unions like the FCUA. It was easy to get the impression that the Clerks Union was being quietly swept under the union movement's carpet and forgotten.

Since 1989, I had become involved in issues relating to vocational training and skill recognition for clerical and administrative workers. The Hawke/Keating governments focused on microeconomic reform to drive productivity and economic performance. These goals were to be achieved in part by improving the skills of employees. Higher skill levels were to be rewarded with higher wages. Improved wages would be provided by skill-based classification structures in industrial awards linked to training inputs and skills recognition. When the FCUA considered these new arrangements, it quickly realised that there was little formal training, skills recognition, or skills development in place for office-based employees. Most industries had industry training committees focussed on blue-collar workers. There was little or nothing in place for clerical and administrative employees. The FCUA determined to create it. In 1990, the Union won agreement from the Australian Government and some employer organisations to form a clerical skills committee of which I became the interim chair. This committee was set up as a formal corporate entity in December 1991 as the National Office Skills Formation Advisory Body [NOSFAB]. I became the first Chair. I have remained on the Board of NOSFAB and its successor bodies for 29 years.

*The Admin Training Company Board in 1996. The ATC was a successor to NOSFAB. Vince Higgins is seated on my left.*

Photo Copyright Aspire Training and Consulting Ltd, used with permission.

As a result of this work, I became involved in a range of committees concerning vocational education and training, including the Employment and Skills Formation Council [EFSC] of the National Board of Employment Education and Training [NBEET]. This high-powered board advised the Federal Government on higher education, schools as well as workplace training and skills [the latter through the ESFC]. During my time on the ESFC, Laurie Carmichael chaired it. He was formerly an ACTU Assistant Secretary and before that a Metal Workers union official and was formerly a Communist Party member. Under his leadership, the ESFC produced what became known as the Carmichael Report recommending a new vocational training system for Australia. I enjoyed working with Carmichael whose passion had now become the industrial transformation of Australia.[206]

This work in vocational education and training also led me to represent the ACTU on several overseas missions and conferences on these matters; in Singapore, Bangkok and Tokyo as well as at the International Labour Conference in Geneva in June 2000. I worked closely with the ACTU Assistant Secretary Bill Mansfield on these issues [he was also a member of the ESFC]. Bill Mansfield was one of the lesser known but tireless workers of the trade union movement. Oddly, the ACTU nominated me to serve on the Prime Minister's Science and Engineering Council although I knew little about either discipline. This body was a high-status Council, which met twice a year in the Cabinet Room at Parliament House, Canberra. The Prime Minister chaired it, at first Bob Hawke and then Paul Keating.

At the new ASU, my role changed from a mainly research and vocational training focus to industrial work. I became a National Industrial Officer and took on the important airline industry [which had quickly burnt out one or two staff]. I did more work as an industrial advocate [learning a lot from Hugh Armstrong, now Joint National Secretary of the ASU] and became involved in training others in advocacy and other aspects of industrial work. Declining union membership and staff numbers put paid to any expectation of becoming an elected official of the ASU. I had a quiet tilt at becoming Assistant Secretary of the ACTU which failed. ACTU Secretary Greg Combet preferred someone else and I declined the consolation prize of an ACTU Industrial Officer's job in lieu, preferring to stay at the ASU.

*Social Action* magazine remained an important interest. I continued to write articles for the journal. This work was a private activity, done in my own time. Michael O'Sullivan, now a joint National President of the ASU, knew of my involvement but he was no longer involved in the work of Social Action. I continued to have the same political interests, that is, in freedom and democracy and opposition to Communism. With the Soviet Union no longer in existence, the Cold War had largely ended. However, the fate of the people of China and Viet Nam still concerned me. Much remained to be done [and still does] in respect of these two Asian countries, but I was no longer able to do much, other than to write about it. *Social Action* reported on trade union politics, domestic policy – especially social security and industrial relations – as well as on the circumstances of workers in the remaining communist countries.

My political focus shifted to support for and a defence of the role of trade unions in society as organised labour came increasingly under attack. This was particularly the case after 1996 when the Howard Government came to power and introduced radical changes via the *Workplace Relations Act*. This interest intensified after the so-called 'WorkChoices' laws were enacted after the 2004 election when Howard gained control of the Senate and was able to pass draconian anti-union and anti-worker legislation. In 2006-7, I was happy to be part of the ACTU's Your Rights at Work [YRAW] campaign and especially in the 'marginal seats' campaign in the Federal seat of Deakin. Under the dynamic leadership of Linda Cargill, the campaign set out to unseat the sitting Liberal member. The ACTU ran a strong public campaign against the Government focusing on the anti-worker nature of the so-called 'WorkChoices' laws. Amongst other activities, Linda Cargill wanted to run what she called a 'Faith Communities' campaign. This would look to engage local churches and their members around industrial legislation as a social justice issue. I recall the campaign meeting when Linda proposed this idea. Possibly, I was the only one in the room at the time who had recently been inside a Church.

In Victoria, there was a deep divide between ALP activists in general and the churches. Many ALP members saw the Churches – especially the Catholic Church – as being opposed to the ALP, doubtless because of the 1950s split in the Party. The mainstream Christian Churches were now seen as conservative forces in society. The churches appeared to have few connections with the Labor side of politics. Linda Cargill knew that I was a Catholic and asked me to coordinate this campaign. This work was immensely enjoyable and rewarding. It both allowed and forced me to hone my ideas about two things of importance to me: faith and social justice at work. A small but hardworking campaign team came together to see what we could do.

## SOCIAL JUSTICE, RELIGION, AND 'SOCIALISM'

This campaign forced me to learn more about the connections between religion, the trade union movement, and the ALP. What I learned surprised me. I had previously assumed that Australian unions had been started by Catholics since they made up the bulk of the working class in early Australia. Reading more deeply about this, it became clear that this assumption was wrong. The early leaders of the trade union movement were much more likely to have been evangelical Protestants, especially Methodists, than Catholics. For example, the union movement in South Australia [SA] had at its core the Cornish-born hard rock miners of the Yorke Peninsula, who were predominantly Methodists of one sort or another, including the so-called Primitive Methodists [PMs].[207]

Methodist preachers worked closely with their people and saw that to improve the lives of working people, unionism was needed. From unionism, the ALP evolved. According to Piggin and Linder:

> *In South Australia, a 'significant proportion' of the members of the United Labour Party [as the ALP in SA was known until 1918] were 'ardent' Methodists. The first Labor men elected to any Australian parliament (May 1891) were Robert Guthrie, a Primitive Methodist, ..., David Charleston from Cornwall who was a member of the Churches of Christ, and worked at that Methodists hothouse, Moonta mines, in the late 1880s, and Andrew Kirkpatrick, an Anglican...* [208]

The first United Labour Party Premier in South Australia was Tom Price, who headed a minority government for four years until his death in 1909. Price was Wesleyan Methodist, a lay preacher and Sunday school superintendent.[209] One of the early Mining union leaders in SA was John Verran, who also worked at Moonta Mines. Verran became the Premier of the first majority ALP government of South Australia in 1910.[210] He famously said, "I am an MP because I am a PM".[211] Both Price and Verran described themselves as Christian Socialists.[212] This was a revelation to me.

Other early union leaders were also practising non-Catholic Christians, including, for example, the AWU's W G Spence, who was a Presbyterian lay preacher and who also preached with Primitive Methodists and other "Bible Christians".[213] In 1892 Spence gave a lecture in Sydney under the auspices of the Australian Socialist League on *'The Ethics of new Unionism'*. This 'new' unionism had several dimensions, not the least of which an interest in the promotion of social change both through unionism and the involvement of workers organisations in the political process through what ultimately became the ALP. Spence became a Labor member in the first Federal parliament elected in 1901. Spence also said:

> "If asked to give a short definition of our aim I should say that is an effort to give practical effect to the teachings of the founder of Christianity,...in taking up this new unionism we must see if it cannot get right back to the level of the founder of Christianity, imbibe some of His spirit and get rid of musty theology, for some of it is very musty" [Laughter and cheers]...Christ taught men that they could and should bring the kingdom of heaven upon earth. New unionism aims at giving practical effect to that...' [Note: the words in brackets are included in the published text][214]

Methodists were also prominent in the early Labor caucuses in NSW. Ross McMullin, in his centenary history of the ALP, records that the NSW

Labor Electoral League was formed in April 1891.²¹⁵ It successfully contested its first election under the new banner in June 1891, just a few weeks after its formation and performed brilliantly, capturing 35 out of 141seats and holding the balance of power. McMullin says:

> *Five of the new members were English born miners who had migrated to Australia during the previous dozen years: all but one were devout Methodists.* ²¹⁶

Linder, writing about the same election, says:

> *The nine Methodists among the first 35 Labor Party representatives were joined by 12 other known evangelicals for a grand total of 21, or 60 percent of the fledgling ALP. Thus evangelical Christians totally dominated the first Parliamentary Labor Party. There were five Roman Catholics among the 35 Laborites in that historic NSW legislative Assembly. The next election in 1894 brought three more Methodists into the legislature as Labor Party representatives while the Catholic contingent shrank to one.* ²¹⁷

The importance of practicing evangelical Christians in the early Labor Party surprised me. It was virtually lost history.²¹⁸ Neither the union movement nor the Churches seemed to want to claim this historical connection but it gave me a great story to tell the Protestant Churches with which the YRAW 'Faith Communities' campaign wanted to engage. Evangelical Christians are the equivalent of modern-day Bible Christians basing every belief in the texts of the Bible. It seemed unlikely to me that the Bible would mention unionism but in the materials I read was this wonderful Bible passage:

> *Two are better than one, they get a good wage for their labor. If the one falls, the other will lift up his companion. Woe to the solitary man! For if he should fall, he has no one to lift him up. So also, if two sleep together, they keep each other warm. How can one alone keep warm? Where a lone man may be overcome, two together can resist. A three-ply cord is not easily broken.*²¹⁹

A simpler, more succinct argument for unionism would be difficult to find. Even Moses disliked harsh work supervisors, so much so that he killed one! This was never mentioned to me at Sunday School [or anywhere else]. Exodus Chapter Two says:

> *11. When Moses had grown up, he went out to visit his people, the Hebrews, and he saw how they were forced to do hard labor. He even saw an Egyptian*

*kill a Hebrew, one of Moses' own people.*

*12. Moses looked all around, and when he saw that no one was watching, he killed the Egyptian and hid his body in the sand.*[220]

The Book of Ecclesiasticus gives a figurative but powerful definition of murder: '*It is murder to deprive someone of his living or to cheat an employee of his wages.*' [221] The YRAW Faith Communities campaign committee developed a Discussion Paper on industrial laws from a religious perspective and used it as the basis for a discussion with local Church leaders. We also prepared leaflets for distribution in Church communities including a Bible-based one for the more evangelical Churches. I expected that talking to Catholic parishes would be relatively easy, but we had mixed success in this quarter. The Box Hill Ministers Fraternal, a loose association of Protestant Church Ministers very readily agreed to host a lunchtime forum entitled 'A Christian perspective on industrial relations in contemporary Australian society.' It attracted a fair crowd. There were four speakers at this event. In addition to me, ALP Senate candidate Jacinta Collins spoke as did Charles Sherlock, an Anglican theologian. This first debate also managed to attract Robert Clark. He was the local Liberal Party MP for the State seat of Box Hill and also held the position of Shadow Minister for Industrial relations.[222] I suspect that Clark did not enjoy the event and would have concluded that the Liberal Party's arguments in support of the Federal 'WorkChoices' policies did not come out on top in the debate. After this first debate, the Committee was unable ever again to get the Liberal Party to supply a speaker to any faith community event discussing industrial relations. One or two Liberals who did initially accept suddenly found that they had 'another commitment' on the night in question.

This boycott limited the campaign's ability to hold faith-based discussions and debates. The Minister at the Mitcham Uniting Church was keen to hold an event but felt he could not do so without a Liberal Party speaker. A planned event was cancelled because a Liberal Party MP who had initially accepted the Minister's invitation pulled out the next day. St John's Catholic Church in Mitcham had an active Social Justice Group which hosted two events for us despite the Liberals again being 'no shows'. The Liberal Party everywhere went into hiding on the industrial relations issue for the rest of the election campaign. I wrote a piece on Industrial Relations policy which was published in Eureka Street, a Jesuit online publication.[223] The Anglican Church newspaper published a supportive piece in their Melbourne diocesan newspaper after the ACTU's John Ryan and I met with their Social Justice Committee. Individual social justice committees in some Uniting Churches, and the Uniting Church's Social justice committee itself, were also supportive.

My research and discussions during the Your Rights at Work campaign confirmed for me that unionism was indeed spiritual work [although I was trying to put it to a very secular purpose; that is, changing the Government]. It was pleasing to see that both unionism and the ALP itself owed a lot to the pioneering activities of Christians and disappointing to realise that the connection had been broken. I knew the Catholic Church's teaching on social justice well enough but drawing largely on work done by American unions it was possible to find statements supporting social justice at work from nearly all mainstream Christian Churches as well as in the teachings of Islam. The US National Interfaith Committee on Worker Justice had produced several statements on social justice at work, including from the Presbyterian, Lutheran, and Methodist Christian Churches, as well as from Muslim leaders. Their leaflet *The Qur'an and Worker Justice* quoted the prophet Muhammad in words spoken 1400 years ago: 'None of you has faith unless you love for your brother what you love for yourself'.[224] This teaching sounded to me a lot like the second of the New Testament's two 'great commandments', that is, to 'love your neighbour as yourself'.[225]

Nevertheless, it seemed to me that the historical connection between the Church and the labour movement had been lost, at least in Victoria. The Faith Communities campaign found as much support in the local Anglican and the Uniting Churches as in the Catholic community. The evangelical Christian Churches remained elusive, one Minister telling me that his congregation was a 'management' Church. Kevin Rudd, who became ALP leader in late 2006, had tried to engage with faith communities. In August 2006, as Shadow Minister for Foreign Affairs and Trade, Rudd spoke to the National Forum on Australia's Christian Heritage in Parliament House in Canberra. He spoke about 'Christianity, The ALP and current challenges in Australian Politics' making some of the same points about the connection between evangelical Christians and the early Labor parties that have been made above.[226] As Opposition leader, he was even prepared to front up to forums convened by the conservative Australian Christian Lobby and performed well.

Tony Abbott, as the Howard Government's most prominent Catholic, was publicly a powerful supporter of the Government's workplace relations agenda. Abbott was Workplace Relations Minister from 2001-2003. An attempt was made to counteract his influence in the Catholic community by developing detailed briefing notes on the WorkChoices legislation from a Catholic social justice perspective. These notes were given to Cardinal George Pell, who was then Archbishop of Sydney and thought to be close to Abbott. A colleague of mine who was knowledgeable about these matters developed a paper which I passed on to YRAW campaigners in Sydney. It is not possible to say whether this was effective in persuading Pell against the legislation. The Australian Catholic Council for Employment Relations [ACCER] did a great deal of particularly good work on this issue. Australia's Catholic Bishops expressed their concern about various aspects of the proposed WorkChoices legislation in 2005, but their good advice was not heeded by the Howard Government.[227]

It is unclear whether the faith communities' campaign in Deakin had a great deal of effect, but I learned a lot about the connection between faith and trade union and Labor Party history and this encouraged me to continue to explore this link. The Deakin Your Rights at Work campaign's more direct activities such as extensive doorknocking of the electorate were undoubtedly much more powerful than what we managed to do with Church communities. I greatly enjoyed the campaigning: both that involving Church communities and the more direct face-to-face work with electors. Knocking on doors and trying to start a conversation about unions and industrial laws can be daunting but there was surprisingly little hostility and often a ready willingness to discuss the political issues of the day. The ALP won the seat of Deakin in the 2007 election and hung on to it for two terms. Prime Minister John Howard lost his seat in the 2007 general election. The Liberal Coalition governments of Tony Abbott and Malcolm Turnbull [2013-18] did little to change the terms and conditions of employment of workers but sought to impose or re-impose tighter and tighter controls over the ability of unions to represent their members. Scott Morrison is continuing this approach.

As a young person, my first political position, as described in Chapter 2, was simply one of anti-communism, or more generally anti-totalitarianism and anti-authoritarianism. It was more difficult to say then what I was for. I had neither a particular philosophy nor any religion. The Your Rights at Work campaign in 2007 helped me to formulate my ideas on what I was for, as much as what I continued to be against. It led me to a better understanding of the connection between religious faith and the rights of working people.

The NCC was, of course, strongly based on the ideas and practice of Catholic Action, that is, both the right and the responsibility of Catholics to act in the world where they saw injustice. But I was not at first a part of this tradition, although during my university days I was mixing with others who were. When I later became a Catholic, I was more exposed to Catholic social thought on a range of issues, including work. The Church's social justice teachings have often been described as 'the Church's best-kept secret'. But they were certainly not unknown to the NCC's activists and supporters in the union movement. Beginning with *Rerum Novarum* issued by Pope Leo XIII in 1891, the Church had forthrightly set out a progressive approach to what was quaintly called 'the labour question'. This papal encyclical may have played some part in influencing early Australian industrial legislation.[228] *Rerum Novarum* built on the development of Catholic social teaching from the mid-1850s. In part, to be fair, the Church's interest in the world of work was also developed in response to efforts by radicals in Europe to win working people to socialism, including Marxism.[229] Marxist socialism did not allow a role for the spiritual in society, that is, the spirit of God working in the world through people. Religion was, infamously in the words of Karl Marx, the 'opium of the masses' lulling them into inaction and submission in response to what he said was the allegedly false promise of eternal reward after death.[230]

At a meeting I had attended many years earlier, B.A. Santamaria had said it was necessary to fight and defeat Marxism as a political philosophy. This question was still a live issue in the 1970s and 1980s and I took his suggestion seriously. I had studied Marxism at university and had continued to take an interest in it. Marxism underpinned Communism in the Soviet Union and elsewhere. To challenge the legitimacy of Communism it was necessary to question its fundamental philosophical and/or intellectual basis. It should have been enough to be able to criticise Soviet and Chinese Communism on their appalling human rights records. However, even as further details of the bitter fruits of communism appeared, Marxism kept its romantic and intellectual appeal for some. As the communist economic model in the Eastern bloc countries and in China and Viet Nam was being increasingly exposed as a failing system during the 1970s and 1980s, some academics and students promoted a 'New Left' form of Marxism. This movement held, in effect, that Marxism had not ever been tried in its proper form but had been corrupted by Stalin and others. This movement emphasised the writings of the 'young Marx' rather than his later economic works or the actions of his successors.

When Peter Singer wrote two long articles on Marxism in the Melbourne Age's short-lived supplement *The Monthly Review* [231] in 1981, I weighed in with a long reply of my own. *The Age* declined to publish my contribution as an article but printed it as a very wordy letter in the November issue [to which they allowed Singer a further right of reply].[232] My letter accused Singer of wanting to breathe new life into a dead philosophy. He denied that this was his intention. Marxism's weakest link is its claim to be scientific. Marx espoused what he called 'scientific socialism' with its 'iron laws' and firm predictions about the course of human history. Marx appropriated the term socialism from other thinkers and turned it into revolutionary communism. He derided other socialists, calling many of them 'utopian' thinkers who did not base their theories on the underpinning realities of economics. One of those socialists that Marx [and Engels] labelled 'utopian' was the eccentric French socialist Charles Fourier, who established socialist communities that he called 'phalanges' – groups of people working together collaboratively rather than in a 'master and servant' relationship. Fourier and his utopian communities are mentioned in the Communist Manifesto, published in 1848.[233]

While doing some family history research in 2016 with my father, I was surprised to find that I had a follower – and financial backer - of Charles Fourier in my family tree. On my paternal grandfather's side of the family, I am descended from merchants from Aberdeen in Scotland, surnamed Young. After the Napoleonic wars concluded, one James Young had moved the family business interests to Rotterdam and became very wealthy. After he died in 1834, one of his sons, Arthur Young, my great great grandmother's brother, developed an interest in the teachings of Fourier and financially supported Fourierist publications and other activities. Arthur Young then tried to set up a new society based on the principle of 'collaborative' work. He bought a former Catholic Abbey at Citeaux in France in 1839 and invited others to come and work with him there. Unfortunately, the attempt to found a utopian society failed, taking with it a considerable sum of Young family money. [234] [235] But I can applaud his intentions and his efforts to respond to the evils of the industrial revolution and uncontrolled capitalism.

*The Abbey at Citeaux in 2019*

The sociologist Max Weber once reputedly said that the Soviet 'experiment' in communism set history back 100 years.²³⁶ It certainly set Russia back by at least that period and still stunts the economic, social, intellectual and cultural progress of China and Viet Nam. Weber's sentiment has been applied to socialism itself, that is to say, that the Soviet experiment in Marxist socialism has set back socialism itself by the same amount of time.²³⁷ George Orwell once wrote that his experience in Spain during the war against Franco was the impulse behind his novel, *Animal Farm* and that "the destruction of the Soviet myth is essential if we want a revival of the Socialist movement." ²³⁸ However, the collapse of the Soviet Union has been viewed as the triumph of capitalism over socialism, the latter being discredited. But the failure of communism does not serve to justify or validate how capitalism works in our society today.

The Communist 'experiment' has certainly seriously damaged attempts to discover and implement alternatives to capitalism and to find and implement more co-operative modes of work. Other possible models were rejected by the Left and crowded out of consideration in a binary world. During the Cold War, the world was polarised between communism and capitalism both politically and economically. Marx's model failed but his most useful legacy lies in his critique of the operation of capitalism in the 19th century [and, by extension, today]. Marx and Engels closely observed the condition of the working people in England. Marx saw this through the medium of objective and factual parliamentary reports [and other sources] available to him in the Library of the British Museum. Engels wrote the seminal book on the subject.[239] The terrible work practices that they described can be seen in Australia today in the exploitation of vulnerable workers in unorganised sectors of the Australian economy. The equivalents of the 'dark Satanic mills' of the industrial north of England in the 1800s exist again in sectors of Australian industry and commerce.[240] Much to our collective shame in this country, we see repeated exposures of shocking work practices in retail, hospitality, agriculture and elsewhere, in some cases amounting to virtual slavery and rampant wage theft. Capitalism is becoming increasingly unfettered and is reverting to some of the forms and practices seen by Marx and Engels. What can be the social justice response to these issues? Is there any form of economic organisation that can deal equitably with these issues?

## THE END OF BELIEF?

In a perceptive essay on his experience of the Cold War, Rodney Cavalier, a Minister in the Wran Labor Government in NSW, wrote:

> *The end of the Cold War meant the end of belief. In the absence of belief, the ALP evolved into a brand...When the adherents of a busted view of the world declined to dissolve themselves, the settings were in place for the emergence of a league of operatives, once Left and Right, believing in nothing except their own careers.* [241]

I first met Rodney Cavalier in the late 1980s/early 1990s when the Australian Language and Literacy Council [ALLC] was created under the auspices of the National Board of Employment, Education and Training. Rodney was appointed Chair of the ALLC, and I was a member of the Council representing the Employment and Skills Formation Council. There is much truth in Rodney's analysis of the present state of the ALP. But, in my opinion, the end of the Cold War should not mean the end of belief for those in the Party. The ALP was formed well before the beginning of the Cold War; indeed, before the Bolshevik Revolution in Russia in 1917. The pioneers of the union movement and the ALP which grew out of it had a set of beliefs that well predated the unfortunate 'Soviet experiment'.

Many of these pioneers described themselves as socialists, and some of them called themselves Christian Socialists. In 1921, the 9th Federal Labor Party Conference debated the form of a 'socialist' objective for the Party. This was proposed as the *'socialisation of industry, production, distribution and exchange'*. Queensland delegate Ted Theodore objected, noting that "No two delegates would agree as to what socialisation of industry means."[242] Do the words socialism or socialisation have any meaning today? There is no single understanding of what these concepts mean. To many US Republicans 'socialism' seems to mean as little as equal rights or Obama Care.[243] During the COVID-19 lockdown in the USA, some libertarian protestors claimed that 'social distancing' equalled Communism![244] This must be the most remarkable definition of communism ever expressed! Those on the left might have a range of ideas as to what socialist policies could entail. When the term socialist was first employed in the 1830s in the United Kingdom by Robert Owen and by some French reformers, the term commonly meant not much more than opposition to the individualism inherent in capitalism and extreme political liberalism. 'Socialists' simply wanted to construct more equal and harmonious societies based on harmony, cooperation and association rather than the bitter conflict, competition and poverty inherent in laissez-faire capitalism. How this goal might be achieved differed widely.[245]

Is there a future for 'socialism' however it might be understood or at least an alternative vision of how society might function more equitably?[246] In my view, there is scope for a range of understandings of 'socialist' belief through which modern society might be made more equal, fair and harmonious. As a political philosophy, and partly because of its association with the failed Soviet system, socialism as a political and economic idea seems to be in permanent decline. Political parties on the left around the world have often called themselves socialist. The Australian Labor Party still describes itself as a *democratic socialist* party and includes in its policy platform its 'socialisation objective', in the following terms:

> *The Australian Labor Party is a democratic socialist party and has the objective of the democratic socialisation of industry, production, distribution and exchange, to the extent necessary to eliminate exploitation and other anti-social features in these fields.*[247]

The last clause in this objective is known as the Blackburn Interpretation, named after Maurice Blackburn, founder of the law firm of the same name, and added to the socialisation objective in order to qualify it.[248] This qualification makes it an extremely limited goal that would only operate to eliminate 'exploitation' and other 'anti-social' features in industry. These features are not defined. The Chifley Labor Government tried to nationalise banking in Australia but was frustrated by a decision of the High Court and was defeated at the 1949 election fought in part on this issue. It is unlikely that any such attempt will ever be made again.[249] The socialisation objective, though prominent in the ALP Constitution, hardly seems to be taken seriously today. On the contrary, during the Hawke/Keating Governments steps were taken to privatise [or de-socialise] government-owned enterprises in banking and airlines. This trend has continued at both the federal and state government level and in local government through the contracting out of municipal services. All this appears contrary to the stated ALP goal of 'socialising' economic activity.

## THE CATHOLIC CHURCH AND 'SOCIALISM'

The 'socialist objective' has been seen as a major problem for Catholics in the ALP since it was known that the Church did not support socialism. In the late 1890s in Australia, as the Labor Party began to emerge, there was a furious debate about what approach the new party should take to socialism. This question proved to be a problem for the Church and for rank-and-file Catholics most of whom were working class at the time. The great Catholic Churchman of the time, Sydney's Cardinal Moran, was pro-worker and pro-union but was concerned about the influence of socialism on the new party.[250] The great encyclical *Rerum Novarum* was pro-union and pro-worker but strongly anti-socialist. Socialism was considered to be opposed to religion, against private property and to favour revolution. Cardinal Moran, however, found a way to distinguish 'European' socialism from that adopted in the antipodes. European socialism was identified as 'state socialism', that is, that the State should own all land and enterprises [as occurred in Russia after the Bolshevik revolution].

Few Christians, Catholic or otherwise, would be likely to describe themselves today as Christian Socialists. Christians seem to be increasingly found on the conservative side of politics, in Australia, the USA and elsewhere.

There are several reasons for this, but conservatism does not have to be the natural home of Christians, and the social teachings of the Catholic Church, properly understood, do not support a conservative political position. However, some explanation of this is required to go beyond the 'headline' opposition of the Church to socialism.

The first social encyclical *Rerum Novarum* noted a real and pressing social problem for working people:

> ... In any case we clearly see, and on this there is general agreement, that some opportune remedy must be found quickly for the misery and wretchedness pressing so unjustly on the majority of the working class...by degrees it has come to pass that working men have been surrendered, isolated and helpless, to the hardheartedness of employers and the greed of unchecked competition... To this must be added that the hiring of labor and the conduct of trade are concentrated in the hands of comparatively few; so that a small number of very rich men have been able to lay upon the teeming masses of the laboring poor a yoke little better than that of slavery itself.[251]

But the remedy was not socialism, according to Leo!

> To remedy these wrongs the socialists, working on the poor man's envy of the rich, are striving to do away with private property, and contend that individual possessions should become the common property of all, to be administered by the State or by municipal bodies.[252]

Socialism is in fact only mentioned once in the encyclical; socialists four times. But a difficulty with understanding this encyclical is to determine what is meant by the term 'socialism'. The main thrust of the encyclical seems to be a defence of the right to own private property, which seems odd in the context of a document primarily concerned with the rights of workers. Leo believes that 'the main tenet' of socialism is the 'community of goods'. The encyclical assumes that under socialism all property would become common or collective property. It is not clear to me why the Pope had this view of socialism. In the encyclical *Centesimus Annus*, written on the centenary of *Rerum Novarum* in 1991, there is a hint that Pope John Paul II also thought that this view of socialism [and private property] was perhaps slightly misdirected [it is worth observing that the term socialism when twice used in this paragraph is in inverted commas, suggesting that the meaning was not clear to the then Pope]:

> It may seem surprising that "socialism" appeared at the beginning of the Pope's critique of solutions to the "question of the working class" at a time when "socialism" was not yet in the form of a strong and powerful State, with all the resources which that implies, as was later to happen. However, he correctly judged the danger posed to the masses by the attractive presentation of this simple and radical solution to the "question of the working class" of the time — all the more so when one considers the terrible situation of injustice in which the working classes of the recently industrialized nations found themselves.[253]

If *Rerum Novarum* had little or nothing in the way of a discussion of socialism, the next social encyclical, *Quadragesimo Anno*, issued by Pope Pius XI in 1931 was dominated by a discussion of socialism. It sought to distinguish at least two different strands: communism and a more moderate form of socialism. Ultimately, neither was acceptable:

> 120. If Socialism, like all errors, contains some truth (which, moreover, the Supreme Pontiffs have never denied), it is based nevertheless on a theory of human society peculiar to itself and irreconcilable with true Christianity. Religious socialism, Christian socialism, are contradictory terms; no one can be at the same time a good Catholic and a true socialist.[254]

Pius XI rejects socialism on the basis that it is a belief that it is only interested in the material world in which there is no place for God. Thus 'socialism' is being rejected on philosophical/theological basis and its claimed exclusion of a role for the divine in the world. Many socialists have described themselves as Christian socialists [although Catholics have faced particular difficulties in doing so]. I see no reason why men and women cannot devote themselves to improving social and economic conditions for all and still have a role for the Spirit in human affairs. "Work as if everything depended on you: pray as if everything depended on God" used to be a common exhortation for those working in the world. I see no incompatibility between the two. "Your will be done on earth as well as heaven" is part of the Lord's Prayer.

In any case, this is not the end of the story. All the Popes have stressed other important social teachings of the Church in these encyclicals – and in particular the notion of the 'common good' and the peculiarly named doctrine of the 'Universal Destination of Goods'. Both these terms mean that the interests of all people must be considered and that the fruits of the earth and the goods and wealth produced must be distributed equitably to all of God's creatures. In *Quadragesimo Anno* – which attacked socialism – we can read:

> 49. It follows from what We have termed the individual and at the same time social character of ownership, that men must consider in this matter not only their own advantage but also the common good. To define these duties in detail when necessity requires and the natural law has not done so, is the function of those in charge of the State. Therefore, public authority, under the guiding light always of the natural and divine law, can determine more accurately upon consideration of the true requirements of the common good, what is permitted and what is not permitted to owners in the use of their property. Moreover, Leo XIII wisely taught "that God has left the limits of private possessions to be fixed by the industry of men and institutions of peoples."
>
> ...Yet when the State brings private ownership into harmony with the needs of the common good, it does not commit a hostile act against private owners but rather does them a friendly service; for it thereby effectively prevents the private possession of goods, which the Author of nature in His most wise providence ordained for the support of human life, from causing intolerable evils and thus rushing to its own destruction; it does not destroy private possessions, but safeguards them; and it does not weaken private property rights, but strengthens them.
>
> Free competition, kept within definite and due limits, and still more economic dictatorship, must be effectively brought under public authority in these matters which pertain to the latter's function. The public institutions themselves, of peoples, moreover, ought to make all human society conform to the needs of the common good; that is, to the norm of social justice. If this is done, that most important division of social life, namely, economic activity, cannot fail likewise to return to right and sound order. [255]

To sum up in plain words what these paragraphs written in 1931 mean, it is fair to say:

- The fruits of the earth are provided for all - *destined for the entire family of mankind*
- As a result of this social dimension to ownership, the common good must be considered
- The State must intervene to ensure that the common good is served

- This action by the State in the regard is not an offence against the right to private property; rather it is necessary to ensure social justice

- Economic competition must be regulated by the State and that public institutions *ought to make all human society conform to the needs of the common good; that is, to the norm of social justice*

This was beginning to sound a lot like socialism! Well, if not socialism exactly, then socialisation! *Laboren Exercens* issued by Pope John Paul II on the 90th anniversary of *Rerum Novarum* in 1981 refers to the relationship between private property and the right of common use of the Earth's goods:

> *The above principle, as it was then stated and as it is still taught by the Church, diverges radically from the programme of collectivism as proclaimed by Marxism and put into practice in various countries in the decades following the time of Leo XIII's Encyclical. At the same time it differs from the programme of capitalism practised by liberalism and by the political systems inspired by it. In the latter case, the difference consists in the way the right to ownership or property is understood.*
>
> *Christian tradition has never upheld this right as absolute and untouchable. On the contrary, it has always understood this right within the broader context of the right common to all to use the goods of the whole of creation: the right to private property is subordinated to the right to common use, to the fact that goods are meant for everyone. Furthermore, in the Church's teaching, ownership has never been understood in a way that could constitute grounds for social conflict in labour. As mentioned above, property is acquired first of all through work in order that it may serve work. This concerns in a special way ownership of the means of production. Isolating these means as a separate property in order to set it up in the form of "capital" in opposition to "labour"-and even to practise exploitation of labour-is contrary to the very nature of these means and their possession. They cannot be possessed against labour, they cannot even be possessed for possession's sake, because the only legitimate title to their possession- whether in the form of private ownership or in the form of public or collective ownership-is that they should serve labour, and thus, by serving labour, that they should make possible the achievement of the first principle of this order, namely, the universal destination of goods and the right to common use of them. From this point*

*of view, therefore, in consideration of human labour and of common access to the goods meant for man, one cannot exclude the socialization, in suitable conditions, of certain means of production.*[256]

From the quotations above [and others found in a range of encyclicals] we can further conclude that:

- *the right to private property is subordinated to the right to common use, to the fact that goods are meant for everyone*

- private property including ownership of the means of production *whether in the form of private ownership or in the form of public or collective ownership* must serve labour, and

- *should make possible the achievement of the first principle of this order, namely, the universal destination of goods and the right to common use of them*

- *socialization, in suitable conditions, of certain means of production* is permissible – and necessary

The ultimate and primary aim – the first principle – of these teachings is to achieve the 'universal destination of goods' – common use of the wealth of this world. Private property is not the ultimate principle, despite the impression created by *Rerum Novarum*.

Most recently Pope Francis has written:

> 119. *In the first Christian centuries, a number of thinkers developed a universal vision in their reflections on the common destination of created goods. This led them to realize that if one person lacks what is necessary to live with dignity, it is because another person is detaining it. Saint John Chrysostom summarizes it in this way: "Not to share our wealth with the poor is to rob them and take away their livelihood. The riches we possess are not our own, but theirs as well". In the words of Saint Gregory the Great, "When we provide the needy with their basic needs, we are giving them what belongs to them, not to us".*

> 120. *Once more, I would like to echo a statement of Saint John Paul II whose forcefulness has perhaps been insufficiently recognized: "God gave the earth to the whole human race for the sustenance of all its members, without excluding or favouring anyone". For my part, I would observe that*

> "the Christian tradition has never recognized the right to private property as absolute or inviolable, and has stressed the social purpose of all forms of private property". The principle of the common use of created goods is the "first principle of the whole ethical and social order"; it is a natural and inherent right that takes priority over others. All other rights having to do with the goods necessary for the integral fulfilment of persons, including that of private property or any other type of property, should – in the words of Saint Paul VI – "in no way hinder [this right], but should actively facilitate its implementation". The right to private property can only be considered a secondary natural right, derived from the principle of the universal destination of created goods. This has concrete consequences that ought to be reflected in the workings of society. Yet it often happens that secondary rights displace primary and overriding rights, in practice making them irrelevant.[257]

Nor are the social encyclicals on socialisation just a view of socially progressive Popes. In 2006 Benedict XVI, a doctrinally conservative Pope, in discussing various developments in Europe, including dominant philosophical and Church/State models, noted:

> But in Europe, in the nineteenth century, the two models were joined by a third, socialism, which quickly split into two different branches, one totalitarian and the other democratic. Democratic socialism managed to fit within the two existing models as a welcome counterweight to the radical liberal positions, which it developed and corrected. It also managed to appeal to various denominations. In England it became the political party of the Catholics, who had never felt at home among either the Protestant conservatives or the liberals. In Wilhelmine Germany, too, Catholic groups felt closer to democratic socialism than to the rigidly Prussian and Protestant conservative forces. In many respects, democratic socialism was and is close to Catholic social doctrine and has in any case made a remarkable contribution to the formation of a social consciousness.[258]

If democratic socialism 'was and is close to Catholic social doctrine' then it should be acceptable for all modern Catholics to describe themselves once more as Christian democratic socialists. There is considerable continuity in the approach of Benedict XVI [and other Popes] with that of Cardinal Moran and despite the apparent rejection of 'socialism' by the social encyclicals, there is much in these texts which is completely in line with the ALP's approach to social and economic questions. Indeed, considered in this light, the ALP's century old 'socialisation' Objective is not only not offensive to Catholic social justice teachings but is, in my view, completely in line with the Church's social teachings.

I find it difficult to conclude other that the social and economic objectives of the ALP align very well with the principles of Catholic social justice. Catholics supporting conservative political parties which do not support interventions in the economy in the interests of the common good should consider this point.[259]

## SOCIALISATION IN AUSTRALIA – AN HISTORICAL FOOTNOTE

In the 1940s, the Chifley Labor Government proposed the introduction of the Pharmaceutical Benefits Scheme to make medicines more widely and more cheaply available. Of all groups, doctors, whose ethical duty was to assist their patients' health and well-being, opposed this measure. They claimed that this measure was 'socialist' and that it was 'civil conscription' of doctors into government service. Of course, it was none of these things but the predecessor to the AMA, the Australian Branch of the British Medical Association, successfully challenged the Government's legislation in the High Court.[260]

The Chifley Government also sought to impose certain controls on the activity of private banks in Australia and, when the banks successfully resisted this in the High Court [and the Privy Council], sought to nationalise the banking and insurance industries as a whole. This legislation also failed in the courts.

Nationalisation of the banks had been a long-standing ALP policy. Banking was considered to be so important to the successful conduct of the nation's economy and to the financial wellbeing of individuals that it could not be left in private hands, which operated in private interests [not the common good].

What might Catholic social teaching have said about this, in the light of the encyclicals *Rerum Novarum* and *Quadragesimo Anno*, which had so emphatically condemned socialism and defended the right to private property? We do not have to speculate about the answer to this question: the Australian Catholic Bishops explicitly supported government control of the banking sector, particularly with respect to 'credit policy'. In 1948, the year after the Chifley

Government sought to acquire all the shares in private banks [and the year the High Court ruled it unconstitutional] the Australian Bishops issued one of their annual 'social justice statements' on 'Socialisation'.

This statement held:

> 76. ( III ) *The Church recognises that, under present conditions, there are certain forms of enterprise and industry which are of quite extraordinary importance to the community, and which may legitimately come under public control in one form or another, although not necessarily by means of nationalisation.*
>
> 77. *Among these are banking and insurance, the manufacture of steel and heavy chemicals; rail, sea and air transport; public utility services (electricity, gas, tramways); armaments. The public utility services and a section of the transport industry are already generally under some form of public control in Australia, whether operated by Federal, State or by municipal bodies. The other industries are, at the moment, generally owned and operated by great private corporations...*
>
> 81. *It is also out of harmony with Christian thought that the control of credit POLICY—as distinct from the administration of credit—should be in private hands. This is a basic function of the public authority. Whether credit is dispensed by banks or by insurance companies—which are today even more powerful financially than the banks — it is opposed to right order that the sovereign economic power which rests in formulating the credit policy of the nation should be in the hands of private individuals.*
>
> 82. *The nationalisation of the trading banks is not, in itself, opposed to the principles of social morality. It becomes so only if intended as one step advancing a system of total Socialism.*
>
> 83. *It is therefore the Christian view that so long as these particular forms of industry and enterprise endure, they should be under public control. Whether public control is exercised by, way of nationalisation, or in some other way, depends upon all the circumstances of each individual case.*[261]

At the time, of course, the Federal Government had much more limited powers over credit creation by the private banks than it does now, even in the absence of nationalisation. However, it is worth noting this statement and the extent to which the Bishops were willing to agree to Government intervention in the economy in the interest of the common good. Also worth remembering, perhaps, is that this Statement was drafted for the Bishops by B A Santamaria. He may have had a range of motives for drafting a Statement supporting 'socialisation' [knowing that it was ALP policy] but it remains a fact that the Bishops agreed to issue this statement.[262]

## UNIONS UNDER ATTACK

Despite the socialisation objective of the Labor party, the policy of the ALP and most of its affiliated unions at the time of Federation was not in favour of the overthrow of capitalism in favour of state economic control and ownership. In practice, the ALP and the unions favoured what became known as "Laborism".[263] This policy meant the gradual improvement of the conditions of working people through the operation of trade unions, conciliation and arbitration of industrial disputes, tariff protection, and parliamentary action by labor-endorsed candidates [as well as by the now discredited and abandoned policy of White Australia]. This was, in the words of Bede Nairn, 'civilising capitalism', not overthrowing it.[264] These policies made up the 'Australian settlement' or the implicit political and social compact made at the time of Federation.

Laborism is still the practical approach of many unions and the ALP today. In practice, it has had many benefits for Australian workers. It is a somewhat prosaic approach and not the stuff of romantic or utopian dreams or the producer of great revolutionary fervour. Many improvements in terms and conditions of employment could only be introduced by legislation, including the framework of conciliation and arbitration itself and common rule awards. The trade union movement created its parliamentary wing for this purpose, and, despite many frustrations, the relationship endures and delivers benefits to workers.

Since the union movement is a key element underpinning the ALP, it has become a target of the conservative political parties in this country. This was always likely to be the case since the conservative parties also represented the interests of big and small businesses, but for many years both sides of politics supported the industrial relations pillar of the 'Australian settlement' described above. This is no longer true. The conservative parties attack the trade union movement and seek to limit its strength and effectiveness because it is the core of the ALP as well as a countervailing force against unfettered capitalism. The union movement has become a victim of partisan politics as played by the conservative political parties in Australia. At the height of the campaign against WorkChoices, Joe Hockey, then Minister for Employment and Workplace Relations, issued a media release in which, to my mind, he appeared to be delighting in a fall in the number of workers who were union members. The headline of the press release trumpeted:

> *More than 150,000 Australians walk away from the unions.*[265]

Reading this media release at the time, I was struck by the implications of this anti-union triumphalism of the Howard government. Unions are non-government, self-funded, self-help community groups. In other words, the sort of entities conservative politicians normally like. Would the Howard government have put out the same media release if the number of scouts and guides had decreased or if the number of volunteers in the Red Cross, St Vincent de Paul or the Brotherhood of St Lawrence had dropped?

Just before Minister Hockey issued his media release, I had had the opportunity to meet a remarkable human being: Han Dongfang. Han was born in mainland China and helped form the Beijing Autonomous Workers Union. This union organisation took part in the 1989 Tiananmen Square protests which were brutally suppressed by the Chinese Communist Party regime on the night of the 3rd/4th June 1989. Han was jailed for 22 months by the Chinese authorities, suffered tuberculosis, and nearly died while in prison. He was released to go to the USA for treatment and although barred from returning to China he established himself in Hong Kong from where he continued to support the development of real and independent trade unions in China.

Han addressed a meeting of Australian trade unionists hosted by the Australian Workers Union in Melbourne. He told those present that he was seeking to build what he called 'civil society' in China. This work started with the creation of genuine workers organisations by building them up through collective bargaining for better wages and working conditions and health and safety standards. Han strongly believed that properly functioning free and independent unions are an essential part of a free and democratic society. Listening to Han speak, I realised from another perspective what was wrong with the Howard Government's approach to industrial relations law. While Han Dongfang was looking to build civil society in China through unionism, the Coalition Government was looking to weaken the union movement in

Australia and in doing so threatening an essential element of Australian civil society.

The implications of the efforts of successive Coalition governments to inhibit unionism are broad and deep. These include declining worker rights, worsening employment practices and flatlining wages growth, all linked to declining union density rates.[266] Incomes inequality is rising, the worst features of unfettered capitalism are returning, and political institutions and societies are breaking down leading to the rise of populist and extremist politicians. Social justice requires that the union movement be revived, not vilified and destroyed. This is one of Australia's most pressing problems, and the trend is in the wrong direction. When I consulted an old university textbook in the preparation of these memoirs, I found the following statement:

> *Australia has always had a high level of unionisation. This has been maintained by the arbitration system, by legal preference to unionists and, in Queensland, by compulsory unionism. There are more than two million union members, representing 56 per cent of the labour force.*[267]

The publication date was 1968, while I was still at school. By 2020, union membership was down to about 14% of the workforce and barely 10% in the private sector. All the supports mentioned in the quote above have been removed or, in the case of arbitration, greatly weakened by successive governments. In my early years in the union movement, I often gave talks on behalf of the Trades Hall Council to school students. A question often asked was 'do unions have too much power?' Now the question is not asked, except by ideologues on the extreme right of politics and for political purposes only. The wage theft scandals in fast food, retail, agriculture and elsewhere point only to one thing: not only do unions have limited power, employees [and other workers] increasingly have none. Unionism must be strengthened, not weakened. The decline in union density and worker power has occurred during my working life, including during periods when the Labor Party was in government federally. We now need national political leaders to speak out in support of unionism, as President Barak Obama did in his election campaigns and key speeches: "We still need laws that strengthen rather than weaken unions, and give American workers a voice."[268] Even during the 2007 election, fought largely on the issue of industrial relations, similar statements were hard to find, even from Kevin Rudd, the biggest beneficiary of the YRAW campaign. We do not need laws designed to weaken unionism further.

## WORKER CO-OPERATIVES – AN ALTERNATIVE MODEL?

Marxist communism has failed. Capitalism, despite its many flaws, appears triumphant. Is there is any possibility in the future for genuine 'socialised' control or ownership of the means of production? Must we be content just to try to civilise capitalism? Is there an alternative to Marxist socialism and liberal capitalism? Before and after the First World War in England, a fierce debate raged between the Fabian Socialists [who favoured the gradual rather than a revolutionary introduction of State socialism] and a group of Catholic intellectuals who called themselves 'Distributists'. George Bernard Shaw was the leading Fabian protagonist and G.K. Chesterton and Hilaire Belloc were the best-known Distributists. The Distributists had initially been socialists but came to reject 'state socialism' as a solution to the problems of capitalism. The best Australian writer on this subject is a local ALP identity with a Fabian background, Race Mathews, former private secretary to Gough Whitlam and later a state and federal MP and state Minister in his own right. Though not a Catholic, Race Mathews has been the best advocate and publicist for this aspect of Catholic social teaching in practice. In his book, *Jobs of Our Own*, Mathews quotes Chesterton describing the contrast between state socialism and distributism:

> *For Gilbert [Chesterton] and Belloc, state socialism, communism and capitalism were for all practical purposes the same system by different names:*
>
> 'Capitalism and communism are twin systems, resting as they do on the same idea – the centralisation of wealth and, its corollary, the abolition of private property. It is immaterial that they differ on where they wish to centralise this wealth – Communism in the State and capitalism in the hands of the most powerful plutocrats; both succeed in crushing the small individual by taking his property from him'.[269]

Distributism did not propose to abolish private property or personal or corporate ownership of economic activity but to *distribute* ownership of it more widely. State socialism meant the transfer all ownership to the State, while capitalism had the effect of concentrating ownership in fewer and fewer hands – most workers had none. Mathews notes that for all their polemical debates with Shaw and others, the Distributists did not say exactly how this wider distribution of ownership of the means of production might come about. But the answer already existed – cooperatively owned enterprises – which had been pioneered in the United Kingdom in the previous century by Robert Owen [another of Marx's so-called 'utopian' socialists].

Cooperatives exist in several forms. The best known in Australia are credit co-operatives [where the members all own shares in the credit union or mutual bank] or producer co-operatives whereby primary producers band together to market their produce.[270] I have been a member of a credit cooperative since 1980. Worker cooperatives can also exist, whereby each worker is an equal owner and shareholder in the enterprise for which they work. These are much less well-known in Australia: the clothing manufacturer from which I bought my first work suits – Fletcher Jones and Staff – was a well-known example in Melbourne. Worker cooperatives exist in many forms and in many places throughout the world.

The best known and most successful cooperatives are those which form the Mondragon Corporation [MC] in the Basque region of Spain. These cooperatives were set up by a Catholic priest, sent to the depressed region in the aftermath of the 1930s Spanish civil war to see what could be done to improve the economic circumstances of the local people. This mission led to the creation of an amazing array of cooperative enterprises that today dominate the economy of the Basque region. They include manufacturing enterprises, consumer and credit co-ops and even include a university formed on cooperative principles. These enterprises form a key part of the wider Spanish economy. The cooperative movement offers the best alternative to either market capitalism or state ownership since it vests full ownership and control of their workplace in the people who work there. This economic model means 'each person is entitled to consider himself a part-owner of the great workbench at which he is working with everyone else' to quote the now archaic-sounding language of the Papal Encyclical *Laboren Exercens [On Human Work]* issued by the Polish Pope John Paul II in 1981, on the 90th Anniversary of *Rerum Novarum*.[271]

Cooperatives operate in a market economy, but each is a free actor guided by those with a direct interest. It is social ownership in its most complete form. In 2008, my wife and I paid a visit to Mondragon including the Mondragon Corporation head office for a briefing on the work of the cooperative movement. It was an effort to get there but we felt privileged to visit this special part of the world. Race Mathews seems to be one of the few people in Australia interested in this form of economic organisation. After his fifth visit to Mondragon in 2012, Mathews wrote about the success of the Mondragon co-ops in weathering the storm of the Global Financial Crisis:

> *A record of so remarkable a character gives rise inevitably to pertinent questions. What contribution to productivity and workplace wellbeing might countries other than Spain have to gain from attitudinal change such as Mondragon has so successfully engendered?*
>
> *And why is the Church in the English-speaking world so largely silent about the Mondragon cooperatives' success in bringing to fruition the long struggle in the cause of its social teachings?* [272]

*Mary and I with Mike Lezamiz, Director Cooperative Dissemination, Mondragon Cooperative Corporation.*

There are at least two answers to the question posed by Race Mathews. The Communist left in Australia was not interested in cooperatives.[273] They were interested only in socialism on the Marxist state ownership model. State socialism on the Marxist/Leninist/Maoist model gave workers zero control over the enterprises in which they worked. Anything short of full state socialism was typically attacked by the extreme Left as 'making capitalism work'. I often heard this slogan at the Victorian Trades Hall Council meetings in the 1970s. Employers and owners of capital were equally not interested in cooperatives since they take control away from the shareholders and vest it in the workers. Some unions themselves were wary of the cooperative enterprise since the workers there were not employees, but part-owners. These owner-workers did not fit the model of the sort of worker that unions represented. The role of unionism in a cooperative system is unclear since unions represent workers as employees. Other unions, such as the Clerks Union, strongly supported the cooperative model, sponsoring a credit union and a number of cooperative building societies that assisted workers, including women workers who often could not get bank loans, to purchase a home.

When I was at Harvard in 1987, one of the case studies discussed in the joint class with the MBA students was that of Mondragon. The American MBA students in the class were extremely hostile to the idea of worker ownership. They thought that there would not be much demand for their MBA-trained skills in these enterprises [this was said in class]. Associate Professor Janice McCormack, who ran the program, disagreed. She tried to reassure the concerned MBA students saying: 'they are all MBAs there'. By this, she meant that they valued management skills greatly in Mondragon.

It is ironic to note that the USA, the 'home' of capitalism, is quite interested in the wider distribution of ownership. Employee Share Ownership programs [ESOPs] are strong there and well promoted.[274] Australia has paid only lip service to this idea and in most cases, employees only get a dividend from their shareholding. They cannot influence the direction of the company they work for. One practical policy response that Australia can adopt is to promote ESOPs and encourage worker buyouts of the firms they work for. In his most recent article on this subject, Race Mathews noted that the US Steelworkers Union has entered into an arrangement with Mondragon which is designed to aid the setting up co-operative enterprises in the United States.[275]

Australians have a range of opportunities to take part in the cooperative movement. The most accessible form is a credit cooperative [or mutual bank]. A number of health funds are member owned. Road service organisations are cooperatives. In fact, there are over 2000 cooperative and mutual enterprises in Australia with a combined membership of over 30 million people.[276] However, it is not likely that in the foreseeable future that many Australians will be able to work in cooperative enterprises as they are rare in commerce and industry generally. But there is no reason at all why all Australians cannot own the bank which holds their savings and lends them money to buy a house. The financial power generated by compulsory superannuation has allowed workers to buy capital in many enterprises through their superannuation savings. This is a form of social ownership but does not usually offer fund members direct influence or control. But there is no reason why all Australians cannot have their retirement savings invested in superannuation funds where all profits are returned to members rather than to private shareholders.[277] Until forms of social ownership are more widespread in the general economy, most Australians will remain wage and salary earners with little or no ownership or influence over the places in which they work. Unions will remain vitally important to them. But there is no reason why we should not renew interest in discovering and encouraging alternative forms of economic organisation which put social justice, decent work and worker dignity at the forefront. The world is now freed from the unhealthy and stultifying effects of the Cold War. The opportunity should be taken to dust off some of the old ideas about more collaborative forms of work and examine whether they have merit for the future. There is a better world of work that can be imagined. The 'gig' economy or Uber form of employment should belong to the past not the future.

I retired from my job with the ASU National Office in June 2011. I was pleasantly surprised earlier that year when the Victorian Private Sector Branch of the Union awarded me Life Membership of the Branch 'in recognition of a lifetime of exceptional service to members.' I had no forewarning of this event. I thought I was attending a celebration of the centenary of the federal registration of the Clerks Union. Unknown to me, the Branch had arranged for my wife, children, and father to attend the event to see the certificate being presented. The fact that the elected Branch officials were the successors of those who had defeated us in 1988 showed a great generosity of spirit. The ASU National Council in 2012 also awarded me Life Membership of the Union, which is a great honour. The same year, my friends and former colleagues in the Victorian Branch of the Clerks Union organised an informal get together and presented me with a certificate of appreciation created by Terry Sullivan's daughter, Anne Di Nardo. It read, in part, "for loyal dedication and service to true Trade Unionism and fervent support of the Clerks Rank and File Team". All these acknowledgments were unexpected, and all greatly appreciated and genuinely humbling.

Since retiring I have kept my contact with the ASU. I still represent the Union on the Board of Aspire Learning, the successor to NOSFAB which I was part of creating in 1991. I have continued to work with some very impressive people there. I have also been nominated by the ASU to serve on the Board of CareSuper, an industry super fund that was initially set up on the initiative of John Maynes in 1986. The staff of the FCUA National Office were the first to join the new fund and I have been a member ever since.

In retirement, I have also been active in the Australian Institute of Employment Rights which seeks to promote an approach to employment that is based on fundamental labour rights as defined by the International Labor Organisation [ILO]. This is a secular, human rights-based, approach to worker rights and important. The ILO does important work to promote human and worker rights, especially the right to decent and safe work. The rights and values promoted by the ILO can also found in both Christian social teaching and religious principles generally. Love of neighbour means treating everybody with decency, justice and compassion. This includes workers of all types and backgrounds. Love of neighbour implies community and solidarity; individualism dies not.

Recently, I came across a novel written in the late 19th century by Edward Bellamy, an American writer. Bellamy's novel is in the form of science fiction in which a resident of Boston goes to sleep in 1887 and wakes up – Rip Van Winkle-like – in the year 2000. Bellamy's character finds himself in an ideal society in which all the social problems – including those relating to employment – have been solved. Bellamy's work was very influential at the time, including in Australia. The AWU's W G Spence was said to have read it.[278] It was called *Looking Backwards: 2000 to 1887*. The book's utopian suggestions about life in the 21st century now appear to be quaint and highly improbable.[279] William Lane, an Englishman who came to Australia from the USA in 1877 and who left Australia in 1893 after the failure of the great strikes of the early 1890s to found a utopian society in Paraguay, was also said to be inspired by Bellamy's novel. Lane reviewed it in the first issue of the trade union-funded journal *The Worker* in 1890 and serialised it over the next nine months.[280] *Looking Backwards* has power as a novel because of its critique of the 19th-century society and the injustices and poverty that were allowed to flourish in a world where free-market economics and unfettered capitalism prevailed. In a fictional sermon in the book given by a minister of religion in the year 2000, the following comment is made about those who professed to be Christians in 1887:

> *The keynote of the literature of the period was one of compassion for the poor and unfortunate, and indignant outcry against the failure of the social machinery to ameliorate the miseries of men. It is plain from these outbursts that the moral hideousness of the spectacle about them was, at least by flashes, fully realized by the best of men of that time...*
>
> *Although the idea of the vital unity of the family of mankind, the reality of human brotherhood, was very far from being apprehended by them as the moral axiom it seems to us, yet it is a mistake to suppose that there was no feeling at all corresponding to it. I could read you passages of great beauty from some of their writers which show that the conception was clearly attained by a few,...*
>
> *Moreover, it must not be forgotten that the nineteenth century was in name Christian, and the fact that the entire commercial and industrial frame of society was the embodiment of the anti-Christian spirit must have had some weight, though I admit it was strangely little, with the nominal followers of Jesus Christ.* [281]

Bellamy was both right and wrong in his criticism of the attitudes of Christians in the 19th century. As we have seen, many Christians were putting their faith into practice by working closely with working people to improve their employment conditions and especially in Australia through the formation of trade unions and the early ALP. Many Christians were also actively engaged in a range of other efforts to improve the economic and social conditions of disadvantaged people in society. Other Christians – the ones Bellamy clearly had in mind - viewed their religion as a private matter with no social expression. These two tendencies still exist in 2021, which Bellamy might have been shocked to discover.

My direct ancestor, Arthur Harvey, was before he migrated to South Africa, a farmer in Aberdeenshire in Scotland. He was Secretary of the Royal Northern Agricultural Society, an association of 'progressive' farmers, interested in improving all aspects of agriculture. In 1858 he won a competition with an essay examining the condition of agricultural workers in Scotland. It is a remarkably progressive treatise, advocating equal and fair treatment for agricultural laborers. Its language is difficult to read, but he essentially advocates the position that 'masters' should treat their 'servants' as required by the precepts of the Gospel.[282]

Arthur Harvey argued that if humans treated each other in accordance with the second of the two 'Great Commandments' of the New Testament, there could be 'heaven on earth' or a new Garden of Eden. This is a high aim, but a worthy one. It calls for practical action in this world, not the next, in line with the Lord's Prayer. Arthur Harvey and the Fourierist Arthur Young were brothers-in-law and cousins [their mothers being sisters]. Each of them, in his own way, was seeking a better world than the one they lived in. They are two people I would like to meet in the next life. Although I have only come across them recently, their example has helped me put some of my thoughts into perspective.

When I began writing these memoirs, I was mostly concerned to tell at least part of the story of the anti-communist struggle in the trade union movement through my small role in it. It is important that this story be known. This work was important and worth doing. The collapse of communism in Eastern Europe and Russia has revealed the full terror and toll of human misery that was totalitarian communism. The past is important, and we should know the truth about it. But the past cannot be changed, and we do not live there anymore. Freed from the constraints of the past it is possible to look at the future with fresh eyes. It is the world that my grandchildren will grow to live and work in that ought to be the focus of our attention and efforts. Authoritarian regimes still threaten the lives of their citizens. In the West, increasingly unfettered capitalism threatens the wellbeing and security of workers and their families. New and better ways of working are possible. I have hope that my grandchildren will live in a world that acknowledges that two are better than one in all aspects of life.

# APPENDIX

# THE SPECTRE OF COMMUNISM

*'A spectre is haunting Europe, the spectre of communism...'*

Communist Manifesto, 1848

It is well beyond the scope of these memoirs to write anything approximating a history of the fight against communist control of the trade union movement, a contest in which I became involved in late 1972. The purpose of this Appendix is simply to give a short appreciation of the atmosphere of the times largely in the words of independent observers illustrated with references from memoirs and other writings of Communists that have since appeared. What appears here is not a personal memoir since many of these events occurred well before my time.

As Graham Freudenberg observed about Communism in the quote at the beginning of Chapter 1, 'the threat was real'. The threat was a harsh and brutal reality for those in the Soviet Union from 1917 and in Eastern Europe post WW2. It is still a reality for those in China and Viet Nam, although the economic systems in those countries do not resemble Marxist socialism today. The dictatorships remain. My concern was never so much about the likelihood of a Communist revolution in Australia or the 'Red hordes' invading Australia from the north, but for the people forced to live under totalitarian dictatorships of the left.

In 1848 Karl Marx and Friedrich Engels published *The Communist Manifesto*.[283] It began: 'A spectre is haunting Europe...the spectre of communism'. Despite this forbidding forecast, the spectre of communism did not come to haunt Europe for nearly 70 years - after the Bolshevik revolution of October/November [284] 1917 in Imperial Russia. Renamed the Union of Soviet Socialist Republics [USSR] by the Bolshevik regime, the Russian empire was rapidly transformed into a one-party totalitarian dictatorship claiming to govern in the name of the working class but in practice serving only the interests of the party elite. Terror became part of the arsenal of the Bolsheviks as early as 1918 on the orders of Lenin. It was known as the 'Red Terror' and its early victims were members of the left.[285] Interestingly, the Bolsheviks seized power from a moderate social democrat-led coalition led by Alexander Kerensky, not from the Tsar.

A Communist Party was established in Australia in the early 1920s, but its influence waxed and waned over the next 20 years. It had waned when Nazi Germany and Soviet Russia signed their infamous non-aggression pact in 1939 and divided Poland between them. Communists initially opposed the Second World War as an imperialist struggle. When Hitler attacked the Soviet Union, Communists around the world changed their position overnight, now backing the fight against fascism. In Australia, during the latter part of the Second World War and in the immediate post-war period, Communism gained ground.

Thus in 1948 – one hundred years after the publication of the Communist manifesto – a spectre was haunting Australia, the spectre of Communism. In 1944, CPA membership had peaked at about 22,052 members.[286] Communists had won a seat in parliament. Most importantly, influence in the union movement was strong. Hagan says

> *Estimates which allege that by 1945 the Party controlled or powerfully influenced about half the Australian workforce are too high, but it is probably not too much to say that Party members exercised a strong influence on executives of unions whose members numbered about a quarter of Australian unionists.*[287]

The CPA's influence within the ACTU at the 1945 and 1947 Congresses was strong. Deery and Redfern state:

> *The Australian [Communist] Party had majorities or near-majorities*

on numerous state and provincial Trades and Labour Councils, had its resolutions adopted at the 1945 Congress of the Australian Council of Trade Unions and was able to dictate the policies of trade unions which covered every basic industry at the federal level except the Australian Workers Union. [288]

In his balanced account of the 1950s Split in the ALP, Robert Murray described the situation in Australia in these terms:

*Observers could argue about the details, but they could hardly deny that communism was a daunting force in Australia between 1935 and 1950. The control of the Brisbane and many provincial Trades halls by dedicated Stalin communists and their ability to wield 'numbers' only slightly fewer than those of the controlling faction in Melbourne and Sydney, are simple recorded facts. The communists were brilliant industrial showmen and often – but certainly not always – union leaders of more than average ability. But they left little doubt in their heyday that they sought to control the machinery of Australian unionism, smash the arbitration system and at least work for violent revolution...Often it seemed in the late 1940's that half of Australia was on strike half of the time....*[289]

What sort of people were these communists? Again, according to Murray:

*Apart from their revolutionary purpose and industrial record, another controversial aspect of the communist penetration of Australian unionisms was the totalitarian, zealously ideological climate that surrounded it. The Communists rigged ballots [if the findings of half a dozen Australian judges are to be believed] they shamelessly smeared their opponents and ran ruthless wars of nerves against them; they lied; they were often physically violent; they revered Stalin and the Soviet Union... they recruited men who were little more than stooges and thugs, ever ready to obey, to employ verbal and physical violence.*[290]

Dinny Lovegrove, a communist turned anti-communist and an Industrial Grouper who remained in the ALP after the 1955 split had no illusions about Communism and Communists. In his memoir, former ALP Senator John Button, who met Lovegrove during the ALP split quotes Lovegrove as telling him:

*You know Jack [John Button], some people find them [the Communists]*

> *idealistic and friendly...I didn't find them too friendly when they belted me with bike chains in the basement of the Fitzroy Town Hall. Still got the marks on my back.*²⁹¹

The influence of Communism was neither benign nor ineffectual. After a period of 'united front' tactics during which they tried to work in collaboration with the Labor Party, the CPA in 1947 decided to confront 'reformism' in the labor movement [that is the ALP] and instead pledged to 'uproot reformism and isolate it from the working-class movement'.²⁹²

Mark Aarons, a member of a prominent Communist family, understood the CPA's position on these issues at that time, squarely seeing these events as a contest between the Communist Party and the ALP for influence and control over the trade union movement:

> *In practical terms, as I learned at meetings of the Junior Eureka Youth league (the Communist organisation for kids aged between ten and sixteen), Australian communists fought for control of the trade union movement. It was a tough fight. The Australian Labor Party (ALP) dominated the trade unions, which not only controlled the party but defined its ideological standpoint. The ALP was dismissed around our dinner table as a 'reformist' party which, while proclaiming socialism as its objective, really aimed to reform and manage capitalism more humanely than the Menzies government.*
>
> *As my knowledge of history developed, I understood how bitter the battle with the reformists had been, and continued to be. Many unions controlled by the communists at the end of the Second World War <u>had been won back by the ALP</u> by the time I was born in late 1951.* [Emphasis added] ²⁹³

In 1950, the Victorian Secretary of the CPA, Ted Hill said that the job of the party was to fight both the federal ALP leader and deputy and the ACTU's President and Secretary:

> *It is clear that the struggle for working class unity is a struggle not only against the Chifleys and the Evatts but against the Monks and the Broadbys.*²⁹⁴

The full story of the Australian Communist Party's assault on the ALP has been well described by Phillip Deery and Neil Redfern, including the CPA's change of position in response to the dictates of the Communist Party of the Soviet Union [CPSU] expressed through the Cominform [the Soviet-aligned Communist parties in Eastern Europe and elsewhere]. In other words, the local

Communist Party was responding to the dictates of Stalin and the foreign policy interests of the Soviet Union:

> ..., but it was only from late 1947 that the Communist Party, shaped by Cominform perspectives, adopted policies and pursued strategies that were ultra-leftist: inflexible, aggressive and deluded. Communist leaders lost touch with reality and slipped into self-confirming dogmas. As a result, the Chifley Labor government was slotted into the same pigeonhole as the reactionaries. Reminiscent of the 'social fascist' typology during the 'class against class' period initiated by the 6th Comintern Congress in 1928, all social democrats became actual or potential traitors to the working class. Dr Evatt became, in the words of [national CPA Secretary Lance] Sharkey, the 'errand boy of the dollar' and his foreign policy the tool of the 'war plans' of American imperialism. But it was not Evatt who was sycophantic but the Australian communist leaders.
>
> Their unquestioning subservience to the Soviet world view meant that slogans and doctrines – appropriate, perhaps, to Eastern Europe – were fastened, with little adaptation, onto the Australian political landscape. Stalin used the Cominform not merely to pull the French and Italian Communist Parties into line and enforce Moscow's hegemony over the emerging 'Iron Curtain' countries but also to establish a new international framework, designed to serve Soviet national interest, to which all communist parties must adhere.[295]

The Clerks Union's Jack Hughes was one of those at that time openly attacking the ALP, of which he had once been a member [and a secret member of the CPA]:

> One of the many communist trade union leaders who testified to the growing militancy of the workers was Jack Hughes, federal vice-president of the Federated Clerks Union. According to Hughes, 'we are witnessing the left swing of the masses in this country, the surge of discontent throughout industry, a lack of faith in the Labor Government'.[296]

Emboldened, the CPA in Australia began a new strategy of confronting the ALP government in a bid to win the support of workers away from the Labor party. This was no idle threat – in 1949, the Communist-led Miners Federation took on the Chifley Labor Party government on the coalfields. This was not an industrial dispute.[297] As Hagan notes, the Communist Party accused the ALP Government of betraying socialism and the workers and presented itself as the only authentic working-class party.[298] This intention was also recorded by Alistair Davidson in his history of the CPA.[299]

Bernie Taft, a long time CPA activist and official confirmed the intention of the CPA in his memoirs:

> *Of all the difficulties and problems that beset the party in 1949, the most damaging was the nation-wide coal strike, which commenced in winter on 27 June. It was the last desperate attempt by the CPA to take over the leadership of the working-class movement. Politically, the strike was a direct challenge to the Chifley Labor Government, and it led to a major national battle between the CPA and the ALP. Industrially, the strike brought a considerable part of the economy to a standstill. It caused mass unemployment, as some industries were forced to close down, and it directly affected hundreds of thousands of people.*
>
> *The Communist Party was clearly and correctly perceived by the public to be the leading force in the strike, because of its dominant position in the Miners' Union...*
>
> *The strike was a disaster...and it contributed significantly to the defeat of the Chifley government at the end of 1949, heralding twenty-three years of conservative national rule. This was the beginning of the Menzies era, which outlasted Menzies and kept Labor out of office for a generation.*
>
> *Incredibly, the CPA perceived the strike to be a great success. Jack Blake wrote a pamphlet in which he explained that the strike was a 'great victory' for the working class because it had, as he put it, 'exposed reformism on a mass scale'. In fact, the communists paid an enormous price for the strike...*[300]

Taft noted that the strike led to "a significant decline in the party's influence in the trade union movement, from which it never recovered".[301] This was a disaster for the party because:

> *...it was precisely its strength in the trade union movement that had made the CPA a force to be reckoned with. At the end of the war, the party had a decisive influence in over one-third of trade unions – among them some of the most important and strategically placed unions in the country. For years, it had several members on the Executive of the Australian Council of Trade Unions. Moreover, it had considerable influence on the overall policies of the trade union movement. Overseas communist leaders visiting Australia...*

*would express their surprise and approbation at our influence. This was unique for a party of our size...*[302]

Faced with this challenge, the Chifley Labor government decided to take on the Miners Union – fining and jailing union leaders and calling in the army to mine coal. The union movement was divided, and the Government won the battle. But the ALP lost the election a few months afterward and Labor did not again win office federally until 1972.

The developments in Australia must also be seen in the context of international developments. The successful conclusion of the war against Germany by the Allies which included Stalin's Red Army soon turned to disaster for the peoples of Eastern Europe. Over a few years, the occupying Soviet forces succeeded in imposing Communist party control and Soviet hegemony over much of Eastern Europe. Berlin was blockaded by the Soviets and non-Communist leaders and Catholic clergy were arrested throughout Communist-controlled territories. In the Soviet Union, the Gulag Archipelago increased in size dramatically. Churchill's 'Iron Curtin' fell across Eastern Europe behind which totalitarian tyranny reigned unchecked.[303]

In China, the Communist Party won a civil war and became the ruler of mainland China in 1949. The west was naturally concerned with the rapid expansion of totalitarian communism, now forming a block from the borders of central Europe to the Sea of Japan. Communism was an international movement from the beginning. For example, shortly after the Communist victory in China, the Australian Communist Party established relations with Mao's regime.

Eric Aarons explains:

> *Our party had decided to establish direct contact with the Chinese party soon after the victory of the revolution in 1949. Our chance came the following year when we were part of a broad peace movement that was organizing a world conference. It was to take place in Sheffield, England but, as part of the Cold War policy of trying to isolate China, the British Government had banned Chinese participation and the venue was changed at short notice to Warsaw. John Hughes, attending that gathering as a delegate from the Clerks' Union, contacted the head of the Chinese delegation, trade union leader Liu Ning-yi. In the ensuing discussion Liu raised the possibility of China receiving a study delegation from Australia, putting the proposition in terms of them*

*sharing, in the Asian-Australasian region, some of the responsibilities that had previously all been borne by the Soviet Union.*[304]

It was not only the Chinese delegates to the 'World Peace Conference' who were banned by the British Government, but a range of other delegates as well. As a result, the conference was moved at short notice to Warsaw, now under Communist [and, therefore, Soviet] control. The 25 Australian delegates who attended did so despite their passports being stamped 'Not valid for Iron Curtin countries' and they experienced difficulties and delays in returning home.[305] When they got to Warsaw, some delegates were surprised by the format and the content of the messages of the so-called "peace conference":

> *Huge pictures of Stalin, Bierut (the Polish President), Joliot-Curie [the French born former Popular Front Minister and Nobel Prize winner] and the now-ubiquitous white dove of peace adorned the low hall. The slogan "Stalin is with us" was displayed but, diplomatically perhaps, only in Polish. To those delegates from Western countries who were for the first time "experience[ing] a real people's democracy" the rituals, quite different from what could be expected in Sheffield, would be a surprise. Between speeches, the Congress organisers regularly brought into the hall groups of dancing boys and girls dressed in peasant costumes who showered the delegates with posies of flowers. Members of the Polish communist youth organisation gave leading speakers gifts such as the head of Stalin in coal. After certain speeches, "Pokoj", the Polish word for peace, was repeated rhythmically to clapping for many minutes. When Pak Den-Ai, the North Korean delegate, spoke — in Russian — delegates "rose as one man" and cheered for a full ten minutes; when Mao and Kim Il Sung were toasted, "again they rose to cheer until they could cheer no more". All of this may have been "intensely moving and inspiring" and its lasting impression "indelible", but it did provoke concern, then unvoiced, in one delegate that "this was meant to be a peace conference not a communist conference.*[306]

The international trade union movement was also divided by the communist issue. The World Federation of Trade Unions [WFTU] had originally been a worldwide union body but was now dominated by Russian and Eastern European communist run [and State-controlled] 'unions' because of their large numbers of members. Western unions had split from the WFTU to create the independent and non-communist International Confederation of Free Trade Unions [ICFTU] in the late 1940s. The ACTU Congress in 1949 voted to disaffiliate from the WFTU, but Communist led Australian unions continued their direct affiliation to the WFTU.[307] The WFTU continued in existence and operated a policy line completely in keeping with the foreign policy objectives of the USSR.

In 1951, the ACTU Executive sought to control a dispute by coal miners led by the Communist controlled Miners Federation which remained an affiliate of the WFTU. When the Miners Union refused to allow the ACTU to take control of the dispute, the ACTU issued a Statement directing the attention of:

> ...the Australian people, particularly trade unionists, members of affiliated unions, to the extreme danger of being involved in the Communist conspiracy launched by the 2nd World Peace Conference and endorsed by the Communist controlled WFTU Executive Bureau. We believe the Communist Party in Australia is utilising the industrial situation in Australia to further the Communist conspiracy...at the behest of the Kominform and The World Federation of Trade Unions.[308]

In 1948, Cecil Sharpley, a communist union official, defected from the Communist Party and made allegations of communist rigging of trade union ballots. These were widely reported in the mainstream media.[309] Not all of Sharpley's allegations were borne out by the report of a Royal Commission established to investigate the activities of the Communist party in Victoria but his story confirmed what the anti-communist forces in the Union movement had suspected and/or experienced. The evidence confirmed a long-held belief that if they were to wrest control of unions away from the Communist Party, free and fair elections would be needed.[310]

This situation led to a significant development in labor history: a willingness by unions to seek necessary Government intervention in the affairs of unions through legislation to ensure that union elections were fair and that the outcomes represented the will of rank and file members. This was pressed by the Industrial Groups and their supporters. Both the ALP and the ACTU took advice from the Industrial Groups as to how best tackle the problem of ballot-rigging by Communist union officials. In his history of the ACTU, Hagan notes the formation in 1947-8 by the ALP of a Federal Labor Advisory Council [FLAC] to consider proposed industrial legislation, including that relating to union ballots. He records that:

> In September 1948, the Executive Committee of the ACTU invited the Industrial Groups in Victoria to advise it on what further amendments they wished to make to the Conciliation and Arbitration Act. The FLAC's view and that of the Executive Committee itself, was that the Communist Party members were rigging union ballots. It proposed that when the Industrial Registrar was satisfied that prima facie that irregularities or malpractices in union ballots had occurred, he be empowered to refer the matter to an Arbitration Court judge. That judge should be enabled to investigate such claims fully and to order a Court supervised ballot if irregularities could be proven. The Executive endorsed the FLAC's proposals.[311]

This policy was narrowly endorsed by the 1949 Congress of the ACTU and enacted by the Chiefly Labor Government by the Arbitration Act [No. 1] 1949 as Hagan notes "in response to pressure from the Industrial Groups and the Movement..."[312] Under the Chiefly legislation, irregularities had to be shown in the conduct of elections before a court-ordered and -controlled ballot could be obtained.[313]

This legislation was first used by the ALP Industrial Groups in the Federated Clerks Union in Victoria in 1949 where the Returning Officer appointed by the incumbent left-wing administration burnt the ballot papers in his back yard rather than count and declare the result which he presumably suspected would be unfavourable to his side.[314] The legislation also led to the defeat of the Communists in the Federated Ironworkers by Industrial Grouper Laurie Short who was declared elected by the court after irregularities were proven.[315]

Under the new Menzies Liberal Party Government, attempts were made to ban the Communist Party – by legislation which was struck down by the High Court and then by a referendum which failed to win enough support. But these 'top down' methods of tackling communist influence and control were never going to be completely successful. There was another and better way to deal with the anti-democratic and anti-labor Communist presence in the trade union movement; that is, by asking union members to win back these working class organisations from the Communists. A group of Australian men and women set out to do just that.

As Ross Martin says, in response to the communist threat:

> There had emerged a counter-organisation dedicated to the destruction of

*Communist influence in the Unions. Its leaders were distinguished by the kind of toughness and sense of purpose found among the Communists themselves. They were to add a new dimension to Australian trade unionism by giving it a right wing with a relatively coherent ideological position centered on anti-communism.*[316]

## THE COUNTER-ORGANISATION

In the early 1940s, B. A. Santamaria – already well known for his interest in Catholic Action, as it was then known, was approached by moderate labor unionists for assistance in battling communist influence in the union movement. In response, Santamaria established the Catholic Social Studies Movement [CSSM] – known in short as the Movement or later as 'The Show' – in 1941-2. The Movement was a Catholic organisation run on a day-to-day basis by lay people but with episcopal oversight by a Committee of bishops. Its basic method was to contact Catholic workers and unionists to encourage them to take an active interest in the affairs of their unions. Most Catholics at the time were working class. The Movement asked its members and supporters to attend union meetings and vote in union elections.

The membership of the ALP itself at the time was strongly Catholic reflecting the working-class nature of the Catholic community. As Patrick O'Farrell, noted historian of the Catholic Church in Australia has written:

*For most Catholics, as Catholics, politics was just not an issue. They voted according to their economic status – that is, mostly Labor.*[317]

Splits in the ALP at the time of the First World War over conscription had cost the Labor Party much of its Protestant Christian support, especially Methodists.[318] Later in the 1940s, the ALP also recognised the threat to the Party itself and authorised the establishment of 'ALP Industrial Groups' – groups of ALP members in particular unions, the aim of which were to wrest control of the Unions away from the Communists and return it to members sympathetic to traditional labor values of moderate reform, parliamentary democracy and arbitration.

While there are some conflicting accounts, it is likely that non-Communist ALP leaders suggested the formation of the Industrial Groups. B.A. Santamaria at times claimed that they were his idea and at other times said that moderate

ALP leaders had proposed their formation. In any case, ALP leaders were happy to seek out and welcomed the assistance of the Movement in tackling Communist penetration of the union movement and the ALP itself. Labor leaders and those representing the Groups and the Movement worked closely together for a period against the Communist party.[319]

This endeavor became a battle, as Murray put it, 'not only about power and jobs, but for the very soul of the Australian labour Movement'. What sort of a battle was waged? A tough one. Murray says:

> *Often with a warped idealism, the communists were hysterically unscrupulous in trying to fend off those they believed to be the tools of capitalism in its last days. They subjected groupers to violence, smears and a persistent war of nerves. The wife of a Group activist might be telephoned while her husband was out on union work and told he was with yet another mistress; Eureka Youth league members would create disturbances outside the home of another absent Grouper. On all sides, the atmosphere was bitter and emotional.* [320]

The establishment of the ALP Industrial Groups was a significant event and a departure from the traditional ALP approach. In fact, it was an extraordinary development. Because of the subsequent history of the Groups, and especially the split in the ALP in the mid-1950s, it has been easy for some to forget that the Industrial Groups were originally a creation of the ALP and involved only ALP members.

As D W Rawson has noted:

> *Why did the Groups appear? The obvious answer, 'In order to remove Communists from union positions,' is substantially the correct one. There is a long-standing tradition, of which vestiges still remain, that the Labour Party was the creation and should be the servant of the industrial wing, and that it had no right to interest itself in the internal affairs of the unions. Attempts to break this tradition, notably by the groups which the supporters of J. T. Lang formed in the unions during an internal dispute within the party in 1938-39, had always been unsuccessful. Nothing short of an attempt by another party to gain control of the unions could have aroused the Labour Party to intervene directly in union affairs.*[321]

Much has been written about who was responsible for the split in the ALP and the reasons behind the action of Federal leader H.V. 'Doc' Evatt in denouncing the Movement and disbanding the Groups. Supporters of the

Industrial Groups and the Movement saw Evatt as the main villain, having gone from a position of support and co-operation with anti-Communists to one where he attacked them publicly, denouncing the Groups and Movement activists as sinister external forces seeking to control the ALP.

In 1947, Evatt had told the Federal ALP Caucus that the Communist Party had "a hymn of hate against Labor and against Australia" during a Caucus discussion on an Australian 'Rocket Bomb range':

> *Dr Evatt stated that the Communist Party had issued a pamphlet opposing the Range Bomb proposals. In his opinion the Communist Party intended to torpedo the defence plan of Australia. There is no evidence that the Soviet Government has issued any instructions to the Communist Party but the Communist Party was acting in the interests of the Soviet in Canada, America and Australia. The Party is fostering animosity against the Australian defence Plan and have a hymn of hate against Labor and against Australia".*[322]

Evatt was Attorney-General in the Chifley Labor Government when in 1949 he introduced the National Coal Emergency Bill which, when enacted, led to the jailing of as many as eight union officials in the coal mining industry for contempt of court.[323] Evatt was also Attorney-General when the Commonwealth Government prosecuted CPA official L.L. Sharkey for sedition, after he was quoted saying that Australian workers would welcome Soviet troops into Australia:

> *If Soviet Forces in pursuit of aggressors entered Australia, Australian workers would welcome them...*[324]

Later, of course, Evatt – as ALP Deputy Federal Leader in Opposition – appeared in the High Court on behalf of the Waterside Workers' Federation to successfully oppose the Menzies Government legislation banning the Communist Party [on not insubstantial human rights grounds] and later campaigned to defeat the referendum to outlaw the CPA. From a previously anti-Communist position, Evatt now appeared to be favouring the CPA through his assistance.

The SDA's Jim Maher, who I knew well and respected, blamed Evatt for introducing what he called a 'sectarian' attack on the Groups and the Movement; that is, charging that they were carrying out a specifically Catholic agenda within the party, not just an anti-Communist one.[325] Some Catholics and non-Catholics maintained their support for the Groups. Some Catholics [and non-Catholics] who were previously Group supporters remained in the ALP led by Evatt. Who was responsible for the Split?

ALP historian Ross McMullin has a measured view:

> The lasting enmity between the ALP and the DLP helped to shape a subsequent ALP tradition that the split was inevitable and justified. According to this doctrine, Evatt was a principled radical who decisively exposed the treacherous conduct and connections of minority elements which were like boils on the body of Labor and had to be lanced sooner or later. This tradition is flawed. Evatt was a tremendous fighter for civil liberties and had other outstanding radical credentials, but he also dabbled in intrigue and power plays. During his first three years as leader he had consistently cultivated labor's right wing, and his flirtation even extended to secret meetings with Santamaria before the 1954 election...Evatt invited suggestions for the ALP policy speech from him...It was the Petrov controversy, and Evatt's response to it, that made a continuation of this cosy concord impossible...
>
> Evatt's leadership aggravated the split. His increasingly erratic behaviour during 1954 – combined with unsettling Evatt characteristics observable for years, such as acute suspiciousness – intensified muted speculation about the Doc's mental stability...[326]

Bill Hayden, former Federal ALP Leader, Minister for Foreign Affairs and later Australia's Governor-General has a similar view, shared by others who lived through these times:

> Evatt was in deep trouble within the Party at the time he precipitated the Split and it was all his own work.[327]

Phillip Deery has a different view of Evatt's motives, suggesting that he may have had rational reasons for seeking to oppose the activities of Santamaria's Movement. However, Deery also notes that in 1954, Evatt had met three times with Santamaria to discuss ALP matters, a strange act for someone who would later attack forces said to be 'outside' the labor movement:

> His [Evatt's] sensational public exposure of the Movement directly triggered the Labor split in March 1955, which in turn changed the course of Australian political history. Evatt's press statement of 5 October his 'hydrogen bomb', as a journalist, Alan Reid, termed it included the now legendary reference to

> "...a small minority group of members, located particularly in the State of Victoria, which has, since 1949, become increasingly disloyal to the Labor Movement and the Labor leadership ... It seems certain that the activities of this small group are largely directed from outside the Labor Movement. The Melbourne News-Weekly appears to act as their organ. A serious position exists."

> Issuing such a statement at that time, according to one historian, 'was like putting a match to tinder-dry scrub in a heatwave'. Evatt's action becomes all the more remarkable when we realise that earlier in that same year, 1954, Evatt met privately with Santamaria to discuss in detail ALP policies and tactics no fewer than three times.[328]

Paul Strangio has written an almost morbidly compelling account of the Split in the Victorian Branch of the ALP.[329] He attributes blame in almost equal portions to B.A. Santamaria, Evatt and the industrial wing of the Victorian Branch of the ALP. Nobody, Strangio suggests, appeared to value the existence of the Cain Labor government in Spring Street. The ALP had been so little in office in Victoria [unlike in NSW and Queensland] that all parties seemed willing to fight 'to the last Victorian' for their objectives and did not seem to concern themselves about the fate of the Cain government. The Victorian ALP machine [and Evatt] appeared to prefer the 'purity of opposition' to the attractions of the Treasury benches.

In any event, serious damage to the labour movement was done by the 1950s Split. Expulsions of those associated with the 'old' Victorian Executive led to the creation of the Australian Labor (Anti-Communist) Party in Victoria [which was later found by court decision to be the continuing legal entity in Victoria]. This organisation eventually became the Democratic Labour Party [DLP]. Interestingly, in the 1955 state election, which swept the Cain Victorian Government out of office, late in the campaign, both the 'new' and 'old' Labor parties decided to preference the conservative parties ahead of the other labor grouping in the majority of cases.[330]

The ALP also split some years later in Queensland when in 1957 the Gair-led Parliamentary Party refused to follow certain directions by the Queensland Executive regarding annual leave and the Queensland Labor Party was formed, eventually also becoming associated with the DLP. This event was of a completely different character to the split in Victoria. Major splits did not occur in other States but DLP Branches emerged and contested parliamentary seats. However, many ALP members in these States, and especially in NSW, who were supportive of the aims of the Industrial Groups and even the Movement itself, remained within the ALP. The NSW ALP was in Government at the time of the split but survived in office. The NSW ALP Branch Executive was reformed by the Federal Executive, but all sides accepted the outcome and unity prevailed. It was reasonably clear that, unlike in Victoria, NSW ALP activists valued the existence of a Labor Government. This view extended to the influential NSW Catholic hierarchy, which indicated to Movement and Industrial Group activists that there should be no split in NSW.[331] The situation in NSW also partly reflected concern in the Church hierarchy in NSW about the work of the Victorian based Movement which became the National Civic Council [NCC] after the NSW church successfully appealed to Rome to remove official church support for and oversight of the work of the Movement.

The emergence of the DLP as a competitor to the ALP for working-class Catholic votes hardened the Split. Splitting the Party and ALP governments is a great offence to loyal Labor party members. The on-going existence of the DLP angered loyal ALP members. This was particularly true because of the decision of the DLP to direct preferences to the Menzies Liberal/Country Party coalition government federally. The Communist Party and the left of the ALP must have rejoiced in the Split. Their strongest opponents had been stripped of their ALP orthodoxy and appeal. They could now be relentlessly portrayed as splitters, rats and traitors to the ALP cause at best and as 'clerical fascists' doing Rome's work at worst.

Former Victorian Premier John Cain, Junior, whose father's Labor Government had been brought down by the Split and who had no sympathy for the Groups or their allies, put the position this way:

> *The 1955 Split cut across the fundamental support base of the ALP. The party's traditionally strong Irish Catholic component was what had provided commitment and workplace support to the emerging trade unions in the second half of the nineteenth century. They were the same elements that led to our being at the forefront of many industrial and political reforms in the last years of that century..."*
>
> *[After the split] ...the Victorian ALP, narrow in outlook and negative in attitude, became less and less politically relevant. Organisationally, the party took on a bunker mentality and sought to crush by whatever means*

*seemed appropriate any elements in its ranks that urged a broader-based party. The views of branch members were largely ignored. Party policy and elections to the executive and key party committees were dominated by a small group within the trade union movement known as the Trade Union Defence Committee. This group did everything it could to keep out of the party elements that might disagree with the current holders of power...*

*One little discussed result of the bitterness of the DLP Split was the virtual exclusion of Catholics from selection as candidates for public office. Strong anti-Catholic feeling persisted in the party power holders in those years... There was in fact no Catholic newly elected as an endorsed ALP member of the State parliamentary party until Pauline Toner won the seat of Greensborough in a by-election in 1977.*[332]

Many people took part in the struggle against communism. I played a minor role. It was work worth doing with lasting beneficial results for human freedom. I was pleased to work alongside many people of integrity and faith and who ran this race to the end. This memoir is dedicated to them.

# · Notes

1. Graham Freudenberg, Foreword to Robert Murray, *Labor and Santamaria*, Australian Scholarly Publishing, 2016, p viii. Freudenberg worked as a speechwriter for 40 years for successive generations of ALP leaders, including federal parliamentary leaders such as Calwell, Whitlam and Hawke, as well as for NSW ALP leaders.
2. These events are recounted in Chapter 4.
3. As well as Robert Murray's two books, see also Fr Bruce Duncan, *Crusade or Conspiracy, Catholics and the Anti-Communist Struggle in Australia*, UNSW Press 2001 and Robert Fitzgerald, *The Pope's Battalions: Santamaria, Catholicism and the labor Split*, University of Queensland Press, 2003, Gavin Duffy, *Demons and Democrats, 1950s Labor at the Crossroads*, Freedom Publishing [an NCC imprint] 2002, P. Ormonde, *The Movement*, Thomas Nelson 1972. B A Santamaria has written several accounts of his life and work. For highly critical views of Santamaria and his methods and beliefs, see Paul Ormonde [Editor], *Santamaria – The Politics of Fear*, Spectrum Publications, 2000.
4. The 'Movement' ceased to be a strictly Catholic organisation in December 1957 following a decision of the Vatican withdrawing official Church support. B A Santamaria then established the National Civic Council, the word 'Civic' implying that the new organisation was a secular one, under the control of laypeople rather than the Bishops. See Bruce Duncan, op. cit., pp 346-7
5. See for example Gerard Henderson, *Santamaria, A Most Unusual Man*, The Miegunyah Press, 2015.
6. Ibid, p 66-7.
7. Ben Schneiders and Royce Millar, "Shopped out", *The Age, Good Weekend* online - http://www.smh.com.au/interactive/2016/shopped-out/.
8. I discovered later that ALP Federal leader Evatt made this comparison in October 1954, in denouncing the Movement, so perhaps this is not an entirely recent development.
9. Mark Aarons with John Grenville, *The Show, Another side of Santamaria's Movement*, Scribe, 2017.
10. Ibid, p 10.
11. Ibid, p 12.
12. Robert Murray, *The Split, Australian Labor in the fifties*, Cheshire, 1970, p23. See also Deery, P. and Redfern, N, *No lasting peace*: "Labor, Communism and the Cominform, Australia and Great Britain, 1945-50". *Labor History*, No. 88, May 2005, p 63.
13. James Hagan, *The History of the ACTU*, Longman Cheshire, 1981, pp 194-5.
14. Eric Aarons, *What's Left?*, Penguin Books, 1993, p 228.
15. David McKnight, "Rethinking Cold War History", *Labor History*, Number 95, November 2008, p 193-4.
16. See David McKnight, *Espionage and the Roots of the Cold War*, Frank Cash Publishers, UK, 2002, 156-7; also Ellem B 1997 "Ideology and union purpose: The Federated

|      |   |
|---|---|
|      | Clerks Union in New South Wales, 1956-58", *Australian Journal of Politics and History*, vol.43:3, pp. 344-360;  Milne, L, *The Clerks, A History of the Federated Clerks Union in NSW*, USU, Sydney, 2008, pp 65 and ff. and Macintyre, S, *The Reds, The Communist party of Australia from origins to illegality*, Allen and Unwin, 1998, p 341. |
| 17   | D. Kenyon, *The Struggle for the Clerks Union*, Mimeograph, September 1966, p 7. |
| 18   | E. Aarons, *What's left?*, Penguin Books, 1993, p 74. The term 'federal secretary' of a union refers to the position of national secretary of a union that consists of a number of State based Branches. Unions usually had an honorary President and the position of Secretary was the full time and key role, akin to that of CEO in a company. |
| 19   | Ibid, p. 125 |
| 20   | This letter is in the possession of the author. |
| 21   | Greg F Walsh, *The Federated Clerks Union of Australia: A Study of Government and Unionism in the 20th Century*, Unpublished Ph.D thesis, Monash University, 1984, p 172. Murray, however, says Maynes was Secretary of the Clerks Industrial Group. Robert Murray, *The Split, Australian labor in the fifties*, Cheshire, 1950, p 19. |
| 22   | Ross Fitzgerald, op.cit., p 79. |
| 23   | See Keith Harvey, "JPM – John Peter Maynes" in *The Recorder*, Issues number 262 and 263 for the life and times of John Maynes. A shorter version also appears in *Labor History*, No 97. |
| 24   | Paul Strangio, *Neither Power Nor Glory, 100 years of Political Labor in Victoria, 1856-1956*, Melbourne University Press, 2012, p 313 |
| 25   | Interview with James Maher, National Library of Australia, Oral History project. Interview recorded in 2003. |
| 26   | Andrei Amalrik, *Will the Soviet Union Survive until 1984?* Penguin Edition, 1980. |
| 27   | George Orwell, *Nineteen Eighty-Four: A Novel*, first published 1949 by Secker & Warburg. An excellent 'biography' of Orwell's book is Dorian Lynskey's *The Ministry of Truth – A Biography of George Orwell's 1984*, Picador, 2019. |
| 28   | Ann Applebaum, *Gulag, A History of the Soviet Camps*, Penguin Books, 2003, p 7. |
| 29   | Evgenia Ginzburg, *Into the Whirlwind*, Penguin Books, 1968 [Hardback edition Collins/Harvill, 1967] and *Within the Whirlwind*, Collins Harvill, 1981. |
| 30   | Applebaum, op.cit., p 4 and Chapter 3. |
| 31   | Russell, a famous English philosopher, despite his criticisms in *The Practice and Theory of Bolshevism* (1920), later developed a more positive view of the Soviet Union, thinking the West was equivalently amoral, a view shared with many intellectuals on the left of European politics. *The God that Failed*, an anthology of contributions by authors who were former Communists or fellow travellers, including Arthur Koestler, had been published in 1949 and should have served as sufficient warning. The volume was edited by Richard Crossman, an English Labor Party MP who was later editor of the left-wing *New Statesman*. *The God that Failed*, Richard Crossman, (Editor), Harper and Brothers, New York, 1949. |
| 32   | Applebaum, op.cit., pp 4-5 and Appendix: *How many?* Pp 515 and ff. |
| 33   | According to Applebaum, estimates vary of between 12 and 20 million who died as a result of forced collectivisation, Stalin's Great Terror of the 1930s and in the camps of the Gulag. Robert Conquest, the historian of the Great Terror gives a figure of 'no fewer than 20 million deaths' as a result of Stalin's rule alone. Robert Conquest, *The Great Terror, A reassessment*, 40th Anniversary Edition, Oxford University press, 2008, p 486. |

34  By 1921, there were already 84 camps – Applebaum, op. cit., p 4 and Chapter 1.
35  Applebaum, p 495. The final camp was closed after the Soviet Union had ceased to exist – p 500.
36  Harry Wu, [with Vecsey, G], *Troublemaker, One Man's Crusade against China's cruelty*, Chatto and Windus, 1996.
37  'Data leak reveals how China 'brainwashes' Uighurs in prison camps', BBC Online, 24 November, 2019.
38  A new DLP was later restarted by others.
39  Gerry Hand, MHR, *To the Committee of Inquiry into the affiliation of certain unions to the Victorian Branch of the Australian Labor Party*, undated, mimeograph, paragraphs 2.5.1 and 2.5.9. Copy in the possession of the author.
40  J.Gillard, G. Lazarus and A Mckenzie – prepared on behalf of the Melbourne FEA, *The NCC, the Students & the Four Unions, A Submission to the Committee of 10 enquiring into the applications for affiliation from the four trade unions*. May 1984, Mimeograph, p 33 and Appendix A30. Copy in the possession of the author.
41  *Report of the Committee of Ten to the Administrative Committee Meeting of the 7$^{th}$ December 1984*, over the name of Ian Mill, Chairperson for the Committee of Ten. Copy in the possession of the author.
42  The 'Pledge' required to be signed by all new applicants for membership of the Party, such as the one I signed in February 1984 required me only to declare that I was not "a member of any other organisation which pledges its members to support candidates for public office". I was able to sign this pledge with a clear conscience.
43  Letter to me from Peter Batchelor, ALP State Secretary, dated 18$^{th}$ January 1985.
44  Letter to me from Peter Batchelor dated 22$^{nd}$ May 1985.
45  This may also have been true of the ASC&J's Jim McLaughlin.
46  Paul Strangio, op.cit., p 313.
47  Ross McMullin, op. cit., p 294.
48  This telephone call is not recorded by John Cain in his otherwise very full account of these events: *John Cain's Years*, op. cit., see Chapter 6.
49  And, in fact, on this issue, the Parliamentary Party completely triumphed over the organisational wing. The Federal ALP Government co-operated with the Victorian and other State Governments and fully succeeded in de-registering the BLF and seizing its assets. Premier John Cain twice told the ALP State Conference that his Government would not implement Conference decisions on the BLF. Cain effectively stared down his opponents with the Party on this issue.
50  Quoted in Tony Judt, *Postwar, A history of Europe since 1945*, William Heinemann, London, 2005, p 197.
51  George Orwell, *Homage to Catalonia and Looking Back on the Spanish War*, Penguin Books, 1974
52  See Short, Susanna, *Laurie Short, A political life*, Allen and Unwin, 1992, pp 91ff.
53  See John N. Button, 'Lovegrove, Denis (1904–1979)', Australian Dictionary of Biography, National Centre of Biography, Australian National University. As a young person, Lovegrove was a militant leader of the Unemployed Workers Movement and an active member of the Communist Party from which he was expelled in 1933. He then became a member of the ALP and the Industrial Groups but remained in the ALP after the split.
54  Frank Hardy, *Journey into the Future*, Australasian Book Society, 1952.

55  Jasper Beck, *Hungry ghosts, China's secret famine*, John Murray, 1996, at page 268 but see especially, Chapter 18, *How many died?* See also Jung Chang and Jon Halliday, whose later work *Mao, The Unknown Story*, Jonathon Cape, 2005, puts the number at 38 million [p 456]. Elizabeth Gooch, "Famine within reach", *History Today*, Vol. 69, Issue 11, November 2019, p 18, puts the figure at between 16.5 and 45 million people and notes that the CCP still refers to the period as "Three Years of Natural Disasters".

56  Jung Chang and Jon Halliday, op.cit., p 569.

57  This 'quote' and variations upon it have been attributed to many people over the years.

58  A 'Nasho', that is a National Serviceman or conscript who had served in Viet Nam was later also invited to speak to even things up.

59  A 1971 play by David Williamson, later made into a movie of the same name.

60  The voting age was 21 at the time, later lowered to 18 by the Whitlam ALP Government.

61  When I traced the origin of the expression the 'Monash Soviet' I discovered that it was probably first applied by the National Civic Council's publication *News Weekly* [for which I would later write] in the mid-1960s, although I have been unable to find a precise citation giving a particular date or issue of *News Weekly* in which this term was used. The history of Monash University written by Graeme Davison and Kate Murphy [*University Unlimited: The Monash Story*, Allen & Unwin, 2012], refers to the term at page 118 and cites Paul Francis Perry's *The Rise and fall of Practically Everybody: an account of student political activity at Monash University, 1965-72* as the source. Perry's mimeograph, of which I have a copy, does not cite a particular issue of *News Weekly* and in fact at page 4 claims that 'Almost as soon as Monash was formed, the NCC through *"Newsweekly"* was referring to the "Monash Soviet" '. Since Monash admitted its first students in 1961, this claim seems unlikely. Perry further quotes *News Weekly* as saying that there was 'more subversion per square foot [at Monash] than at any other Australian university', again without citing a specific reference for this statement. Daniel Robbins, in his Fourth Year Honours Thesis *Melbourne's Maoists: The Rise of the Monash University Labor Club 1965-1967*, Victoria University, November 2005 cites *News-Weekly*, Wednesday, 2 August 1967. p. 2 as the source for the latter quote but also does not give a specific reference for the 'Monash Soviet' statement. It was however, in my experience, a term in common use at the time.

62  See for example *The Family File* by Mark Aarons, Black Inc, 2010 which the author says is based on 209 volumes of intelligence services files totalling 32,000 pages and including photographs, films and tapes as well as transcripts of recorded conversations.

63  C. Wright Mills, *The Power Elite* (1956).

64  See Michael Hyde, [editor], *It is Right to Rebel*, The Diplomat, 1972, pp 5-11 [It is possible that this book was written by Albert Langer and others as much as by Michael Hyde]. Michael Hyde has also published a personal memoir of this period *All Along the Watchtower* [The Vulgar Press, 2010] although this has been criticised by one of his colleagues from the era as being only part memoir and partly a work of fiction.

65  See for example Daniel Robins, *Melbourne's Maoists: The Rise of the Monash University Labor Club 1965-1967* School of Social Sciences Faculty of Arts Victoria University Fourth Year Honours Thesis November 2005.

66  Officially known as the Menzies building, we only ever called it by its nickname.

67    DVA (Department of Veterans' Affairs) (2021), The Birthday Ballot, DVA Anzac Portal, accessed 10 March 2021, http://anzacportal.dva.gov.au/wars-and-missions/vietnam-war-1962-1975/events/conscription/birthday-ballot

68    This is my view but shared by others: see for example Russell Marks, "1968 in Australia – The student movement and the New left", in *The far left in Australia since 1945*, J. Piccini, E. Smith and M. Worley [eds.] Routledge, 2019, at pp 138-9.

69    Michael Hyde, *It is right to Rebel*, op.cit., pp 19-22.

70    Graeme Davison and Kate Murphy, *University Unlimited: The Monash Story*, Allen & Unwin, 2012, pp 124-5.

71    Senate *Hansard*, 5$^{th}$ September 1967 at page 513. See also Jon Piccini: *A whole new world: Global revolution and Australian social movements in the long Sixties*, A thesis submitted for the degree of Doctor of Philosophy at The University of Queensland in 2013, especially at pp 57-65.

72    Mark Aarons, *The Family File*, Black Inc., 2010, p 268. See also pp 1-11 for a brief description of the career of Laurie Aarons in the CPA.

73    Michael Hyde, *All Along the Watchtower*, op.cit., pp 104-5.

74    ASIO collected copies of *Print* and these and they can be read in the National Archives, some of them online.

75    In fact, the Democrats did have one member who was formerly in the communist Eureka Youth League who had participated in demonstrations against US President Lyndon Johnson when he visited Australia in 1966.

76    Jill Jolliffe, *Run for your life, A memoir*, Affirm press, 2014, p 87. See also Davison and Murphy, op. cit., p 121.

77    This phrase, a parody of Mao's dictum "power grows out of the barrel of a gun" is attributed to Darce Cassidy, a Labor Club activist at Monash University in the late 1960s and featured prominently on the masthead of *Print* when he was involved. Cassidy died in 2019. See Piccini, op. cit., p 68.

78    Daniel Robins, *Melbourne's Maoists: The Rise of the Monash University Labor Club 1965-1967*, Fourth Year Honours Thesis November 2005, p 38.

79    Published January 1971. I did not in this letter then [nor do I now] intend to suggest that Michael Hyde himself was involved in any violence, theft or damage to property or that he was charged in connection with any such offence. To the best of my knowledge, the students concerned were only ever charged by the university authorities with refusing to obey a direction to end the occupation.

80    Hyde, M, *All along the watchtower*, op.cit., p 236.

81    G. Henderson, op.cit., pp 366-7.

82    Nelson Mandela, *Long Walk to Freedom*, Abacus, 1995, pp 518-9.

83    Helen Suzman describes her first meeting with Nelson Mandela in almost identical terms in her memoir, *In No Uncertain terms, Memoirs*, Mandarin, 1994, pp 152-3.

84    Letter to the author from Helen Suzman, May 14, 1971.

85    *Lot's Wife*, August 5, 1971, p 3.

86    Jill Jolliffe, *Run for Your Life*, Affirm press, 2014, p 116. See also: Ken Mansell - *Vale Darce Cassidy (1941-2019) – Journalist, Agitator, Organiser*, May 13, 2019. (online).

87    The State Library of Victoria has a reasonable collection, particularly for the years 1970-3.

88    *Free Speech*, Vol 7, No 1. 1/3/72. Membership cost 50 cents!

89    Jim Bacon was later a successful ALP Premier of Tasmania.

90. Mark Taft left the CPA in the 1980s and later became a County Court Judge in Victoria.
91. Milorad M. Drachkovitch and Lewis H. Gann, *Yearbook on International Communist Affairs*, Hoover Institution Press., 1981, p. 122.
92. *Lot's Wife*, June 1971.
93. Free Speech, Vol 6, No 16.
94. Paul Francis Perry, *The Rise and Fall of Practically Everybody, an account of student political activity at Monash University, 1965-1972*, p. 95, mimeograph, undated, copy held by author. Perry's work is an independent account of student politics at Monash and concentrates on the activities of the left factions, especially the Labor Club. Its timeline is at times hard to follow but gives in places a detailed account of the operation of student general meetings and the tactics employed by the left.
95. Free Speech, Vol 6, No 16.
96. George Orwell, *Animal Farm*, Chapter 10.
97. Perry, op.cit, p 95.
98. *Free Speech*, Vol 6, No 16.
99. Mark LaPirow has a different recollection of the place at which we served the writ on the Vice Chancellor.
100. *Lot's Wife*, Vol 12, No. 4.
101. *Lot's Wife*, Vol 12, No. 6.
102. *Free Speech*, Vol 6, No. 22.
103. Perry, op.cit., p 97.
104. Letter from Albert Langer, Lot's Wife, Vol. X1, No 14, p 3.
105. Euphemistically "Fight the Draft". The "F" might have stood for something else.
106. The Tolpuddle Martyrs were a group of six farm laborers from Dorset in the UK who in 1831 formed a trade union to oppose wage reductions. Convicted on a charge of administering illegal oaths, they were transported to NSW and Van Diemen's Land for seven years. They were pardoned after an outcry and massive public campaign in England and allowed to return home. See: Tom Mead, *Man is never Free*, Dolphin Books, Sydney, 1946.
107. John Button, *As it happened*, Text Publishing, 1998, pp 138-140.
108. Jim Beggs, *Proud to be a wharfie*, Arcadia, 2103, p 130.
109. Ross McMullin, *The Light on the Hill, The Australian Labor Party, 1891-1991*, Oxford University Press, 1992, pp 320-2.
110. Published by the AFL-CIO, Publication No 152, *Solzhenitsyn, The Voice of Freedom*.
111. See Jim Hagan, *The history of the ACTU*, Longman Cheshire, 1981, pp 253-255.
112. Letter in the VTHC files regarding this trip, VTHC Archives, Melbourne University library.
113. Transcribed note in the VTHC files regarding the proposed trip. VTHC Archives, Melbourne University Library.
114. Ibid.
115. Matthew Ouimet, *The Rise and Fall of the Brezhnev Doctrine in Soviet Foreign Policy*. London, The University of North Carolina Press, 2003, p 67.
116. "Stakhanovites: In 1935 a coal miner called Alexei Stakhanov was reported to have dug 102 tons of coal in a single 6-hour shift. This was many times more than a miner was expected to cut. Stakhanov was rewarded and praised as an example

to all other workers. The public were not told that the story was an invention: Stakhanov had two co-workers, plus machinery in perfect working order, to help him achieve so much. Russians were told to model themselves on Stakhanov", http://www.nationalarchives.gov.uk/education/heroesvillains/background/g4_background.htm#2.

117 Judt, op. cit., p 569.
118 Judt, op. cit., p 569-70.
119 See the quote at the beginning of Chapter 2.
120 *The Age*, May 19, 1978.
121 Ibid.
122 Melbourne *Sun*, May 23, 1978.
123 Melbourne *Herald*, May 26, 1978.
124 Sinatra said: 'And as for the broads who work for the press, they're the hookers of the press. I might offer them a buck and a half, I'm not sure.' ACTU President Bob Hawke had to intervene to resolve the stand-off that ensued: https://thenewdaily.com.au/news/people/2015/12/11/frank-sinatra-despised-australia/
125 After an interview with the Committee and some correspondence between them and me and between the VTHC and the Committee, the Committee eventually dismissed my complaint in November 1978. They held that there was no job discrimination as there was an 'inherent job requirement' of some sort that I had not been able to satisfy. Ken Stone wrote twice to the Committee outlining a fair summary of the events and concluding that he had sacked me because the Council was not functioning, which was true enough.
126 For the ebb and flow of control of the Trades Hall Executive see Cathy Brigden, Exploring Power, Space and Scale in the Aftermath of the Trades Hall Council 'Split' in, *Proceedings of AIRAANZ, Australia*, Julian Teicher, Peter Holland and Sarah Tuberville (ed.), (The 16th Conference of the Association of Industrial Relations Academics of Australia and New Zealand).
127 Maynes polled the highest number of primary votes in this election but was defeated on preferences. Adam Carr: http://psephos.adam-carr.net/countries/a/australia/states/vic/historic/1952assembly.txt
128 See for example JPM- John Peter Maynes, Parts 1 and 2, *The Recorder*, Official organ of the Melbourne Branch of the Australian Society for the Study of Labour History, Issues No 262 and 263. A shorter version of this story also appeared in Labor History published by the national ASSLH.
129 See Mark Aarons, "Scenes from my Cold War", in Ann Curthoys and Joy Damousi, [eds.] *What did you do in the Cold War, Daddy? - Personal Stories from a Troubled Time*, NewSouth Publishing, 2014, Kindle Edition, Location 2973 and the biographical note about John Grenville in Mark Aarons with John Grenville, *The Show – Another side of Santamaria's Movement, op.cit.*
130 John Grenville's reasons are now set out in *The Show, op.cit.*, co-authored with Mark Aarons.
131 I eventually found the article on about page 50 in the Melbourne *Sun* under the heading ' "Bob Hawke" elected Singapore President', referring to the fact that the President of the Singapore trade union movement, Devan Nair, had been elected as the country's President. John knew him and wanted to write to congratulate him.
132 'Preference to unionists' could be obtained where employers were unduly frustrating union organising efforts. In certain circumstances, the Federal Concilia-

tion and Arbitration Commission could insert clauses into awards providing that, all other things being equal, preference to union members over non-union members should be given at hiring and firing and in other limited respects. Employers often sought to avoid these obligations by encouraging rather than discouraging employees to join their union. Preference clauses are no longer possible.

133  Federated Clerks' Union of Australia v Victorian Employers' Federation [1984] HCA 53; (1984) 154 CLR 472; (1984) 54 ALR 489; (1984) 58 ALJR 475; (1984) 8 IR 157 (20 August 1984). The Chief Justice ruled that that parts of the clause agreed to by the Victorian Commission was beyond power, but his four colleagues allowed the appeal without reservation and the entire clause stood.

134  Termination, change and Redundancy Case, Melbourne, August 2, 1984. https://www.fwc.gov.au/documents/documents/archives/1984tcrcase.pdf

135  "Keep the Hours, Spend the Years" was the catchphrase for this idea which was promoted by the Union over many years.

136  Possibly only because of the election of the Whitlam ALP Government which was elected to office after the case had concluded and successfully argued that the new Government should be able to make additional submissions, supporting the ACTU's case. See 1969 Equal Pay Case The Australasian Meat Industry Employees Union & Others v Meat and Allied Trades Federation of Australia & Others (Equal Pay Cases) (1969) 127 CAR 1142 – Moore and Williams JJ., Chambers Public Service Arbitrator and Gough C, Judgment, 19 June 1969. 1972 Equal Pay Case National Wage and Equal Pay Cases 1972 (1972) 147 CAR 172 – Moore J, (Acting President) Robinson J, Coldham J Deputy Presidents, Taylor Public Service Arbitrator and Brack Commissioner, Decision issued December 15, 1972, No. B8506.

137  "*Facing Multinationals in 1974*", Paper prepared for ASIA-FIET Seminar, Kuala Lumpur, June 27 to the July 3, 1974, by J.P. Maynes, Federal President, FCUA. Mimeograph. Copy in the possession of the author.

138  See Patrick Morgan, *B.A. Santamaria, Running the Show, Selected Documents: 1939-1996*, The Miegunyah press in association with the State Library of Victoria, 2008; Gerard Henderson, *Santamaria, A Most Unusual man*, The Miegunyah Press, 2016; Mark Considine, "The National Civic Council: Politics Inside Out", *Politics*, Journal of the Australasian Political Studies Association, Volume 20 No 1, May 1985.

139  Morgan, P. *op. cit.*, p 377 and ff.

140  Ibid, p 380.

141  Ibid.

142  Henderson, op. cit., Chapter 17.

143  Ibid, pp 401-2, 405.

144  Considine, op. cit., pp 48-58 at 52.

145  Morgan, op.cit, p 378.

146  https://www.australianbiography.gov.au/subjects/santamaria/

147  Ibid, Tape 9.

148  The new Hawke Labor Government introduced the Family Income Supplement [FIS] in May 1983 which was renamed the Family Allowance (FA) in 1984 and the Family Allowance Supplement in 1987. These policies can be traced directly to policies promoted by the FCUA amongst others, adopted by the ACTU and especially promoted by former ACTU President Martin Ferguson. https://www.aph.gov.au/About_Parliament/Parliamentary_Departments/Parliamentary_Library/pubs/BN/0809/childrenpartc.

149  Noel Tennison, *The Life of Every Party*, Primrose Hall Publishing Group, 2014, pp 252-3. Noel Tennison was asked by John Maynes to do media publicity to promote the tour, a task he clearly enjoyed.

150  Morgan, op.cit, Doc 90, p 382-3.

151  Australian Biography interview, Tape 9.

152  An excellent account of the years 1980-81 in Poland is John Burgess's *The Solidarity Challenge: Poland 1980-91 – An Australian Diary*, Connor Court 2019. In his *Foreword* to this book, Professor Geoffrey Blainey, AC, writes: "We now tend to see the Cold War as ending largely by the efforts of President Reagan of the United States, the mistakes of Moscow's leaders and the widening weaknesses in their armed forces and economic life, and the growing influence of a remarkable Polish Pope who happened to be a Polish Patriot. But the eventual collapse of Soviet communism was also foreshadowed and hastened by the determination and courage of the Solidarity Movement in Poland."

153  In its report of the Solidarnosc visit *The Clerk*, the journal of the Victorian Branch of the FCUA, reported that at a meeting at the Victorian Trades Hall Council, Magda Wojcik was "subjected to a barrage of questions and innuendos from Communist delegates of various unions. One delegate asked her to justify Solidarity's support from the [conservative Australian] Fraser Government. *The Clerk*, Vol 14 No. 4, September 1984.

154  For a survey of European trade union responses to the rise of Solidarnosc see Stefan Berger, "Solidarnosc, Western Solidarity and Détente – A transnational approach" in *European Review*, Vol 16, No. 1, February 2008, pp 75 and ff.

155  *The Clerk*, Vol 14, No 4, September 1982, pp 11-14.

156  In 1982, after the crack-down, the military regime in Poland had to try and explain away the absence of Solidarnosc from the tripartite Polish delegation to that year's ILO meetings.

157  See photo in Morgan, *op.cit.*, between pages 240 and 241.

158  Poland in Australia webpage: http://www.canberra.msz.gov.pl/en/p/canberra_au_a_en/c/MOBILE/news/the_history_of_polish_australian_relations

159  I was staggered when I asked what the left unions proposed instead of the UK's EU membership. "Commonwealth preference" I was told, that is preferential trade arrangements with members of the Commonwealth of Nations. The UK has now left the EU, this time in response to the demands of conservatives.

160  Christopher Ng was a remarkable unionist who did ground-breaking work in assisting the unionisation of workers in the Asia-Pacific region. I was fortunate to meet Christopher many times during my years in the union movement.

161  Quoted in Bark and Harries, eds. *The Red Orchestra – The case of the Southwest Pacific*. Hoover Institution, 1989, p xx. In 1983, Chernenko was responsible for the ideological party work of the CPSU. The following year he became Communist Party Secretary.

162  In 2021, China has become the new security threat in the Pacific.

163  Rand Corporation, *Security Trends in the South Pacific, Vanuatu and Fiji*, May 1989, p 6.

164  Hagan, op.cit., p 238.

165  Peter Franks. 'Knox, Walter James', Dictionary of New Zealand Biography, first published in 2000. Te Ara - the Encyclopedia of New Zealand, https://teara.govt.nz/en/biographies/5k13/knox-walter-james (accessed 15 February 2021)

166  Rand Corporation, op.cit.

167     Rand Corporation, op.cit.

168     Rand Corp, op. cit., p 6. See also John Whitehall, *The Nuclear Free and Independent Pacific Movement*, in Bark and Harries, op. cit., pp 51-73 and Michael Easson, *Labor and the Left in the Pacific*, also in Bark and Harries, op.cit, pp 74-118.

169     Rand Corp, op.cit., p 6.

170     This remains an issue, although in 2018 and again in 2020 [by a smaller margin], voters in New Caledonia voted to remain part of France. A third vote may be held by 2022.

171     In 2019, as part of the settlement of this conflict, residents of Bougainville were able to vote in a referendum on independence from Papua New Guinea. Nearly 100% of Bouganvillians voted for independence. I expect that Joe Kabui would be very pleased.

172     However, there had been. The Association of Catholic Trade Unionists, founded by John Cort and which also grew out of the Catholic Worker movement of Dorothy Day, was active in assisting the organising efforts of workers and combatting communist influence in the 1940s and 1950s in the USA. I heard nothing of this group in the US nor had I heard it mentioned in Australia.

173     So named by the Portuguese/Spanish explorer Pedro Fernandes de Queirós in 1606. He visited the region 164 years before Cook arrived on the East Coast of Australia. De Queirós named the island La Austrialia del Espiritu Santo or "The Southern Land of the Holy Spirit", believing he had arrived in Terra Australis or Australia.

174     Rand Corporation, op.cit., p 30ff

175     Shelley Harford, *A Trans-Tasman Union Community: Growing Global Solidarity*, Labor History, No 95, Nov 2005, 133 ff at p 143.

176     No Airbnb or online booking sites in 1987!

177     Because American unions often had members in Canada, their national unions were usually called internationals.

178     For this story see: Gavin Souter, *Heralds and Angels – The House of Fairfax, 1841-1992*, Penguin Books, esp. Chapter 8.

179     Dennis L. Bark and Owen Harries [eds], *The Red Orchestra, Vol III, The case of the Southwest Pacific*, Hoover Institution, Stanford University 1989.

180     Noam Chomsky remained on the HTUP faculty list until 2018. His daughter Aviva Chomsky is a current faculty member.

181     In 2021, the KMU is now an affiliate of the International Trade Union Confederation [ITUC], the successor to the ICFTU, along with the TUCP.

182     A local, or local union, was a unit of the international union, usually based in a relatively small geographic area or industry sector.

183     American Federation of State, County and Municipal Employees.

184     Ann and Melena Barkman from the United Steelworkers in Pittsburgh both became friends and visited and stayed with us in our home later. We met up with them again in 2004 when we spent time in Pittsburgh and at the Steelworkers training college in upstate Pennsylvania.

185     No GPS either.

186     See Keith Harvey, 'JPM – John Peter Maynes' in *The Recorder*, Issues number 262 and 263 for the life and times of John Maynes. A shorter version also appears in *Labor History*, No 97.

187     Lindsay Tanner, *The Last Battle*, Kokkino Press, 1996.

188  Christendom Press, 1995.
189  William Heineman 2005.
190  By the mid-1980s, the CWIG ran under the public banner of the "Clerks Rank and File Team" or CRAFT. The terms are used interchangeably in this chapter although the two groups were not identical.
191  Tanner, *op.cit.*, pp 58-9.
192  Lindsay Tanner, Sideshow – *dumbing down democracy*, Scribe Publications, 2011, p 114.
193  'Minister abused office to help allies', The Australian, May 13th, 1988, p 8.
194  Tanner, *The last battle*, op.cit., p 40ff.
195  Union elections were conducted by an independent Returning Officer, a government employee in the Industrial Elections section of the Australian Electoral Commission. Counting of the ballot papers took place in the AEC offices and candidates could appoint scrutineers to observe the count.
196  As were some other benefits such a greatly discounted staff travel, but large numbers of members worked shift work at airports and in call centres where the work was less than glamorous and often very demanding.
197  CRAFT lost this position by way of a draw from a hat.
198  Although in Tanner's book he notes that "the situation wasn't helped when a Qantas member and friend of Manny's was overheard while drunk in a pub boasting that he had filled in a hundred ballot papers. It was all nonsense...." Tanner, *The last battle*, op.cit., p 132. Manny was Manny Lambrou, new Assistant Branch Secretary.
199  Re An Application By Rosemary Patricia Carter of An Inquiry Into Elections In the Federated Clerks Union of Australia Victorian Branch [1989] FCA 192; 32 IR 1 (31 May 1989).
200  Re An Application By Rosemary Patricia Carter of An Inquiry Into Elections In the Federated Clerks Union of Australia Victorian Branch [1989] FCA 225; 32 IR 30 (21 June 1989).
201  Tanner, *The last battle*, op.cit. pp 174-5.
202  My relationship was quickly restored after the 1991 elections, and I remained a friend of Vince until his death in 2018. I co-authored an Obituary for Vince published in the *Sydney Morning Herald*. He was a man of faith.
203  Tanner, *The last battle*, op cit., p 206.
204  Ibid, p 208.
205  In fact, there was another contest in North Queensland Branch, where Les Hauff, a Maynes supporter and deal participant was challenged by a maverick, James O'Donnell, who won in a surprising result.
206  Laurie Carmichael astounded me once in a one-on-one conversation at Adelaide Airport by telling me that the trouble with Stalin was his early training to be a Russian Orthodox priest. This had given him all the wrong ideas, according to Laurie. It does not matter who it is, the Church is always to blame!
207  For more detail on the role of evangelical Christians, especially Methodists, in the union movement and the ALP, see Robert Linder, The Methodist Love Affair with the Australian Labor Party, 1891-1929, *in Lucas: An Evangelical History Review* [Lucas 23&24 (1997-1998)], pp 35-61 and Stuart Piggin and Robert Linder, *The Fountain of Public Prosperity, Evangelical Christians in Australian History 1740-1914*, Chapter 16, pp 455 and ff, Monash University Publishing, 2018. For the role of Methodists and other evangelicals in South Australia see the excellent: *One and all – Labor and the*

*radical Tradition in South Australia*, by Philip Payton, Wakefield Press, 2016.

208 Piggin and Linder, op.cit, p 466.

209 Steven Weeks, 'Price, Thomas (Tom) (1852–1909)', Australian Dictionary of Biography, National Centre of Biography, Australian National University, http://adb.anu.edu.au/biography/price-thomas-tom-8109/text14157, published first in hardcopy 1988, accessed online 21 October 2018. See also Piggin and Linder, op.cit., pp 457-460.

210 Former SA ALP Premier Don Dunstan says that Verran's government was the first "Labor Government to govern with a majority in its own right in the world." Don Dunstan, *Felicia, The political memoirs of Don Dunstan*, MacMillian, 1981, p 10.

211 Arnold D. Hunt, 'Verran, John (1856–1932)', Australian Dictionary of Biography, National Centre of Biography, Australian National University, https://adb.anu.edu.au/biography/verran-john-8917/text15669, published first in hardcopy 1990. I also have a family connection with the Moonta and Wallaroo mines, but unfortunately it was on the management side!

212 Payton, op.cit., p 172.

213 Coral Lansbury and Bede Nairn, 'Spence, William Guthrie (1846–1926)', Australian Dictionary of Biography, National Centre of Biography, Australian National University, https://adb.anu.edu.au/biography/spence-william-guthrie-4628/text7623, published first in hardcopy 1976.

214 William Spence, *The Ethics of new Unionism*, p 8. Available on line at http://digital.slv.vic.gov.au

215 Ross McMullin, *The Light on the Hill – The Australian Labor Party 1891-1991*, Oxford University Press, Melbourne, 1992, p 11. Rodney Cavalier says that the name was the Labour Electoral Leagues. The name Political Labor League [PLL] was also used following a merger between the LEL and the Australian Labour Federation [McMullin, p 19]. The name Australian Labor Party was not universally adopted until the early 1900s. Labor parties in various colonies prior to 1901 had a variety of names.

216 Ross McMullin, op.cit., p 12.

217 Linder, op.cit., p 42

218 Although Associate Professor Stuart Piggin, who was in 2007 Director of the Centre for the History of Christian Thought and Experience at Macquarie University had done much to tell this story and I used his writings extensively. More recently, Dr Adrian Pabst has also drawn attention to some of this history, drawing on some of the same sources as I discovered during the YRAW campaign: Adrian Pabst, *The Story of our Country*, Connor Court, 2019. In South Australia Philip Payton's 2016 work previously cited has detailed this story in that State.

219 New American Bible, Ecclesiastes, Ch 4, Verses 9-12.

220 Good News Bible, Exodus, 2:11-12.

221 Ecclesiastics 34:22 [Good News Bible]. This would not have impressed the Protestant Ministers to who I spoke since this book – also known as Sirach – is only in the Catholic Bible. It has many statements, many of them odd.

222 Clark was defeated in the ALP's landslide victory in the November 2018 elections.

223 Keith Harvey, 'Who has the fairest IR policy?' *Eureka Street*, June 27, 2007. https://www.eurekastreet.com.au/article/who-has-the-fairest-ir-policy

224 *The Qur'an and Worker Justice*, National Interfaith Committee for Worker Justice, p 1, https://www.wpusa.org/Interfaith-Council/Resources_quran.pdf

225 Matthew 22:35-40/

226 Kevin Rudd, *Christianity, The Australian Labor Party and Current Challenges in Australian Politics, A Contribution to the National Forum on Australia's Christian heritage*, Parliament House, Canberra, 7 August 2006, copy in the possession of the author.

227 ACCER, *Workplace Relations: A Catholic Perspective"*, 2007, p 6.

228 This claim should not be overstated but compulsory arbitration of industrial disputes via wages boards or industrial tribunals arose in part from the failure of the great strikes of the early 1890s. The NSW Government appointed a Royal Commission into these strikes in November 1890. The Commission's Report was published in 1891 and had a summary of the main points of Rerum Novarum published in May 1891, towards the end of the work of the Commission. The encyclical mentioned without elaboration that it may be "advisable that recourse be had to Societies or Boards…, or some other mode of safeguarding the interests of the wage-earner; the State being appealed to, should the circumstances require, for its sanction and protection". The Report also had summaries of the views of Karl Marx, Henry George and others. See: Murtagh, J G, *Australia: The Catholic Chapter*, Sheed and Ward, New York, 1946 at page 151. A stronger case can be made for the influence of Rerum Novarum on Justice Higgins's 1907 Harvester decision establishing a living wage, using terminology like that in the encyclical. This link has been made in many places, for example see Isaac and Macintryre, *A New province For Law and Order: 100 years of Australian Conciliation and Arbitration*, Cambridge University Press, 2004 and by Adrian Pabst, op. cit.

229 Rerum Novarum itself notes in its opening sentence that there was a "spirit of revolutionary change" in the spheres of both politics and economics. The encyclical is written as a response and as a repudiation of the socialist solution of abolishing private property in favour of State ownership.

230 This was not true, of course, since Christians, as shown above, were highly active in working to improve the lot of working-class people in this world, including through unionism and political action.

231 Peter Singer, *The Age Monthly Review*, August and September 1981.

232 The Age *Monthly Review*, November 1981.

233 Karl Marx and Friedrich Engels, *The Communist Manifesto*, 1848, Chapter III: Socialist and Communist Literature.

234 Arthur Young seems to have been supported in these activities by his brothers, especially James Hadden Young. Young paid 1,350,000 French francs to buy a former abbey at Citeaux. One of his collaborators was another Fourierist, and early feminist, Zoe Gatti de Gamond. The de Gamond family also lost money through the Citeaux phalange.

235 Jean Forneserio, A Fourierist in South Australia. *The Colonial Adventures of Arthur Young*, in The *Regenerative Spirit, Vol 2*, Lythrum Press 2004.

236 Peter Beilharz, Socialism in Europe: After the Fall, *International Journal of Politics, Culture and Society*, Vol. 11, No. 1, 1997 pp 50-51.

237 Peter Beilharz, The Weekend Australian Review, 11-12 February 2017, page 20. This appears to be Beilharz misquoting himself from his review of Donald Sasson's major work, *100 Years of Socialism: The West European Left in the Twentieth Century*, I. B. Tauris, London & New York, 1996, Socialism in Europe: After the Fall, *International Journal of Politics, Culture and Society*, Vol. 11, No. 1, 1997.

238 George Orwell, *Preface to the Ukrainian Edition of Animal farm*, March 1947, p 88 quoted in Dorian Lynskey, *The Ministry of truth – A Biography of George Orwell's 1984*, Picador, 2019, p 138.

239    Friedrich Engels, *The Condition of the Working Class in England*, first published in German in 1845 but not in English not until 1887.
240    The phrase 'dark satanic mills' is taken from a poem by William Blake, a radical Christian. It may not have initially been meant to apply to factories but has been adopted as a phrase that refers to the worst features of industrial life during the Industrial Revolution.
241    Rodney Cavalier, *A war I did not know much about that influenced me so much*, in *What did you do in the Cold War, Daddy?, Personal stories from a Troubled Time*, Ann Curthoys and Joy Damousi, [eds.], NewSouth Publishing, 2014, Kindle eBook edition, final paragraph Chapter 7.
242    Ross Fitzgerald, *"Red Ted" – The Life of E G Theodore*, UQP, 1994, pp 146-7.
243    Frank Newport, 'The Meaning of "Socialism" to Americans Today', Gallup, October 4, 2018. In this survey 23% of Republicans thought socialism meant equality for all and another 23% thought it meant "Government ownership or control, government ownership of utilities, everything controlled by the government, state control of business". Seven per cent said it meant social services and free medicine. At least this is more perceptive than the five per cent who thought it meant "Talking to people, being social, social media, getting along with people". Even six per cent of Democrats thought this as well!
244    *Sunday Age*, April 25, 2020, p. 23.
245    Pamela Pilbeam, *French Socialists before Marx*, Acumen, 2000, Chapter 1, especially pp 8-9; and Leszek Kolakowski, *Main Currents of Marxism, Vol 1, The Founders*, OUP, 1981, Chapter 10.
246    I am using the term 'socialism' for want of a better alternative term to describe a different economic and social structure.
247    ALP National Constitution, adopted December 18, 2018; https://www.alp.org.au/media/1574/alp_national_constitution.pdf. See Clause 4. This objective has been under review.
248    The history of how the Blackburn Interpretation came to be added is quite involved but also very interesting, with suggestions that B A Santamaria or others associated with him 'rediscovering' this addendum which was not formally added to the Objective in 1921. It was officially added later. See: Frank McManus, *The Tumult and the Shouting*, Rigby, 1977, pp140-145 and Gerard Henderson, *op.cit*, pp 193-197.
249    Rodney Cavalier disagrees with me on this point [among many others], believing that the economic crisis of 2008-9 and the pandemic of 2020 has meant that nationalisation, and greater government intervention in the economy, is now more likely than ever. He may be correct.
250    See Patrick Ford, *Cardinal Moran and the A.L.P., A study in the Encounter between Moran and Socialism 1890-1907*, MUP, 1966 or, more briefly, either Race Mathews, *Of Labour and Liberty, Distributism in Victoria 1891-1966*, Chapter 4, Monash University Publishing, 2017 or James Murtagh, *Australia: The Catholic Chapter*, Sheed and Ward, New York, 1946, Chapter VIII.
251    Leo XIII, *Rerum Novarum*, Par. 3.
252    Ibid, Par. 4.
253    John Paul II, *Centesimus Annus*, Par 12, p 10.
254    Pope Pius XI, *Quadragesimo Anno*, Par 120, P 23.
255    Ibid, Par 49.

256 John Paul II, *Laborem Exercens*, Par 14, P 20-21.

257 Encyclical Letter Fratelli Tutti Of The Holy Father Francis On Fraternity And Social Friendship, Pars 119 1nd 120.

258 Benedict XVI, *Europe And Its Discontents*, First Things, January 2006, I am indebted to a column by Michael Sean Winters in the US National Catholic Reporter for drawing my attention to this remark.

259 This is not to say that there are not other problems for Catholics wishing to support the ALP. Policies on a range of ethical issues such as abortion and euthanasia do present serious concerns for Catholic voters.

260 Martyn S Goddard, 'How the Pharmaceutical Benefits Scheme began', *Medical Journal of Australia*, 2014; 201 (1): S23-S25. Published online: 7 July 2014 https://www.mja.com.au/journal/2014/201/1/how-pharmaceutical-benefits-scheme-began

261 *Socialisation, Social Justice Statement 1948*, Published by the Archbishops and Bishops Of the catholic Church in Australia, http://handle.slv.vic.gov.au/10381/127297.

262 See Gerard Henderson, *op.cit.*, pp 193-197.

263 James Hagan, *History of the ACTU*, *op.cit*, p 14ff.

264 Bede Nairn, *Civilising Capitalism, The Labor Movement in NSW 1870-1900*, ANU Press, 1973.

265 The Hon. Joe Hockey, MP, Media Release, April 3, 2007.

266 See AIER [authors Clare Ozich, Mary Lambert, and Keith Harvey], *Inequality and Insecurity. Responding to the challenge of precarious work*, The Ron McCallum Debate 2016 Discussion Paper, AIER Inc, 2016 and AIER [Authors Keith Harvey and Clare Ozich], *Justice @ Work: Free to Associate?* The Ron McCallum Debate 2015 Discussion Paper, AIER Inc, p 10.

267 James Jupp, *Australian Party Politics*, Melbourne University Press, Second Edition 1968, p 31.

268 Remarks by the President in State of the Union Address, January 20, 2015.

269 Race Mathews, *Jobs of our own, Building a Stakeholder Society: Alternatives to the Market and the State*, The Distributist Review press, Irving, Texas, Second Edition, 2009, p 94.

270 In particular, agricultural and fishing co-ops.

271 *Laborem Exercens - On human work*, part 14.

272 Race Mathews: *Catholic social solutions to workplace fairness*, *Eureka Street*, February 1, 2012.

273 This was not the case for the moderate left which did support the development of co-operatives.

274 *ESOP (Employee Stock Ownership Plan) Facts* https://www.esop.org/.

275 Race Mathews: *Catholic social solutions to workplace fairness*, *Eureka Street*, February 1, 2012.

276 Business Council of Co-Operatives and Mutuals, *2019 National Mutual Economy Report*, p 21.

277 Disclosure: at the time of writing these memoirs, I was a Director of an industry superannuation fund.

278 Stuart Piggin and Robert Linder, *op.cit.*, p 461.

279 And a lot like what would happen if you merged American corporate capitalism with Soviet-style state socialism!

280 James Murtagh, *op.cit.*, p 134. See also John Kellett, William Lane and 'New Australia': A Reassessment, *Labour History*, No 72, pp 1- 18 at p 5. See also Bradley

Bowden, 'The Rise and Decline of Australian Unionism', *Labour History*, No 100, p 57. Also, R. McMullin, *The Light on the Hill*, p 4.

281  Edward Bellamy, *Looking Backwards: 2000 to 1987*, Kindle edition, Chapter 26.

282  Arthur Harvey, *The Agricultural labourer: His present condition and means for his amelioration*, A Brown & Co, Aberdeen, 1858, p 47.

283  Manifesto of the Communist Party by Karl Marx and Frederick Engels, February 1848; https://www.marxists.org/archive/marx/works/download/pdf/Manifesto.pdf.

284  Depending on which calendar is used.

285  Jennifer Llewellyn, Michael McConnell, Steve Thompson, 'The Red Terror', Alpha History, August 11, 2019, https://alphahistory.com/russianrevolution/red-terror. See also Robert Conquest, op.cit., p 3ff.

286  Phillip Deery and Neil Redfern, 'No lasting peace: Labor, Communism and the Cominform, Australia and Great Britain, 1945-50'. *Labor History*, No. 88, May 2005, p 63.

287  James Hagan, *The History of the A.C.T.U.*, Longman Chesire, 1981, p 122.

288  Deery and Redfern, op.cit., p 63. See also T. Bramble, *Trade Unionism in Australia: A history from flood to ebb tide*. Cambridge University Press, 2008, pp 8-11. In his introduction to this book, the author says that it is "framed within a Marxist perspective".

289  Robert Murray, *The Split, Australian Labor in the fifties*, Cheshire, 1970, p23. See also Deery and Redfern, op.cit. p 63.

290  Ibid, p 24.

291  John Button, *As It happened*, Text Publishing, 1998, p 73.

292  James Hagan, *op.cit.*, p 445.

293  Mark Aarons, *Scenes from my Cold War*, in *What did you do in the Cold War, Daddy? Personal Stories from a Troubled Time*, Curthoys and Damousi, [Eds] New South Publishing 2014 Kindle Edition – Chapter 8, Loc 2792-2803.

294  Don Rawson, *Unions and Unionists in Australia*, George Allen & Unwin, 1979, p 105.

295  Deery and Redfern, op.cit., p 71.

296  Ibid, p 70.

297  Hagan, *op.cit.*, p 196 A detailed account of the dispute and the events leading up to it can be found in Tom Sheridan, *Division of Labour, Industrial Relations in the Chifley years, 1945-1949*, OUP Australia, 1989.

298  Hagan, *op.cit.*, p 204.

299  Alastair Davidson, *The Communist Party of Australia, A Short History*, Hoover Institution Press, Stanford, 1969, pp 133ff.

300  B. Taft, *Crossing the Party Line – Memoirs of Bernie Taft*, Scribe Publications, 1994, pp 63-4.

301  Ibid, p 64.

302  Ibid.

303  Winston Churchill, "Sinews of Peace" (Iron Curtain Speech), March 5 1946 at Westminster College, Fulton, Missouri; https://www.nationalchurchillmuseum.org/sinews-of-peace-iron-curtain-speech.html

304  Aarons, op.cit., pp 80-81.

305  Phillip Deery, 'The Dove Flies East: Whitehall, Warsaw and the 1950 World Peace Congress', *Australian Journal of Politics and History*, Vol.48, No.4, 2002, pp. 449-468,

464 and footnote 97.

306 Deery, op.cit, at p 466. The White Dove of Peace was an image created by Pablo Picasso for the First world 'peace' Conference held in 1949: https://www.pablopicasso.org/dove-of-peace.jsp

307 Hagan, *op.cit.*, p 238.

308 Hagan, *op.cit.*, p 240. The Kominform [or more usually Cominform] was the Communist Information Bureau established by the Soviet Union and its Eastern European satellite communist parties [plus those of France and Italy] in 1947 to co-ordinate communist propaganda and activities around the world. Ref.: https://www.britannica.com/topic/Cominform. The 2nd World peace Conference was the conference attended by Jack Hughes from the FCUA at which he met Chinese communist party officials as described by Eric Aarons.

309 L. S. Merrifield, 'Regulation of Union Elections in Australia', *Industrial and Labor Relations Review*, 1957, Vol 10, p 252.

310 Royal Commission Inquiring into the Origins, Aims, Objects and Funds of the Communist Party in Victoria and Other Related Matters, 1950 https://www.parliament.vic.gov.au/papers/govpub/VPARL1950-51No12.pdf.

311 Hagan, *op.cit.*, pp 194-5.

312 *Ibid*, p 195.

313 Merrifield, op.cit., pp 259-260.

314 See Federal Court decision: *FCUA: ex parte Henry* [1949] 66 Commonwealth Arbitration Reports [CAR] at page 281. The Returning Officer was F T [Fred] Farrell, who was named in the Report of the Royal Commission into the Communist Party in Victoria as a person who was or had been a member of the Communist Party in Victoria. Source: Report of the Royal Commission, p 138.

315 Susanna Short, *Laurie Short – A Political Life*, Allen & Unwin, 1992, Chapters 9 and 10.

316 Ross Martin, *Trade Unions in Australia*, Pelican Books, Revised Edition 1980, p 12.

317 Patrick O'Farrell, *The Catholic Church in Australia – a short history 1788-1967*, Thomas Nelson, *Melbourne*, 1972, p 258.

318 For more detail on the role of evangelical Christians, especially Methodists, in the union movement and the ALP, see Robert Linder, *The Methodist Love Affair with the Australian Labor Party, 1891-1929*, in Lucas: An Evangelical History Review [Lucas 23&24 (1997-1998)], pp 35-61 and Stuart Piggin and Robert Linder, *The Fountain of Public Prosperity, Evangelical Christians in Australian History 1740-1914*, Chapter 16, pp 455 and ff, Monash University Publishing, 2018.

319 Murray, *op.cit.*, pp 14-15.

320 Murray, *op.cit.*, p 29.

321 Don Rawson, The A.L.P. Industrial Groups - An Assessment, *The Australian Quarterly*, Vol. 26, No. 4 (Dec. 1954), pp. 30-46.

322 Minutes of meeting of Federal Parliamentary Labor Party, Thursday 15/5/1947 at 10.30 am, quoted in Brian McKinlay, *Australian Labor History in Documents, Vol 2, The Labor Party*, Collins Dove, 1979, p 124.

323 Alastair Buchan, The Impact of the 1949 Coal Strike on the Illawarra community and its responses, Bachelor of Arts (Hons.) Thesis, Department of History and Politics, University of Wollongong, 1998, pp 15-16.

324 R v Sharkey [1949] HCA 46; (1949) 79 CLR 121; [1949] ALR 828; 23 ALJ 435.

325 Interview with James Maher, National Library of Australia, Oral History project. Interview recorded in 2003.

326  Ross McMullin, *The Light on the Hill, The Australian Labor Party 1891-1991*, Oxford University Press Australia, 1992, p 276.

327  Bill Hayden, *Hayden, An autobiography*, Angus & Robertson, 1996, p 83. See also James McClelland, *Stirring the Possum*, Viking, 1988 for a similar view pp 101-109. McClelland knew Santamaria at school and University, enlisted his support to help Laurie Short defeat Communist control of the Ironworkers but remained an ALP member and was briefly a Minister in the Whitlam Government.

328  Phillip Deery, Santamaria, 'The Movement And The Labor Split Of 1954-55 - A Re-Examination', *Journal of the Australian Catholic Historical Society*, Vol 22, 2001, pp 47-8

329  Strangio, *op.cit.*, Chapters 9 and 10.

330  The 'new' ALP Executive [also known as the 'Stout-Cain' party acted first and preferenced the Liberal and Country Party and the Country Party [two separate conservative parties] in 19 out of 32 seats. The 'old' Executive then preferenced the conservative parties in most seats, but three 'Stout-Cain' ALP members were elected on 'old' Executive preferences. These decisions guaranteed a win by the Bolte-led Liberal and Country Party. Robert Murray, *The Split*, op. cit., p 252 and Adam Carr, http://psephos.adam-carr.net/countries/a/australia/states/vic/historic/1955assembly.txt

331  Interview with Vince Higgins, former NSW Branch Secretary of the FCUA and NSW Movement Organiser.

332  J. Cain, *John Cain's years*, Melbourne University Press, 1995, pp 7-10. Paul Strangio notes the same phenomenon.

# Index

Aarons, Eric 12, 225
Aarons, Laurie 39
Aarons, Mark 10, 39, 222
Abbott, Tony 191-2
Abrams, Peter 174-175
Agee, Phillip 149-150
ALP Industrial Groups 8-9, 11, 16, 130, 156, 228-230
Amalgamated Society of Carpenters and Joiners [ASC&J] 7, 104
Amalrik, Andrei 18
Armstrong, Hugh 156-157, 161, 174-6, 177, 186
Asian American Free Labour Institute [AAFLI] 137
Australian Council of Trade Unions [ACTU] 12, 14-15, 76, 79-80, 83, 85, 99, 113-114, 121, 126, 134-6, 143-4, 152, 185-7, 220-1, 225, 227-8, 216, 221, 242n, 243n
Australian Labor Party [ALP] 7, 12, 15-17, 20-25, 29, 31-32, 34, 38-40, 62-5, 69-70, 76, 78-81, 85, 93, 96-98, 103, 105-8, 123, 130, 135, 149, 150, 156, 158-60, 180, 182-3, 187-92, 196-8, 205, 207-8, 210, 216, 221-5, 227-8, 229-35, 236n, 238n, 239n, 243n, 249n, 250n, 253n
Australian Rope and Cordage Workers Union 17, 62, 64-76, 78, 82, 91-2, 94, 99-100, 103-4, 106
Bacon, Jim 34, 52, 240n
Bailey, John 40, 46
Barassi, Ron 66
Batchelor, Peter 23
Bellamy, Edward 215-6
Betros, Lance 160
Betts, Bob 69-70, 90
Blackburn Interpretation 198, 249n
Bolsheviks 11, 35, 81, 220

Brezhnev, Leonid 88, 161
Builders Laborers Federation [BLF] 24, 35, 238n
Burns, Maud 69-71, 82
Cahill, Les 95-6
Cain, John [Junior] 17, 24, 160, 234, 238n, 253n
Cain Government [John Cain Senior] 8, 17, 233
Cairns, Dr Jim 38-9, 76, 80
Cameron, Duncan 108-9, 112
Cameron, Clyde 79
Cargill, Linda 187
Carmichael, Laurie 185, 246n
Carter, Rosemary 161, 163
Cashman, Mike 161, 163-5, 178, 180
Catholic Action 140, 193, 229
Catholic Social encyclicals 193, 198-205
Cavalier, Rodney 196, 247n, 249n
Catholic Social Studies Movement [the Movement] 8-11, 16-17, 64, 78, 116-7, 120, 228-34, 236n
Chaudry, Mahendra 139
Chernenko, Victor 18, 133, 244n
Chesterton, G K 210
Chifley, Ben 198, 205, 206, 222-5, 231
Chinese Communist Party 13, 19, 30, 208, 252n
Chomsky, Noam 150, 245n
Christian Socialists 188, 197-8, 200
Clancy, Pat 134, 165
Clarke, Ralph 175
Clerical Workers Industrial Group [CWIG] 16, 107, 156, 178, 246,
Clerks Rank and File Team [CRAFT] 156, 158-9, 161-4, 166-8, 171, 174-81, 214, 246n
Coal Strike 224
'Committee of 10' 21-2

Committee of Inquiry Into Technological Change in Australia [CITCA] 105-6, 115, 127
Communist Party of Australia [CPA] 10-13, 15, 35, 39, 52, 134, 180, 220, 222-4, 231, 240n
Communist Party of the Soviet Union [CPSU] 18-20, 87-8, 133, 165, 180, 223, 244n
Cragg, David 25
Crean, Simon 135-6
Danby, Michael 149
Darroch, Harry 109, 112, 161, 163-4
Davidson, Alistair 34, 224
Davies, Kevin 85, 101
Democratic Labour Party [DLP] 8, 20-1, 40-1, 46, 50, 55, 64, 78, 80, 85, 92-3, 103, 232-5, 238n
Distributism/Distributists 210-11
Donaghy's Ropes 67, 69, 72, 74
Doncaster Travel 115, 160
Donovan, Michael 25
Douglas, Ken 134
Downs and Son 67
Easson, Michael 4, 149
Engels, Friedrich 194, 196, 220
Evatt, H.V. [Doc] 8, 16, 223, 231-3, 236n
Fairfax, Warwick 146, 148
Federated Clerks Union of Australia [FCUA] 7, 10, 13, 15-16, 105-8, 111-15, 121, 123-7, 129, 131, 135, 137, 144, 154, 167, 176-7, 182, 184, 215, 243n, 244n, 252n
Federated Ironworkers Association [FIA] 7, 13, 16
FEDSDA Pty Ltd 111, 115, 159-60, 164
Fourier, Charles 194
*Free Speech* 40, 42-3, 49-52, 57-8, 92
Gillard, Julia 22
Ginsburg, Evgenia 18-19
Goldschlager, Les 58
Gorbachev, Mikhail 19, 159, 161, 173, 180
Gramsci, Antonio 34
Green, James [Jim] 150
Grenville, John 10, 22, 108, 242n
Gulag Archipelago 18-19, 80, 225
Hagan, James (Jim) 220, 224, 227-8
Halfpenny, John 84-5, 96, 105, 134-6
Han, Dongfang 208
Hand, Gerry 22
Hardy, Frank 30
Harradine, Brian 80, 97
Harvard Trade Union Program [HTUP] 80, 144-52, 245n
Harvey, Arthur Young 216-7
Hawke, R.J. [Bob] 17, 80, 114, 121, 184, 186, 198, 236n, 242n, 243n
Hayden, Bill 232
Henderson, Gerard 46, 117-8
Hewat, James [Jim] 164, 176
Higgins, Vince 160, 169, 174-5, 185
Hockey, Joe 208
Hogan, Ray 96
Hughes, John [Jack] 12-15, 223, 225, 252n
Hughes, Robert 148
Hunt, Jim 72
Hunt, Ken 72
Hyde, Michael 34, 39, 43-4, 53, 79, 239n
Imparato, Ann 152
Industrial Action Fund [IAF] 21-2, 123, 159
Industrial Groups 8-9, 11, 16-17, 26, 130, 156, 227-31, 234, 238n
International Confederation of Free Trade Unions [ICFTU] 134, 143, 152, 227, 245n
International Labour Organisation [ILO] 102, 126-32, 215, 244n
Kabui, Joseph 138-9, 245n
Kelly, Sean 80
Kim Il Sung 226
Kinnears Ropes 66-7, 69-71
Knox, Jim 134, 143
Labor Committee for Pacific Affairs [LCPA] 137-43, 149
Landeryou, Bill 23
Langer, Albert 34, 52, 58, 239n
Lanigan, Jim 164
LaPirow, Mark 41, 44, 55-7, 241n

256

# Index

Launder, John 177-9
Lee, Frank 23, 176-7
Lenin, Vladimir 18-19, 35, 61, 220
Lewis, Barbara 163, 171, 177
*Lot's Wife* 40-2, 49, 51-2, 54-6, 58, 92, 102
Lovegrove, Denis [Dinny] 27, 221, 238n
Maher, J.B. [Jim] 17, 23, 85, 111, 125, 160, 231
Maier, Heribert 127, 129
Mao Tse Tung 13
Marsh, Peter 91, 94-5, 105
Marx, Karl 61, 193-4, 196, 220, 248n
Marxism/Marxists 34, 155, 193-5, 202, 210, 212-13, 219
Matheson, Louis 44, 53, 55
Mathews, Race 210-13,
May, Tom 53
Maynes, John 13, 16-17, 62, 105-19, 121, 123, 125-7, 130-1, 144, 155, 158, 160-1, 163-5, 168-9, 172-8, 180-2, 215, 237n, 242n, 244n
MacBean, John 135-6, 140, 144-5,
McCormack, Janice 147, 213
McPhillips, L.J. [Jack] 13-14
Medlicott, Tony 162-3
Melbourne Rope Works 67, 73
Melksham, John 99
Mercer, Gerald 117, 123, 176
Methodists 187-9, 229, 246n, 252n
Milewski, Jerzy 124
Miller, Kerry 34
Millers Ropes 66-7, 69, 73-4
Miners Federation 223, 227
Monash Association of Students [MAS] 35, 38, 41, 51-3, 55-7
Monash DLP Club, a.k.a. Monash Democrats 40-3, 46-7, 51, 53, 57, 64, 81-2, 92
Monash Labor Club 34, 38, 40, 50
Mondragon Cooperative Community [MCC] 211-13
Morgan, Patrick 117-20, 122
Moses 189-90
Murray, Robert 221, 230, 237n
National Civic Council [NCC] 8-9, 10, 17, 20-2, 26, 46, 50, 61-5, 76-8, 80-1, 85, 92, 96-7, 103, 108, 111, 116-25, 130, 159, 176, 183, 193, 234, 236n, 239n
National Office Skills Formation Advisory Body [NOSFAB]/Admin Training Company/Aspire Learning 184-5, 215
Neenan, Frank 85, 109
*News Weekly* 76-8, 233, 239n
Ng, Christopher 130-1, 244n
Nolan, Peter 79, 83
Norris, Terry 98
NZ Federation of Labour 134, 143
Obama, Barak 209
O'Brien, Fr Denis 81
O'Brien, Tony 166,
O'Sullivan, Michael 23, 62, 69, 75-6, 78, 85, 99, 109, 111, 117-8, 123, 161, 163-4, 171-2, 174, 176, 178, 181, 182
Orwell, George 18-9, 27, 53, 195, 237n
Pacific Trade Union Forum [PTUC] 133-4, 137, 141
Pell, George 192
Perry, Paul Francis 53, 239n, 241n
Petrov, Vladimir 14-15, 232
Porritt, Clive 52
*Rerum Novarum* 193, 198-200, 202-3, 205, 211, 248n
Richardson, Bill 134-5, 136
Ridge, Brian 53
Riordan, Joan 111
Riordan, Joe 108, 112
Roulston, Jim 84, 95
Rubenstein, Linda 52
Rudd, Kevin 191, 209
Ryan, John 191
Salameh, Linda 161, 164-5
Santamaria, B.A. [Bob] 8-10, 20, 46, 62, 76-8, 92-3, 115-23, 125, 193, 207, 229, 230, 232-3, 236n, 249n, 253n
Satungia, Kenneth 140-2
Sharpley, Cecil 227
Shop Assistants Union [SDA] 7, 10, 23, 17, 85, 111, 121, 124-5, 159
Short, Laurie 27, 228, 253n

Sinatra, Frank 101, 242n
Singer, Peter 194
Slape, Paul 124
Social Action [magazine, organisation] 123, 148-9, 159, 166, 176, 186
Social Democrats, USA 140
Socialisation 197-8, 202, 204-7
Socialism 88-9, 187, 193-5, 197-202, 204-5, 206, 210, 212-3, 219, 222, 224, 249n, 250n
Socialist Left [SL] 21, 23-4, 156, 158, 183
Socialist Objective 197-8
Socialist Party of Australia 35, 134
Solidarity/Solidarnosc [Polish trade union] 20, 123-26, 161, 165, 170, 244n
Solzhenitsyn, Alexander 18-9, 30, 80, 85, 89
Specht, Larry 140-3
Spence, W. G. 188, 215
Stackpoole, Herbert J 64-5, 71
Stalin, Joseph/Stalinism 10-12, 18-19, 27, 39, 61, 159, 193, 221, 223, 225-6, 237n, 246n
Steinkulher, Irma 171
Stinear, Grant 52-3
Stone, Ken 75-6, 78-9, 82-8, 91-101, 103, 105, 125, 242
Strangio, Paul 233, 253
Sullivan, T. W. [Terry] 65, 69, 73-4, 106, 108-9, 156, 158, 174
Suzman, Helen 47-9, 240n
Taft, Bernie 224
Taft, Mark 52, 55, 240n
Tanner, Lindsay 155-61, 163-5, 167-9, 172-3, 175, 177-82, 246n
Technical Services Guild [TSG] 104
Theodore, Ted 197
Thornton, Ernest [Ernie] 13
Union of Kanak and Exploited Workers [USTKE] 136
Union of Soviet Socialist Republics/Soviet Union [USSR] 7, 10, 12, 15, 18-20, 30, 35, 52, 79-81, 85-9, 124-5, 130, 133-5, 138, 141, 148-9, 155, 159, 161, 165, 170, 173, 180, 186, 193, 195, 219-21, 223, 225-7, 237n, 238n, 252n
Universal Destination of Goods 200, 203-4
Uzbekistan 85-6, 89
Vanuatu Trade Union Congress 140
Vella, Tony 83-4, 91, 94-5, 135-6
Verran, John 188
Victorian Mothercraft Nurses Association 104
Victorian Trades Hall Council [VTHC] 17, 21, 25, 47, 75-6, 79, 82-9, 91-9, 103-5, 125, 135,152, 213, 242, 244
Viet Cong 31, 38-9,
W.E. Green [Weg] 101, 103
Walesa, Lech 20, 124-5
Waters, Jack 85, 102
Whitlam, Gough 25, 31-2, 36-8, 51, 75-6, 79-80, 102, 210, 236n, 239n, 243n, 253n
Wojcik, Mugda 124, 244n
Worker cooperatives 210-14
World Federation of Trade Unions [WFTU] 13, 134, 226-7,
Wu, Harry 20
Young, Arthur 194, 217, 248n
Your Rights at Work [YRAW] 186, 189, 190-2, 209, 247n

www.ingramcontent.com/pod-product-compliance
Lightning Source LLC
Chambersburg PA
CBHW051114230426
43667CB00014B/2570